T0324171

Progress in IS

More information about this series at http://www.springer.com/series/10440

Kai Spohrer

Collaborative Quality Assurance in Information Systems Development

The Interaction of Software Development Techniques and Team Cognition

Springer

Kai Spohrer
University of Mannheim
Mannheim, Germany

This book is based on a doctoral thesis successfully defended at the Business School of the
University of Mannheim.

ISSN 2196-8705   ISSN 2196-8713   (electronic)
Progress in IS
ISBN 978-3-319-25161-5   ISBN 978-3-319-25163-9   (eBook)
DOI 10.1007/978-3-319-25163-9

Library of Congress Control Number: 2015956833

Springer Cham Heidelberg New York Dordrecht London

Printed on acid-free paper

Springer International Publishing AG Switzerland is part of Springer Science+Business Media
(www.springer.com)

Foreword

For more than a decade, agile software development with its principles, methods, and techniques has been challenging the traditional, plan-driven, and mechanistic ways of developing software. In fact, it has led to an enormous change in the way how software is developed in industry today, and nearly all software companies are cherry-picking one or the other agile element in order to improve in their daily routines. In the scholarly literature, however, this important trend is heavily underrepresented and only little understood, leaving us with open questions. In particular, there is little evidence whether and how agile practices actually result in beneficial development outcomes. This lack of research may well be rooted in the heterogeneity, fuzziness, and variability of aspects that are subsumed under the label "agile software development" in industry.

Therefore, it appears reasonable to unveil the drivers of agile software development by focusing on focal and frequently observed elements. This is what Dr. Kai Spohrer attempts in his dissertation when he examines the quality effects and detailed work pattern of pair programming and peer code review, two extremely widespread and popular agile development techniques. His book highlights that prior research on the effectiveness of these techniques has overlooked a decisive aspect: these techniques are typically used in the context of entire development teams rather than between single developers only. Theory-based empirical results show that these techniques thereby also influence teams' joint cognitive accomplishments and not only in beneficial ways!

Kai Spohrer's work presented in this book helps to understand that team cognition plays a tremendously important role in how pair programming and peer code review are applied in software development teams in the first place and that the long-term application of these techniques changes the ways how teams work together and how effectively they produce high-quality software. This includes the unwanted and negative side effects that may arise when teams rely unconditionally on such techniques without reflecting their long-term impact.

The monograph delivers contributions to both theory and practice. It offers a comprehensive overview for industry in the form of negative and positive effects of pair programming and peer code review which need to be kept in mind when adopting these techniques. I am confident that this book provides a valuable source of information to a large and diverse audience, and I would like to wish its many readers an insightful experience.

Mannheim, Germany   Prof. Dr. Armin Heinzl
August 2015

Acknowledgments

This book presents the essence of my research on collaborative quality assurance in software development teams that I conducted as a doctoral student during the last five years. Pursuing a Ph.D. at the University of Mannheim was often an interesting, sometimes a challenging, but always a rewarding endeavor for me. It enriched my life in many more ways than are obvious from a dissertation and a new title. Both successes and failures on this path allowed me to grow personally and helped me to develop the ways in which I work, think, and interact with others. I would like to thank many people for the encouragement, support, and inspiration I have received in this process.

First of all, I am deeply grateful to my advisor Professor Dr. Armin Heinzl for giving me the support, the guidance, and also the freedom to develop my skills in research and teaching. He not only supported me in pursuing research in relevant areas of my interest; he also provided productive academic guidance and encouraged me to discuss my work at various international conferences and workshops with other scholars of the discipline.

Professor Heinzl also enabled me to follow an invitation of Professor Suprateek Sarker to spend more than 2 months as a Visiting Scholar at Washington State University (WSU) in Pullman, Washington. At WSU, I had the chance to participate in doctoral courses and was honored to discuss my work at various occasions with international top researchers. In particular, I want to express my deep gratitude to Professor Suprateek Sarker and Professor Saonee Sarker for their time, for their critical and inspirational comments, and for their enormous warmth and hospitality. I also want to give special thanks to Christopher Califf, Tanya Beaulieu, and Leal Gatewood for making my time there so equally productive and enjoyable.

Furthermore, I highly appreciate the support of our Administrative Staff Luise Bühler and Ingrid Distelrath and of the student assistants Nina Jaeger, Melanie Marnet, Olga Oster, Lea Offermann, Santana Overath, Kathrin Teupe, Stefan Eckhardt, Alexandra Lang, and Pascal Kunz.

My research strongly benefited from discussions with academic and industrial researchers and with experienced software development experts. As such, I want to thank Tobias Hildenbrand, Jürgen Heymann, and Markus Berg for their valuable input that helped me to keep always an eye on the practical relevance of my work. Moreover, I am very grateful for the productive and entertaining debates with Professor Dr. Christian Becker and the valuable analyses and suggestions provided by Professor Dr. Michael Woywode as a member of my dissertation committee.

The strongest influence on both my work and my personal development, however, came from my colleagues at the Chair of General Management and Information Systems. With Thomas Kude and Christoph Schmidt, I was fortunate to have two friends as fellow researchers who also enjoyed working in my field of research and had different but equally justified perspectives on the same problems. Among other things, we conducted a large quantitative study together that yielded data sets and results for Christoph's dissertation, this book, and several further publications. Working with and learning from Thomas and Christoph was a great and very productive pleasure. But I also want to express my deep gratitude to my other current and former colleagues Okan Aydingül, Saskia Bick, Jens Förderer, Erik Hemmer, Lars Klimpke, Tommi Kramer, Miroslav Lazic, Nele Lüker, Tillmann Neben, Marko Nöhren, Alexander Scheerer, Sven Scheibmayr, Sebastian Stuckenberg, and Aliona von der Trenck who created an excellent atmosphere at the chair where I enjoyed coming to work every day.

My deepest gratitude goes to my closest friends and family for their advice and encouragement, especially to my uncle Gerd and my aunt Sabine, to my brother Nicolai, to my brother Andreas and his partner Kathrin, and to my parents Ralf and Christa. Above all, I thank my partner Simone for her patience and unconditional support during the past years.

Mannheim, Germany   Kai Spohrer
August 2015

Abbreviations

AFVIF	Average full collinearity variance inflation factor
AVE	Average variance extracted
AVIF	Average block variance inflation factor
CI	Continuous integration
COORD	Coordination
Cr.α	Cronbach's α
CRED	Credibility
DIV	Task diversity
ES	Effect size
EXTQ	External software quality
ICC	Intraclass correlation
INTQ	Internal software quality
IS	Information systems
ISD	Information systems development
IT	Information technology
MOD	Software modularity
NOV	Task novelty
OLS	Ordinary least squares
OS	Open source
OWNSHP	Code ownership
PCR	Peer code review
PLS	Partial least squares
PP	Pair programming
QUAL	Software quality
REF	Refactoring
REL	Relationship quality
RQ	Research question
SPEC	Specialization
TMS	Transactive memory system
VIF	Variance inflation factor
VOL	Task volatility

Contents

List of Figures

List of Tables

Chapter 1
Introduction

1.1 Problem Statement

"Two heads are better than one" may well be the most discussed proverb in information systems research (e.g., Balijepally et al. 2009; Dybå et al. 2007; Mangalaraj et al. 2014). Whereas information systems development (ISD) traditionally relied on well-defined processes, extensive documentation, and numerous distinctive roles, the movement of Agile Software Development overthrew this paradigm (Dingsøyr et al. 2012). It aimed for more flexibility and higher quality in ISD by radically embracing collaboration and empowerment of developers, active involvement of customers, and short development cycles (Cockburn and Williams 2002; Highsmith and Cockburn 2001). Today, these principles are widely adopted in industry (Dingsøyr et al. 2012) and the altered paradigm now regards teams of empowered developers as the decisive entities, also with respect to the quality of software. Consequently, contemporary ISD teams have accommodated quality assurance techniques in their daily routine that are based on the collaborative interactions of several developers on the same piece of source code (Dybå and Dingsøyr 2008). Such additional work on a single piece of code constitutes a major effort for developers and software developing companies. Numerous scholars have therefore investigated the question whether the application of collaborative quality assurance techniques is more effective than the task work of single developers, that is whether two heads are indeed better than one (Balijepally et al. 2009; Hannay et al. 2009; Mangalaraj et al. 2014; Vanhanen and Mäntylä 2013).

Findings of prior research on collaborative quality assurance techniques are contradictory and for this reason no conclusive judgment has been made about their effectiveness and efficiency (Vanhanen and Mäntylä 2013). The present study rests on the premise that these inconsistencies may result from an important shortcoming of extant literature: this stream of research has largely neglected the fact that collaborative quality assurance techniques are typically applied within the scope of an entire ISD team that is larger and more durable than the sub-group

© Springer International Publishing Switzerland 2016   1
K. Spohrer, *Collaborative Quality Assurance in Information Systems Development*,
Progress in IS, DOI 10.1007/978-3-319-25163-9_1

collaborating on a single task for quality assurance (Coman et al. 2014; Vanhanen 2011). Collaborative quality assurance techniques aim at capitalizing on the joint cognitive accomplishments of single developers, assuming that together they find more defects and achieve better solutions (Mangalaraj et al. 2014). At the same time, scholars have often argued that single developers may actually benefit from collaborative quality assurance by learning from their peers and even generating new knowledge (Salleh et al. 2011). Arguably, collaborative quality assurance may therefore not only impact the knowledge of individual developers but also how they coordinate their knowledge as a team, that is team cognition.

Research on team cognition and ISD techniques has grown over the last years but is still an emerging stream of literature (Mangalaraj et al. 2014). In fact, scholars have recently declared the connection of ISD techniques and the distributed cognition in ISD teams to one of the most enduring open questions in the information systems discipline (Davern et al. 2012). Nevertheless, team cognition is of paramount importance for ISD teams and their performance of knowledge-intensive work (Faraj and Sproull 2000; He et al. 2007; Kotlarsky and Oshri 2005; Maruping et al. 2009b). At the same time, prior research on collaborative quality assurance techniques has only rarely focused on team level effects and even less on team cognition. Rigorous examinations of collaborative quality assurance techniques were mostly centered around dyads of developers and focused on performance effects within these dyads. Particularly, studies on pair programming and peer code review provided very mixed results regarding the question whether these techniques lead to effective quality improvements or not (Arisholm et al. 2007; Balijepally et al. 2009; Hannay et al. 2009; Mangalaraj et al. 2014; Müller 2004, 2007; Rigby et al. 2008; Salleh et al. 2011; Williams et al. 2000). Aside from performance impacts, scholars have argued that collaborative quality assurance techniques have also other effects; more specifically, learnings of single team members and knowledge sharing between individual developers are broadly seen as positive outcomes of these techniques (e.g., Bacchelli and Bird 2013; Cockburn and Williams 2002; Dawande et al. 2008; Hulkko and Abrahamsson 2005; Rigby et al. 2012; Salleh et al. 2014, 2011; Vanhanen and Lassenius 2007; Vidgen and Wang 2009). However, rigorous investigations into such socio-cognitive effects and their, implicitly assumed, positive outcomes beyond the individual level are rare. Studies that approached the topic examined primarily relative expertise levels between members of dyads without deeper theoretical anchoring (cf. Chong and Hurlbutt 2007; Hannay et al. 2009; Mangalaraj et al. 2014; Plonka et al. 2015; Salleh et al. 2011). By consequence, it is still unclear whether and how team cognition is affected by the application of collaborative quality assurance techniques in ISD teams.

Aside from this gap in research, Conboy and Fitzgerald (2010) show that ISD practice rarely adopts entire ISD methods which incorporate several techniques. Although ISD teams evaluate the techniques they use against one another, there are no such things as inseparable clusters of techniques that only appear or disappear together (Conboy and Fitzgerald 2010). Instead, single techniques are applied selectively to complete specific tasks when teams deem them appropriate for doing so (Dybå and Dingsøyr 2008). Scholars have therefore argued for studying not entire methods but single ISD techniques in order to understand which activities of ISD teams really impact their performance (Erickson et al. 2005; Maruping et al. 2009b). However, prior research suggests that not even techniques are adopted in the same way by every team (Fitzgerald et al. 2006). Instead, ISD teams adapt single techniques to their needs and often go beyond applying a technique in its textbook version (Fitzgerald et al. 2006; Wang et al. 2012). In spite of this, many teams apparently end up with few distinct but similar patterns how they apply specific techniques (Wang et al. 2012). Whereas numerous prior studies have proposed adaptation patterns for entire ISD methods on an organizational level (cf. Dingsøyr et al. 2012), it is hitherto unclear why and how ISD teams adapt the application of specific ISD techniques to their needs. This appears even more important as scholars have argued that adapting techniques and other work practices is an essential feature of successful ISD teams (Lee and Xia 2010; Vidgen and Wang 2009). Research has also stated that contemporary ISD actually relies on the idea that ISD teams "have experience needed to define and adapt their processes appropriately" (Domino et al. 2007, p. 297). In light of this, team cognition may also play a major role in ISD teams' decision whether and how to apply ISD techniques. However, such assertions have not been investigated in detail. There is consequently considerable reason to discuss the role of team cognition in ISD teams with respect to the application of collaborative quality assurance techniques.

1.2 Research Objective

Based on the aforementioned gaps in research, this study seeks to answer recent calls for work that helps understand how ISD techniques relate to team cognition and how this relation affects the outcome of teamwork in ISD (Davern et al. 2012). In doing so, it focuses on collaborative quality assurance techniques as important ISD techniques that have frequently been argued to affect ISD teams' knowledge distribution and that depend on the knowledge of involved developers. First, this study seeks to explain the role of team cognition in the decision whether and how to apply ISD techniques. In particular, developers make such decisions on a task-by-task basis (Hulkko and Abrahamsson 2005), but why and how this happens is unclear. The present study consequently aims to answer the following research question:

1) How does team cognition affect the application of collaborative quality assurance techniques to tasks of ISD teams?

Moreover, the application of collaborative quality assurance techniques constitutes a major investment for ISD companies, but prior research has provided inconsistent results on whether these techniques do indeed improve software quality. This study argues that the neglect of the role of the team as a collective entity may actually be one reason for these inconsistencies and may have left important effects unaccounted for. According to extant research, each instance of collaborative quality assurance may change the knowledge distribution between involved developers (Salleh et al. 2011). Continuously applied over time and between different team members, collaborative quality assurance techniques may therefore possibly alter an entire ISD team's ability to collectively acquire, organize, and use knowledge for its tasks. This study therefore seeks to identify and explain the effects of collaborative quality assurance techniques on software quality and ISD team cognition. It therefore aims to explain the team level effects captured in the following questions:

2a) Why and how does the continued application of collaborative quality assurance techniques affect team cognition in ISD teams?
2b) Why and how does the continued application of collaborative quality assurance techniques affect ISD teams' software quality?

Answering these research questions, which are depicted graphically in Fig. 1.1, aims to provide a number of insights to research and practice. This study is one of the first to overcome the dearth of research on team cognition in relation to ISD techniques that was recently lamented by Davern et al. (2012). Combining two theoretical lenses, namely transactive memory systems theory and the concept of functional affordances, it provides an explanation how team cognition impacts the adoption of two specific and most popular collaborative quality assurance techniques, namely pair programming and peer code review. In doing so, this study attempts to understand why team cognition and properties of ISD techniques create the enabling and constraining factors for teams that decide whether to apply a technique. The present study also intends to add to literature on collaborative quality assurance techniques by considering the role of team cognition in the creation of quality effects. Creating and corroborating a mid-range theory which explains the emergent effects of collaborative quality assurance techniques, this study identifies and explains important and previously neglected influences on the effectiveness of these costly techniques. This supports research in further investigations and practice in the decision whether and how to conduct collaborative quality assurance.

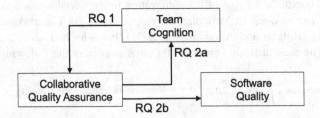

Fig. 1.1 Research questions

1.3   Research Focus and Design

In order to address the research questions stated above, this study focuses on *two widely adopted collaborative quality assurance techniques* and their use in *collocated ISD teams:* pair programming and peer code review. Pair programming is an ISD technique in which two developers work collaboratively on the same piece of software, sitting at a single workstation and communicating intensively (Balijepally et al. 2009; Coman et al. 2014; Wray 2010). Alternately, one of them takes the role of a *driver* who actively writes source code using the hardware while the other is "observing the work of the driver and identifying tactical and strategic deficiencies in their work" (Williams 2000, p. 3). Pair programming is by far the most widely adopted agile software development technique on a team level (Dybå and Dingsøyr 2008).

Using peer code review, source code is developed by one software engineer, the *author*, who submits this code to an electronic review system. Fellow developers then examine the code for its quality and correctness, propose changes, highlight defects, and recommend improvements (Bacchelli and Bird 2013; Rigby et al. 2012). Several rounds of reviews and revisions may be required before the *reviewers* are satisfied with the result. For many years, peer code review has been a central quality assurance technique in open-source communities (Liang and Mizuno 2011; Rigby and Storey 2011), and it has rapidly been gaining popularity in for-profit software companies such as Microsoft, Google, SAP, and AMD during the last years (Bacchelli and Bird 2013; Rigby et al. 2012; Rigby and Bird 2013; Sutherland and Venolia 2009). Both pair programming and peer code review come at a huge expense of resources invested in observing or reviewing, which has led to questions regarding their efficiency (Arisholm et al. 2007; Balijepally et al. 2009). Consequently, it appears crucial for ISD teams to understand the preconditions and consequences of applying these collaborative quality assurance techniques in order to determine how to use their resources effectively.

Focusing on these two techniques is particularly interesting for the present study because: (1) pair programming represents the most popular and widely-adopted collaborative quality assurance technique (Dybå and Dingsøyr 2008) whereas peer code review is used in the majority of open source software projects (Lee and Cole 2003; Rigby and Storey 2011); (2) practice and research have explored the proposition that peer code review may constitute a less costly substitute for pair programming (Müller 2004; Paulk 2001; Rigby et al. 2012); (3) research on either technique has proposed that it may cause learning effects that go beyond the individual level (Bacchelli and Bird 2013; Coman et al. 2014; Rigby and Bird 2013; Salleh et al. 2011); (4) whereas distributed teams may not be able to conduct all collaborative quality assurance techniques due to physical separation, collocated ISD teams can freely choose which technique to apply and may therefore help understand differential impacts.

This study takes the ontological and epistemological stance of critical realism and follows a sequential mixed-methods research design in which two qualitative investigations are followed by a phase of quantitative corroboration (for details see Sect. 3.2). Such a sequence of different research phases is recommendable as it allows the particular methods of single phases to compensate for shortcomings of methods in other phases (Mingers 2001; Venkatesh et al. 2013). Moreover, there is only a very limited body of knowledge applicable to answer the research questions of this study. For research streams in such an intermediate state, a mix of methods with a focus on qualitative elements appears most promising (Edmondson and McManus 2007). This entire study is further conducted with employees and ISD teams of a single, large enterprise software company which reduces the number and complexity of external factors involved in the study (Zachariadis et al. 2013). In a first phase of initial exploration, literature is reviewed and appropriate theoretical lenses are selected that guide subsequent steps. Qualitative data is collected from interviews with developers and from the attendance of trainings in collaborative quality assurance techniques at the case company. On this basis, an initial understanding is achieved how team cognition impacts the application of pair programming and peer code review on a task level. In a second phase, four in-depth case studies with ISD teams are conducted based on a variety of data sources including participatory observations, interviews with team members and stakeholders, and archival analyses of peer code review systems. This phase leads to a refined explanation how the adoption of pair programming and peer code review is affected by team cognition and the techniques' characteristics. Moreover, this phase serves to create a comprehensive mid-range theory that explains the emergent effects of the application of the techniques on team cognition. The third phase builds on this mid-range theory and incorporates it into research model for quantitative corroboration. Results from a questionnaire-based survey of more than 600 individuals associated with 81 ISD teams serve to reexamine the model and explain the quality effects of pair programming and peer code review. Figure 1.2 depicts these phases.

1.4   Study Organization

This study is divided into six chapters and reflects the research design outlined before. Chapter 2 first provides definitions of several core concepts of this study, including team cognition and collaborative quality assurance techniques. Subsequently, extant research on collaborative quality assurance techniques and team cognition is summarized and lays the foundation for the selection of two theoretical lenses: whereas transactive memory systems theory is immediately applicable to the research questions of this study, the concept of functional affordances is adapted to the examination of ISD techniques as opposed to technologies.

In Chap. 3, critical realism is introduced as an ontological and epistemological perspective that also guides the selection of an appropriate research design. Afterwards, the chapter gives a more detailed description of the single phases belonging to the mixed-methods research design.

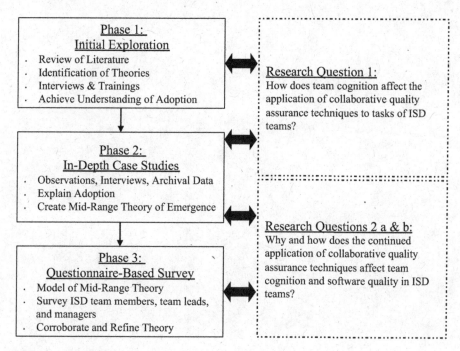

Fig. 1.2   Research design

Chapter 4 provides the findings of the research phases in their sequence, starting with results of the initial exploration. After presenting the results of the in-depth case studies and the resulting mid-range theory, hypotheses are developed and tested in the survey study.

Chapter 5 first summarizes and integrates the results of the three research phases into a coherent picture. Subsequently, implications and limitations of this study are discussed emphasizing on potential avenues for future research.

The study concludes with a brief summary in Chap. 6.

Chapter 2
Theoretical Foundations

In the following, this chapter provides the conceptual and theoretical foundations to investigate how team cognition affects the application of collaborative quality assurance techniques in ISD teams and how continued use of collaborative quality assurance techniques affects team cognition and team performance in turn. In a first step, core concepts of the investigation are defined. Subsequently, analyses of extant research on collaborative quality assurance techniques and team cognition in ISD teams are conducted. Based on these analyses, the theoretical lenses are selected that constitute the basis for the further investigations, namely the theory of transactive memory systems and the concept of functional affordances.

2.1 Definition of Core Concepts

Information systems development is concerned with the development of technologies that support people in gathering and processing information in various business contexts (Avison and Fitzgerald 2006; Heinrich et al. 2011). By consequence, it is a necessary requirement for this research endeavor to define the terms that relate to information and information systems precisely.

2.1.1 Information, Knowledge, and Team Cognition

The conceptual definition of information and knowledge has been subject to long, and yet ongoing, discussions in the information systems (IS) discipline. In fact, there is even dissent about the categories of different conceptualizations of information and knowledge (Alavi and Leidner 2001; Kettinger and Li 2010; McKinney et al. 2010). Some argue that the ongoing variety of conceptions of a core entity of

© Springer International Publishing Switzerland 2016   9
K. Spohrer, *Collaborative Quality Assurance in Information Systems Development*,
Progress in IS, DOI 10.1007/978-3-319-25163-9_2

the discipline actually blurs the meaning of scholarly work in IS and decreases the relevance of IS research (Hemmer and Heinzl 2011; Mingers 1995). Scholars often try to circumvent discussions about their perspective on information by not taking any position at all. Consequently, McKinney et al. (2010) argue that "[v]irtually all the extant IS literature fails to explicitly specify meaning for the very label that identifies it" (McKinney et al. 2010, p. 329). In the meanwhile, other disciplines established entire new research streams that are primarily concerned with philosophical questions of what information is and how it is used in today's society (Floridi 2002, 2005, 2011; Floridi and Illari 2014). Although Mingers (2013) shows that many of those philosophers' theoretical arguments have been discussed in IS literature decades ago, IS research may be in danger to lose the sovereignty of interpretation regarding one of its core concepts to the increasingly popular stream of information philosophy (cf. Floridi 2011).[1]

This study adopts a prominent view in IS research that takes a realist perspective on information (Alavi and Leidner 2001; Floridi 2008; Kettinger and Li 2010; Mingers 1995). In contrast to conceptualizations that consider information as data with meaning (McKinney et al. 2010), this study conforms to a viewpoint that grants information an objective existence in its own right without ontological dependencies on human interpretation (Alavi and Leidner 2001; Mingers 1995, 2013). As such, *information* is defined as the propositional content of a sign (Mingers 1995). Information is thereby seen as objective and as a property of a physical sign of events in reality. In other words, physical signs carry and transmit information about their causes and the consequences of their causes. Mingers (1995) describes this in the following way: "[information] exists whether or not there are people to observe or extract it, and it can be stored and transmitted by artifacts, e.g. books, newspapers, TV sets and computers. Information is different from the sign [...] The knock on the door causes someone to open it not because of its physical sound but because it carries the information that someone is there knocking" (Mingers 1995, p. 290). This implies that human beings generate meaning from information which is carried by signs. While there is objective, existing information, human beings cannot access this objective information directly because they are bound to their senses and cognition (Mingers 1995). When these actors process information in their minds, when they generate meaning from information, information becomes knowledge (Alavi and Leidner 2001). *Knowledge* is therefore the "result of cognitive processing triggered by the inflow of new stimuli" (Alavi and Leidner 2001, p. 109). While this knowledge, the meaning of information to a person, may not necessarily capture information entirely and exactly, it can be expressed in words, text, graphics or other symbolic forms, thereby becoming new information (Alavi and Leidner 2001). Actors interpret information based on their various backgrounds and dispositions.

---

[1]There are several summaries of extant definitions as well as conceptual discussions of these definitions and their consequences (e.g., Alavi and Leidner 2001; Floridi 2005, 2011; Hemmer and Heinzl 2011; Kettinger and Li 2010; McKinney et al. 2010; Mingers 1995, 2013). However, this discussion is not at the core of the present study and is therefore not addressed any further.

If these are similar, the actors also create similar knowledge or meaning from the same information. That is, knowledge is confined to individuals' minds but it is *intersubjective* in the sense that individuals can generate similar meaning from the same information (Mingers 1995).

Prior research distinguishes most prominently two social activities that refer to the intentional communication of knowledge between individuals. As such, Tiwana and Mclean (2005) define *knowledge transfer* as the "transmission of knowledge from one individual to another" and *knowledge sharing* as "a more limited instance of knowledge transfer: It involves revealing the presence of pertinent knowledge without necessarily transmitting it in its entirety" (Tiwana and Mclean 2005, p. 18). This study acknowledges that, based on the above definition of knowledge, a transfer of knowledge is strictly speaking impossible for two reasons: (1) knowledge is subjective and confined to the mind of a single actor; (2) even if communication between two actors, a sender and a receiver, succeeds in creating similar meaning of information for the receiver, extant knowledge does not immediately leave the sender. Nevertheless, individuals can express themselves in the intent to communicate the meaning of a piece of information to another individual. Converting knowledge of a sender to information and information to knowledge of a receiver is conceivably more complex than the definition given by Tiwana and Mclean (2005). Importantly, there is no guarantee that the same meaning is conceived by both individuals, but common experience and background make it possible to grasp intersubjectively nearly equal meanings. This study therefore adopts the terms of knowledge transfer and knowledge sharing but acknowledges the mentioned restrictions and their inherently higher complexity than some prior literature suggests.

Prior research also differentiates specific *types of knowledge*, either by their prag-matic value or by content domains. For example, Floridi (2010, p. 49) distinguishes factual and instructional information, whereas Heinrich et al. (2011) delineate factual from procedural knowledge. For these authors, the differentiating element of different knowledge types lies in their pragmatic impact: while adding information to one's factual knowledge stock only keeps actors informed about the state of the world, procedural knowledge allows actors to apply more generic problem-solving strategies to multiple concrete problems (Heinrich et al. 2011, p. 158). Differentiating by content domains, researchers in ISD contrastingly propose that software development requires specific types of knowledge as opposed to other business activities (Kang and Hahn 2009). As such, Faraj and Sproull (2000) state that software developers need knowledge about technologies they work with, knowledge about the development process or method they follow, and application domain knowledge of their customers' needs and their products. Several other scholars also rely on this conceptualization (Kang and Hahn 2009). Tiwana (2004) differentiates only technical and domain knowledge, whereas Espinosa et al. (2007) conceptualize knowledge about one's team and knowledge about one's tasks as the central knowledge types for software developers. When referring to knowledge in ISD, this study refers to technical knowledge, domain knowledge, and process knowledge in line with Faraj and Sproull (2000). However, for the behaviors and events investigated in this study, a differentiation between the three does not appear necessary and is not made in the following. What Espinosa et al. (2007) describe as team knowledge is to large extents knowledge about team members' knowledge. The present study refers to the latter as *meta-knowledge*.

A concept closely related to knowledge is expertise. *Expertise* is defined as "the specialized skills and knowledge that an individual brings to the team's task" (Faraj and Sproull 2000, p. 1555). It is thereby a relational concept between the tasks of a work group and different actors, who possess qualitatively and quantitatively different skills and knowledge. A group member who has expertise consequently stands out in the group for being particularly equipped to perform a specific task successfully. Other group members may have less or no skills and knowledge that allow for performing this task. The present study refers to *specialized expertise* when talking about task-relevant skills and knowledge that are held exclusively by a single team member whereas *expertise* is used as an expression to signify that single other group members (i.e., a minority of members of a group) may possess equal resources.

Lastly, the term *cognition* refers to "the activity of knowing: the acquisition, organization and use of knowledge [...] involving both processes and knowledge structures" (Davern et al. 2012, p. 292). According to this view on cognition as an individual level phenomenon, scholars argue that groups of actors develop a collective form of cognition that allows them to benefit from the cognitive accomplishments of their single members (Edmondson et al. 2007; Goodman and Dabbish 2011; Spohrer et al. 2012). This study refers to *team cognition* as an interpersonal mechanism for collectively acquiring, organizing, and using knowledge to perform tasks in a work group. Extant literature contains several different conceptualizations of team cognition that are analyzed in more detail in Sect. 2.3.

2.1.2 Information Systems Development

Information systems are defined as the "means by which people and organizations, utilizing technology, gather, process, store, use and disseminate information" (Ward and Peppard 2002, p. 3). Information systems are therefore complex, socio-technical systems that encompass the interactions of information technologies, organizational tasks, and human actors (Heinrich et al. 2011; Krcmar 2005). In this context, information technologies refer to the hardware, software, and computer networks to which human actors attribute qualities that make them appropriate means to achieve the actors' goals. Information systems development then constitutes the process of creating technological solutions that support human actors in achieving their goals with respect to their organizational tasks.

Commonly, ISD is seen as a sequence of steps that are conducted by a number of different actors and range from the elicitation of customer requirements over the design of a technological solution, its implementation and validation, to the delivery of the solution to a customer (Avison and Fitzgerald 2006). While the development of an information system can also encompass the creation of hardware, this study focuses on the development of software artefacts as part of an information system. In particular, this study concentrates on the phase of software implementation.[2]

ISD requires a broad variety of knowledge about the problem domain, technologies, as well as the software development process (Faraj and Sproull 2000). Consequently, software developers are grouped in ISD teams to combine their cognitive abilities for a joint creation of software products (Sawyer et al. 2010). While much research on ISD emphasizes on the technical aspects of the process, some scholars also acknowledge that social and cognitive activities reside at the core of ISD (Sawyer et al. 2010). Davern et al. put it as follows: "Creating a software system is fundamentally a cognitive endeavor; software itself has been described as 'pure thought-stuff, infinitely malleable' [...]. By implication, software is an outgrowth of human cognition" (Davern et al. 2012, p. 278). In the light of such assertions, it appears promising to examine ISD teams and their activities from a perspective of team cognition. In fact, Davern et al. (2012) ask for exactly that.

In more detail, this study examines the use and the effects of collaborative quality assurance techniques in ISD teams, namely of pair programming and peer code review. Avison and Fitzgerald (2006) define an ISD technique as a way of doing a particular activity in the ISD process. A combination of several ISD techniques is then called a *method*. The authors highlight that techniques may involve the use of information technology (IT) artifacts such as software, that have often been developed for a specific technique (Avison and Fitzgerald 2006, p. 21). Less broadly than this definition of an ISD technique, Mingers (2001) defines what constitutes a technique in research. As such, research techniques, for example the analysis of a survey, are seen as basic research activities that "are generally well-defined sequences of operations that if carried out proficiently yield predictable results" (Mingers 2001, p. 241). This study adapts the latter perspective and defines an *ISD technique* as a well-defined sequence of operations in the ISD process which may rely on specific technologies and which, if carried out proficiently, yields predictable results.

Practice often groups ISD techniques into bundles with guidelines for their application that are called ISD methods (Avison and Fitzgerald 2006). Exemplary famous ISD methods include Extreme Programming and Scrum (Beck 2000; Cockburn and Williams 2002; Schwaber and Beedle 2002). However, some scholars argue that these bundles are seldom adopted in their entirety and that the study of single ISD techniques may therefore be more beneficial (Conboy and Fitzgerald 2010; Maruping et al. 2009b). In line with this reasoning, the present study is primarily interested in the application and the effects of collaborative quality assurance techniques.

---

[2]For reasons of simplicity and in line with much prior research, this study uses the term *ISD* from here on to refer to software development only, ignoring that also hardware and data can be subject to development in ISD.

2.1.3 Software Quality

The definition of software quality is a controversial topic in practice (e.g., Mc Connell 2004) and research (e.g., Balzert 2009; Ravichandran and Rai 2000). Early intents to measure software quality date back to the 1970s when Mc Call et al. (1977) and Boehm et al. (1978) provided their software quality models. Essentially, these models define taxonomies and metrics for software characteristics that are argued to represent software quality. As such, Boehm et al. (1978) define seven quality factors, or high level quality attributes, that are broken down further to be measured on a lower level. These quality factors are: portability, reliability, efficiency, usability, testability, understandability, and flexibility (Boehm et al. 1978). Further developments of this work resulted in the ISO standard for software product quality ISO 9126 (Ambrose and Chiravuri 2010). From this perspective, software quality is a bundle of measurable attributes of a software product for which the customer holds a positive value (Ambrose and Chiravuri 2010; Gopal et al. 2011). Software quality is therefore clearly more than the absence of defects and not only depends on explicitly specified functional customer requirements but also depends on explicit and implicit non-functional requirements (Sommerville 2012, p. 712). Additionally, software quality can be conceptualized very differently on different levels of abstraction and from different organizational viewpoints (Rai et al. 1998; Ravichandran and Rai 2000; von Hellens 1997). This study defines *software quality* as the compliance to the requirements of external as well as internal stakeholders of a software under development, i.e. as the sum of internal and external software quality (Mc Connell 2004). Internal software quality refers to properties of a software product's source code that facilitate its maintenance over time and flexibility for future changes (Mc Connell 2004, p. 483). This includes that source code be written, formatted, and documented in a way that allows for grasping its purpose and implementation specifics, thereby facilitating the identification of hidden flaws, changes, and extensions in the future. In addition, external quality refers to the fulfillment of customer demands in that it is responsive to user needs and is efficient in its operation (Liang et al. 2010).

Other scholars, moreover, acknowledge that the total quality of an information system is not solely determined by product quality characteristics of the end result but also by the process quality during its development (Heinrich et al. 2011, p. 242). For example, intermediary activities and documents such as the requirements specification of a software strongly influence the final product and whether it complies to the customer's needs (Schmitz et al. 1982, p. 18). Based on this reasoning, *software quality assurance* does not focus exclusively on controlling the characteristics of the final software product but also comprises measures for managing the software development process (Ravichandran and Rai 2000; Ambrose and Chiravuri 2010; Rai et al. 1998). In literature, some scholars refer to software quality assurance as the procedures, processes, and standards that assure the achievement of software quality during software implementation, whereas others see software quality assurance as activities such as product verification and validation that are typically conducted after an ISD team has delivered the result of its work (Sommerville 2012, p. 709). In fact, the latter is the more traditional view, particularly in software engineering literature; it holds that software quality assurance is an activity of the ISD function that is separate from actual software development and is conducted by experts outside the single ISD teams (Balzert 2009, p. 19). The contemporary ISD paradigm of agile software development, by contrast, emphasizes much more on the responsibility of ISD teams for assuring software quality throughout the different activities of ISD (Beck 2000; Dingsøyr et al. 2012; Schmidt et al. 2012). While literature on software quality assurance contains numerous valuable technical, managerial, and organizational insights into and solutions for different aspects of quality assurance (for comprehensive reviews see Ambrose and Chiravuri 2010; Rai et al. 1998), the question of how to balance the significant efforts for software quality assurance with investments in other value-creating activities is still pressing for research and practice (Karg et al. 2011). This study aims to contribute to software quality assurance literature by shedding light on the effects of two widely adopted collaborative quality assurance techniques on software quality and team cognition.

2.1.4 Collaborative Quality Assurance Techniques

Based on the above definitions of ISD techniques and software quality, the present study refers to *collaborative quality assurance techniques* as ISD techniques that are jointly carried out by two or more software developers from the same team during daily routine in order to ensure the acceptable quality of one another's source code. Collaborative quality assurance techniques became necessary, and actually desired, with the appearance of agile software development (Dybå and Dingsøyr 2008). In traditional ISD, assuring the quality of newly implemented source code was primarily the task of dedicated testers and quality managers (cf. Balzert 2009). Contemporary ISD, based on the ideas of agile software development, by contrast, regards teams of empowered developers as the decisive entities, also with respect to quality. Consequently, agile ISD teams need to take care of assuring the quality of the source code produced by their single members. On the one hand, this may be done based on technical solutions such as extensive test suits, adequate testing processes, and supportive technology (Beck 2000; Hildenbrand 2008). On the other hand, teams may rely on techniques based more on human interaction and collaboration such as pair programming and peer code review.

In fact, pair programming is one of the most prominent techniques in agile software development literature and is part of a bundle of techniques in the most popular development method *Extreme Programming* (Beck 2000; Dingsøyr et al. 2012; Erickson et al. 2005). Pair programming is an ISD technique in which two developers work collaboratively on the same piece of software, located at a single computer and using a single set of input devices (Balijepally et al. 2009). Alternately, one of them takes the role of a *driver* who actively writes source code using the hardware while the other is "observing the work of the driver and identifying tactical and strategic deficiencies in their work" (Williams 2000, p. 3). While pair programming is by far the most widely adopted agile software development technique on a team level (Balijepally et al. 2009), it is not applied homogeneously in all teams. Scholars emphasize that pair programming does not always "follow all the constraints of formal pair programming" (Coman et al. 2014, p. 131). Wray (2010) argues that a variety of practices has been labeled as pair programming, but he states that there is a common core to all these instances of pair programming. This view of a common core is recognized today by most scholars (e.g., Coman et al. 2014; Mangalaraj et al. 2014; Vanhanen and Mäntylä 2013; Wray 2010) and it is also the working definition of pair programming of this study. *Pair programming* is an ISD technique in which two software developers design, code, and test a piece of software at one computer actively communicating with each other.

Peer code review is the second collaborative quality assurance technique in the focus of this study. It constitutes an ISD technique that allows for critically discussing newly developed code before it is included in the shared code base of an ISD team. This technique is not dissimilar to academic peer review (Beller et al. 2014). Peer code review originates from the open source context where communities apply peer code review as a central quality assurance mechanism and as a mechanism for organizational learning (Lee and Cole 2003; McIntosh et al. 2014). It is therefore conducted asynchronously and based on a mediating information system for peer code reviews (i.e., a peer code review system). Similar to pair programming, research on peer code review highlights that peer code review is often instantiated differently, but some key characteristics are argued to exist in general (Rigby and Bird 2013). According to Rigby and Bird (2013), the core of *peer code review*, and hereby also the working definition for this study, consists of three sequential operations: first, when a developer (i.e., the author) has created a piece of software (i.e., a code change) he or she submits it to an ISD team's peer code review system for review. Second, one or more other developers (i.e., the reviewers) review the code change and note their critique in the system in written text, giving the author the chance to revise the code change and resubmit it if necessary. This sequence of review and revision can take several iterations until, third, the reviewers either accept the code change and include it in the team's shared code base or reject it entirely.

Peer code review is therefore different from classical code inspections as defined by Fagan (1986). It is less formal than code inspections and does not require large physical meetings but is instead part of ISD teams' daily routine and conducted via a peer code review system (Wang and Carroll 2011). Extant research accordingly uses a number of synonyms for peer code review that include *lightweight code review* (Rigby and Storey 2011), and *modern code review* (Beller et al. 2014; Pangsakulyanont et al. 2014). In fact, some scholars argue that peer code review shares more commonalities with pair programming than with traditional code inspections (Rigby et al. 2012).

This study focuses on collocated ISD teams; the members of these teams work physically close to one another, typically in the same office. By consequence, such teams can basically apply either collaborative quality assurance technique without restrictions of physical distribution. In spite of calls from research and practice (Müller 2004; Paulk 2001), surprisingly few scholars have endeavored to compare the two techniques for their effects on ISD teams. Moreover, it is unclear why there appear to be large differences in the ways that ISD techniques are applied in different contexts on the one hand (Conboy and Fitzgerald 2010) whereas there are frequent patterns of similar applications, a common core, on the other hand (Rigby and Bird 2013; Wray 2010). In order to shed light on these questions, this study subsequently presents extant research on collaborative quality assurance techniques.

2.2 Prior Work on Collaborative Quality Assurance Techniques

There is quite a substantive and yet growing amount of publications on pair programming. It draws attention in the fields of IS (Balijepally et al. 2009; Erickson et al. 2005; Mangalaraj et al. 2014), empirical software engineering (Dingsøyr et al. 2012; Dybå and Dingsøyr 2008; Dybå et al. 2007; Vanhanen and Mäntylä 2013) as well as in education (Hanks et al. 2011; Salleh et al. 2011). In fact, there are decade-old calls for structuring and aggregating the abundance of results in pair programming research (Gallis et al. 2003; Hulkko and Abrahamsson 2005). Following these calls, Salleh et al. (2011) and Hanks et al. (2011) review more than 75 studies on pair programming in educational settings. Hannay et al. (2009), Di Bella et al. (2013), and Mangalaraj et al. (2014) review more than 30 experimental studies in educational settings as well as with professional software developers. Vanhanen and Mäntylä (2013) summarize results from more than 170 quantitative and qualitative empirical studies conducted with professional ISD personnel. Lastly, a number of dissertations focuses on pair programming (Sun 2011; Vanhanen 2011; Williams 2000).

In stark contrast to this extensive body of literature on pair programming, peer code review traditionally receives only little but increasing attention (Beller et al. 2014; Bosu and Carver 2014; Rigby 2011; Rigby and Bird 2013; Thongtanunam et al. 2015). Peer code review has found broad reception in industry in ISD teams of numerous software developing companies such as Google, SAP, Erickson, Sony, Facebook, Microsoft, and AMD to name but a few (Bacchelli and Bird 2013; Rigby and Bird 2013). Despite of this adoption in industry, extant research on peer code review primarily focuses on the open source context, the setting from which this technique originates and where it constitutes a central and successful mechanism to assure the quality of source code developed by globally distributed and loosely connected individuals (Beller et al. 2014; Liang and Mizuno 2011; McIntosh et al. 2014; Rigby et al. 2008; Rigby and Storey 2011; Sutherland and Venolia 2009).

However, open source communities differ from for-profit work groups in many characteristics (Daniel et al. 2012). Consequently, extant studies are often concerned with aspects of peer code review that are idiosyncratic to the open source context such as gaining reputation in a community (Bosu and Carver 2014), examining the structure of large developer networks (Yang 2014), and managing the sheer amount of review comments in huge open source communities (Pangsakulyanont et al. 2014; Thongtanunam et al. 2014, 2015). Table A.1 of the appendix provides a brief overview of the small extant stream of literature on peer code review.

Traditionally, software engineering research does not draw strongly on existing theory to explain or hypothesize empirical findings (Hannay et al. 2007). This is also reflected in research on pair programming and peer code review. By and large, this body of empirical investigations is free of theory in that the studies do not provide causal explanations why the events they observe empirically actually occur.[3] Extremely few of the studies incorporate theoretical arguments that go beyond ad-hoc reasoning; only the authors of literature reviews and meta-studies cited above partially rely on group work theory to justify their aggregations of extant results (e.g., Gallis et al. 2003; Hannay et al. 2009). In the following, this study presents the results of prior work on pair programming and peer code review that are of relevance to its research questions. While not all results of prior empirical work are presented in detail, the few exceptions that rely on theoretical arguments in their investigations are mentioned explicitly.

2.2.1 Adoption and Appropriation

While the ISD technique of pair programming has been proposed more than two decades ago, adoption in industry has increased strongly during the first years of the trend of agile ISD and especially with the advent of the *Extreme Programming* method (Balijepally et al. 2009; Beck 2000; Dingsøyr et al. 2012; Dybå and Dingsøyr 2008; Erickson et al. 2005; Flor and Hutchins 1991; Nosek 1998; Williams et al. 2000). Today, pair programming is one of the most wide-spread ISD techniques in industry and has gained extensive attention of both practitioners and researchers (Dingsøyr et al. 2012; Erickson et al. 2005). Especially during the early years of this millennium, many researchers were engaged with studies on the adoption of agile ISD methods (Dybå and Dingsøyr 2008). However, ISD teams and organizations do not necessarily adopt entire methods in an all-or-none fashion. Instead, these actors may carefully decide about every single technique whether it

---

[3]While there has been a long and ongoing debate of what constitutes strong theory, causal mechanisms are an important element of nearly all definitions of theory (cf. Avgerou 2013; Bacharach 1989; Gregor 2006; Sutton and Straw 1995; Whetten 1989). This study conforms to a critical realist view of ontology and epistemology and seeks theory that explains the causal relationships of events in the domain of the real (Mingers et al. 2013).

suits their needs, and "an a la carte selection and tailoring of practices can work very well" (Fitzgerald et al. 2006, p. 200). Research nevertheless often focuses on entire development methods such as Extreme Programming that consist of a variety of different techniques, values, goals, and artifacts (Conboy and Fitzgerald 2010) to examine their introduction, effects, but also their adaptation (cf. Conboy and Fitzgerald 2010; Lee and Xia 2010; Maruping et al. 2009a). Thereby, scholars often concentrate on conglomerates of techniques and produce normative results regarding the adaptation during initial adoption of these conglomerates (for an overview see Conboy and Fitzgerald 2010, pp. 6–7).

However, teams that have at least minimal levels of autonomy, which is common in ISD industry (Janz and Prasarnphanich 2003, 2009), can actively decide whether and when to apply a specific technique and can react to changes in their needs by applying techniques accordingly. In fact, some scholars argue that adapting techniques and work practices is an essential feature of successful ISD teams (Lee and Xia 2010; Vidgen and Wang 2009). Research shows, for example, that adopting pair programming is not a dichotomous decision, but can be done gradually, and is consciously reflected on by ISD teams (Domino et al. 2007; Vanhanen 2011). This is in line with the commonly held statement that ISD teams decide on a task-by-task basis whether to apply pair programming (Hulkko and Abrahamsson 2005). Wang et al. (2012) accordingly examine the adoption of several development techniques clustered under the labels of Extreme Programming and Scrum, pair programming being one of them. These scholars show, based on literature on innovation assimilation, that the respective techniques can be adopted to varying degrees. They conceptualize the strongest form of adoption of a certain technique as its routinized use in a "comprehensive or sophisticated manner" (Wang et al. 2012, p. 450) where sophistication refers to a strong adaption of the technique to the ISD team's needs or using it for tasks that it was not preconceived for.

Much prior literature refers to this behavior as *appropriation*, and also technology is often found to be appropriated in such a way (DeSanctis and Poole 1994; Markus and Silver 2008). Dourish (2003) defines appropriation as "the way in which technologies are adopted, adapted and incorporated into working practice. This might involve customisation [. . .], but it might also simply involve making use of the technology for purposes beyond those for which it was originally designed, or to serve new ends" (Dourish 2003, p. 466). Accordingly, this study refers to the adoption of ISD techniques, their adaptation and their application towards new ends as *appropriation*.

While frequently acknowledged, the actual *appropriation of pair programming* is not often a topic in literature (Vanhanen 2011). Bahli (2005) relies on the technology acceptance model and theory on knowledge creation to study the adoption of Extreme Programming. He finds that techniques of Extreme Programming, such as pair programming, facilitate task-based communication between single developers as well as between developers and users. Bahli (2005) suggests that developers adopt and adapt techniques to a large degree depending on their perceived needs for knowledge. Domino et al. (2007) find that adapting pair programming to the needs of single teams is common in practice and has a large impact on the effectiveness of pair programming in each setting. In fact, they see the freedom to adapt techniques as a core part of agile ISD, arguing that "developers have experience needed to define and adapt their processes appropriately" (Domino et al. 2007, p. 297). Vanhanen et al. (2007) show that on the one hand unfavorable organizational settings can discourage developers from making use of pair programming (e.g., by reward systems that explicitly value only solo work); on the other hand, they show that simply rephrasing descriptions of pair programming given to developers to create "a more positive atmosphere" can alone increase adoption rates (Vanhanen et al. 2007, p. 6). Looking specifically at backup behaviors in developer interactions, Coman et al. (2014) find that developers can become involved in pair programming sessions to different degrees: while developers are sometimes found to collaboratively invest major efforts to fully solve a problem as a pair, there are also situations of cooperative pair programming in which one developer only adds small pieces to the solution of the partner's task. The authors emphasize that interaction patterns between developers can conform more or less to the formal definition of pair programming, but some characteristic elements apparently always stay the same: "they certainly shared between them the same computer, monitor, keyboard and mouse, focusing on the same particular issue that they wanted to solve" (Coman et al. 2014, p. 131). Similarly, Hulkko and Abrahamsson (2005) explicate the motivations for pair programming that are recurrently found in ISD practice and cited in literature: developers apply pair programming because they find it suitable for learning, discovering little mistakes, and solving problems together in ways they would not go alone. This pattern is quite recurrent across pair programming literature (Arisholm et al. 2007; Hannay et al. 2009; Vanhanen and Lassenius 2005; Williams and Kessler 2000).

Empirical research on *peer code review appropriation* remains largely in a descriptive state and is to the largest part based on data from open source communities. However, some scholars indeed scrutinize the specific appropriation patterns that can be found in different communities (Beller et al. 2014; Liang and Mizuno 2011; McIntosh et al. 2014; Rigby 2011; Rigby et al. 2008; Rigby and Storey 2011; Yang 2014). Others compare these patterns to peer code review appropriation in professional ISD teams (Bacchelli and Bird 2013; Rigby and Bird 2013), and try to transfer knowledge from open source communities to industry based on lessons learned (Rigby et al. 2012). The single open source communities are found to differ with regard to several characteristic details in their use of peer code review. These details include the timing and frequency of peer code reviews, the size and modularity of contributions to review, the number of reviewers, the additional roles that reviewers take, and the selection process for reviewers (Beller et al. 2014; Bettenburg et al. 2013; Rigby et al. 2008; Yang 2014). Thongtanunam et al. (2015) acknowledge that finding reviewers with appropriate expertise can be a complicated task in open source communities. Rigby and Storey (2011) highlight that reviewer participation in all open source projects is voluntary, but the mechanisms for stimulating reviewers differ. While some communities rely on invitations that authors send to renown experts, other communities rely purely on broadcast review requests. That is, once a code change is uploaded to the review system, an entire list of developers is automatically notified of this situation, thereby creating very a large group of potential reviewers. Based on their expertise and personal interest in a piece of code, these developers make a decision whether to review a change personally or leave others to do it (Rigby and Storey 2011). Bosu and Carver (2014) show that an author's reputation in an open source community, which is indicated by his/her position in the community's social network structure, influences whether and how fast reviewers respond to review requests. Peer code review can take significantly longer for contributions from peripheral authors because reviewers do not volunteer quickly to examine their code (Bosu and Carver 2014). As one of the scarce studies in organizational contexts, Bacchelli and Bird (2013) examine motivations, challenges, and outcomes of peer code review based on a broad analysis of quantitative and qualitative data. Research on collocated teams has emphasized that developers heavily adapt their review strategies depending on their a-priori understanding of a code change: where reviewers have expertise in the code areas of a software in which a code change is situated, they are found to engage in more in-depth and critical reviews than in code areas where they possess only passing knowledge (Bacchelli and Bird 2013; Sutherland and Venolia 2009). When reviewers cannot satisfy their need for understanding specifics of a code change, they may even cancel the code review and try to engage in face-to-face communication with the author instead (Sutherland and Venolia 2009). This is in line with the arguments of Rigby et al. (2012) who make an effort of transferring lessons learned from open source settings to code review in ISD companies. They stress the need for appropriate expertise of a reviewer and recommend that developers should decide themselves if their expertise is helpful for a given code change (Rigby et al. 2012). Bacchelli and Bird (2013) further show that developers' primary motivation to engage in peer code review, both as authors and as reviewers, concerns the elicitation of defects and the improvement of the solutions codified in a piece of source code. However, they also highlight that developers appear to be motivated by the knowledge gains they can draw from reviews and expertise they can provide to colleagues (Bacchelli and Bird 2013). Interestingly, this is also in line with the motivational reasons of peer code review provided in open source communities (Rigby 2011; Rigby et al. 2012). Lastly, Rigby and Bird (2013) emphasize on the broad diversity of ways how peer code review is conducted in open source and commercial projects they study, but they also show that across all areas, a core of a lightweight peer code review process has apparently emerged which is common to open source as well as for-profit settings. In line with such reasoning, Beller et al. (2014) state: "Surprisingly, results show that the types of changes due to the MCR [modern code review] process in OSS are strikingly similar to those in the industry and academic systems from literature" (Beller et al. 2014, p. 202).

There is consequently evidence as well as frequent acknowledgement that pair programming and peer code review, like other ISD techniques, can be appropriated in different ways by professional ISD teams. Scholars state that these appropriations appear to be closely related to task and team characteristics (Bacchelli and Bird 2013; Rigby and Bird 2013; Coman et al. 2014). In fact, appropriations are often mentioned together with expertise and knowledge requirements of single developers (e.g., Coman et al. 2014; Rigby et al. 2012). Prior research suggests that there appear to be consciously reflected elements (Domino et al. 2007) as well as subconsciously enacted elements (Vanhanen et al. 2007) to these appropriation behaviors. Moreover, scholars highlight that, despite all freedom for appropriation, there are patterns of appropriation that are found recurrently. Some elements of the techniques appear even to be stable and generally present in all settings (Coman et al. 2014; Hulkko and Abrahamsson 2005; Rigby and Dird 2013). Extant research, however, does not consider the theoretical question why this is actually the case for collaborative quality assurance techniques or any other ISD techniques. It appears consequently necessary to investigate more closely why and how collaborative quality assurance techniques are appropriated in different ways and why there are stable elements that are not subject to appropriation.

2.2.2   Application and Outcome Effects

Research on pair programming follows a long empirical tradition of searching for outcome effects (e.g., Balijepally et al. 2009; Müller 2006, 2007; Nosek 1998). In particular, large numbers of studies engage in comparing pairs of programmers to solo programmers with respect to a number of outcome variables (Mangalaraj et al. 2014). Together these investigations constitute a broad and inconsistent body of results (for reviews see Di Bella et al. 2013; Hannay et al. 2009; Salleh et al. 2011; Vanhanen and Mäntylä 2013). Many scholars lament the absence of a true cumulative tradition and the lack of an underlying theoretical lens that would allow for putting contradicting results into context (e.g., Di Bella et al. 2013; Gallis et al. 2003). Due to these shortcomings, inconsistent results can to date not be traced back to causal differences, and proposed explanations remain primarily ad-hoc.

For example, Di Bella et al. (2013) review 30 rigorous empirical studies on pair programming for identified quality effects. They find that no general conclusions can be drawn about the effects of pair programming on the quality of produced results due to empirical diversity with respect to: (1) the consisting of students on the one and professional developers on the other hand; (2) performed tasks of software development, primarily design, coding, maintenance or testing; and (3) a number of further context variables (Di Bella et al. 2013). Di Bella et al. (2013) further add to this literature by conducting a longitudinal case study in a professional ISD team. They find that pair programming leads to only slightly less defects than solo programming but to increased effort. Hannay et al. (2009) conduct a meta-analysis of 18 experimental studies. Their results suggest that task complexity constitutes a relevant moderator of the outcome effects that pair programming is frequently argued to exhibit. The authors find pair programming to lead to faster task completion at lower quality than solo programming if a task exhibits only low complexity. In case of high task complexity, pairs of developers are found to create higher quality results which however require significantly higher effort than solo programming. At the same time, the authors state that pair programming simply seems to work well in some settings whereas it does not work well in others (Hannay et al. 2009). Salleh et al. (2011) review 74 studies on pair programming as a pedagogical technique that aims at improving not necessarily only task outcomes during pair programming but also at individual learning of students beyond a single task. They find a very mixed picture of pair programming effectiveness in educational research. While they clearly show that pair programming students are more satisfied with both their work results as well as the way of achieving them, findings regarding technical or academic performance are inconsistent: for nearly all measures of effectiveness, Salleh et al. (2011) find prior results to be inconsistent with some studies claiming positive and some claiming negative effects. Effectiveness measures include the time spent for task solution, the number of defects produced, expert opinions on code quality, functional correctness as well as a number of indicators for short-term academic performance (e.g., course and exam grades). However, the authors find that results are consistently supporting the assertion that pair programming can be used to educate less knowledgeable students relying on knowledge and programming skills of more knowledgeable partners. Salleh et al. (2011) emphasize that relative expertise and programming skills of pair programming partners appears to be a strong predictor of pair performance. Where expertise levels differ strongly, pairs are found to perform significantly worse than solo programmers (Salleh et al. 2011). This finding is also corroborated by prior meta-analyses and direct experiments (Arisholm et al. 2007; Hannay et al. 2009). Similarly, Vanhanen and Mäntylä (2013) examine more than 150 empirical studies with professional software developers. They show that the vast majority of empirical industry studies reports on pair programming as affecting knowledge distributions. However, rigorous empirical studies on this topic, let alone studies with a theoretical underpinning, are nearly non-existent (Mangalaraj et al. 2014; Plonka et al. 2015).

Focusing more on these knowledge effects, Plonka et al. (2015) study knowledge sharing behaviors between pair programmers based on the theory of cognitive apprenticeship. They emphasize on the existence of learning opportunities for individuals, independent of their expertise levels. Even expert developers who pair program with novice colleagues are found to learn from reflection during pair programming as they verbalize and explain their strategies to their partners. Plonka et al. (2015) theorize that specific, inherently adopted teaching behaviors foster cognitive impacts and knowledge transfer between pair programmers but also account for much of the frequently mentioned efforts that make pair programming across expertise levels less productive and more tiring for the pair (e.g., Salleh et al. 2011; Vanhanen 2011).

Authors of more recent studies on pair programming strive to create a better, theory-based understanding of the mechanisms that underlie pair programmers' activities and knowledge exchange to resolve issues of prior, inconsistent results. As such, Balijepally et al. (2009) and Mangalaraj et al. (2014) work in the tradition of Flor and Hutchins (1991), studying pair programming from a perspective of distributed cognition. They theorize that by relying on each other as well as on additional artifacts, pair programmers extend their individual cognitive capacities.

As this helps less proficient pair programmers more than their experienced partners, pairs are found to achieve better quality than their weaker but not better than their stronger individual members (Balijepally et al. 2009; Mangalaraj et al. 2014). Coman et al. (2014) look at pair programming in ISD teams from a backup behavior perspective. Their results suggest that task and team characteristics are decisive for the outcome effects of pair programming: where tasks require cooperative interaction of team members (i.e., major pieces of one team member's but only small pieces of another's knowledge), pair programming incurs more costs than benefits (Coman et al. 2014).

With regard to the *application and outcome of peer code review*, the majority of valuable findings stems from open source communities. As such, studies show that software quality in several open source projects significantly depends on both the code coverage of peer code review and the participation of community members in peer code review that allow the code to evolve and become better over time (Lee and Cole 2003; McIntosh et al. 2014). However, scholars have also criticized peer code review in open source communities as lacking behind the quality standards of ISD industry and taking too long as compared to agile ISD in industry (Bernhart et al. 2010; Stamelos et al. 2002). Extant studies show that the majority of revisions does not help improve the functionality of source code but ensures that it can easily be extended by other developers later on (Beller et al. 2014; Rigby 2011). As such, most open source review comments focus on the structure, visual representation, and understandable documentation of a piece of code (Beller et al. 2014). Lee and Cole (2003) theorize that this extensive culture of criticism, which materializes in the peer code review activities, allows open source communities to create community-wide knowledge and helps them to establish an evolutionary mechanism of code improvement over time.

Only three extant studies focus on peer code review in for-profit organizations (Bacchelli and Bird 2013; Rigby and Bird 2013; Sutherland and Venolia 2009). All three primarily study individual level motivations and specifics of appropriated peer code review. Rigby and Bird (2013) emphasize that, despite all differences, the core elements of peer code review are the same in all settings. Findings by Bacchelli and Bird (2013) suggest that peer code review in for-profit organizations often not only reduces defects but also helps to develop alternative solutions to the original one proposed for review. A common pattern to studies in an industry context is their emphasis on the side effects of peer code review that relate to the combination of different developers' knowledge and go beyond the elimination of defects in source code (Bacchelli and Bird 2013; Rigby et al. 2012; Rigby and Bird 2013). As such, scholars argue that reviewers on the one hand need expertise in a specific area of code in order to review it effectively (Bacchelli and Bird 2013; Rigby et al. 2012; Wang and Carroll 2011); on the other hand, findings suggest that authors as well as reviewers learn to know new code areas during their peer code review activities (Bacchelli and Bird 2013; Rigby and Bird 2013). Moreover, prior work highlights that there appears to be another learning effect of peer code review that deserves further research: developers may not only learn from review comments and source code, but they may also become aware of one another's activities. Consequently, they become able to draw on team members' expertise which they deduce from their members' activity in a certain area (Bacchelli and Bird 2013; Hildenbrand 2008; Schmidt et al. 2014).

In sum, literature on both techniques emphasizes on their quality impacts and the efforts that incur when conducting them. While findings for pair programming are mixed, peer code review is known to be a central quality mechanism in open source communities. However, there are no comparable results on quality impacts in for-profit ISD organizations (cf. Table A.1 of the appendix). Regarding both techniques, literature highlights that expertise and knowledge of involved developers appear to play a central role both as a success factor for their application and as an element affected by the techniques. Deeper investigations into these assertions are however scarce and are therefore addressed in the remainder of this study.

2.2.3 Transferability to Team Level

Extant literature contains studies on the comparison of *pair programming* and solo programming in abundance. They focus on a vast number of different variables on an individual level or on a dyadic level. However, little research takes into account that pair programming is typically not applied in a single pair on a single task only. That is not to say that there is only laboratory research. On the contrary, Vanhanen and Mäntylä (2013) state that of the more than 150 papers they review, "83 % of the papers came from a typical, industrial software development context, where the pairs (1) worked within a team larger than two developers (2) performed tasks related to a large project, and (3) developed the software for real use instead of it being an exercise" (Vanhanen and Mäntylä 2013, p. 20). However, this stream of research does not make use of this context as a source of explanations or even as the level that may actually be affected by pair programming. The larger ISD team is traditionally ignored in pair programming research (Coman et al. 2014; Flor and Hutchins 1991).

Studies that focus on a team level rarely look at pair programming as a distinctive technique, but they rather investigate ISD methods as bundles of techniques that may contain pair programming. As such, Maruping et al. (2009a) find that the use of a joint set of agile ISD methods (containing amongst others pair programming, coding standards, continuous integration, and unit testing) reduces the number of severe bugs and the complexity of software produced by ISD teams. Vidgen and Wang (2009) argue that pair programming, applied in a canon of other agile techniques, fosters sharing and team learning in ISD. Schmidt et al. (2014) show that team-wide applications of multiple agile ISD practices, including pair programming, improve software quality in ISD teams by fostering shared mental models and backup behaviors. Sharp and Robinson (2006) take a perspective of distributed cognition and find that frequent pair programming with oft-changing partners primarily breaks common ground and creates shared knowledge across the entire ISD team. The few studies that focus on pair programming while also taking the team level into account either suggest that frequently assumed, unconditional performance gains on a dyadic level do not necessarily translate to a team level (e.g., Coman et al. 2014; Dawande et al. 2008) or underline the importance of distributed knowledge for pair programming in teams (Plonka and van der Linden 2012). As such, Coman et al. (2014) show that team and task characteristics are influential factors on the effectiveness of pair programming on a team level. Based on analytical modeling, Dawande et al. (2008) emphasize on the finding that teams need to balance knowledge sharing, which is easier achieved through pair programming, and adherence to time constraints, which is easier achieved through solo programming. On the one hand, findings of Plonka and van der Linden (2012) support these claims by showing that individual developers can become discouraged from pair programming by time pressure. On the other hand, their findings question whether knowledge sharing may generally be facilitated by pair programming because they show there can be "no pairing opportunities due to a special field of expertise" (Plonka and van der Linden 2012, p. 125).

Although acknowledging the need to study socio-technical effects and team level knowledge exchange (Bacchelli and Bird 2013), extant *peer code review* research in for-profit organizations does not focus on team level factors or include theory to inform such investigations. Nevertheless, literature suggests that peer code review may affect how teams can make use of their single members' knowledge as they gain access to new knowledge about one another and their current doings (Bacchelli and Bird 2013). While individuals apply peer code review also with the aim to extend their personal skills or knowledge (Rigby et al. 2012; Rigby and Bird 2013; Sutherland and Venolia 2009), it is hitherto unclear what that means for ISD teams that conduct peer code review.

These diverse but related findings suggest that there are team level effects of expertise distribution that impact the way in which collaborative quality assurance techniques are applied on a task level and that the application of the techniques may somehow affect the body of knowledge in ISD teams. Literature holds that individual developers learn from their peers during pair programming and peer code review (e.g., Rigby et al. 2012; Salleh et al. 2011). Scholars often conjecture that collaborative quality assurance must therefore also lead to team learning (Begel and Nagappan 2008; Cockburn and Williams 2002). In the light of the above studies, it is however questionable whether such learning also transfers to improved team cognition in larger groups.

2.2.4 Substituting Pair Programming with Peer Code Review

The large amount of studies that try to ascertain whether pair programming is more effective than solo programming shows that this technique is not uncontroversial. In fact, pair programming incurs significant efforts for developers and personnel costs for organizations (Müller 2006). Scholars and practitioners are therefore interested

Table 2.1 Studies on substitution of pair programming by peer code review

Study	Type	Compared to pair programming	
		Reduced defects	Reduced effort
Tomayko (2002)	E	−	
Müller (2004)	E	0	0
Müller (2005)	E	0	0
Phongpaibul and Boehm (2006)	E	−	+
Winkler and Biffl (2006)	E	−	
Phongpaibul and Boehm (2007)	E	0	0
Keeling (2010)	E	−	−
Rigby et al. (2012)	C	0	+

E experiment; C conceptual; − negative effect; 0 equal; + positive effect

in the question whether pair programming can be substituted with a less costly way of quality assurance (Paulk 2001; Tomayko 2002); a question that has not yet received conclusive answers (Mangalaraj et al. 2014).

In particular, a number of experimental studies addresses the question whether code review can lead to lower efforts and better results (Di Bella et al. 2013). Importantly, these studies do not address an ongoing way of conducting peer code review as part of developers daily routine; they investigate formal inspections as proposed by Fagan (1986). Overall, some studies find weak support for pair programming being more effective in detecting defects at slightly increased efforts (Keeling 2010; Phongpaibul and Boehm 2006; Tomayko 2002; Winkler and Biffl 2006) whereas other studies find that both techniques are comparable with regard to effectiveness (Müller 2004, 2005; Phongpaibul and Boehm 2007). Table 2.1 depicts the results in detail.

There are no empirical studies on the effectiveness of contemporary peer code review compared to pair programming.[4] Nevertheless, pair programming enthusiasts traditionally state that pair programming incorporates a continuous process of reviewing written code (e.g., Cockburn and Williams 2002; Williams and Kessler 2000), implicitly indicating that this substitutes further reviews. Moreover, Rigby et al. (2012) conceptually compare pair programming to peer code review in their collection of lessons learned from open source peer code review. They argue that peer code review creates slightly lower costs and requires less effort of reviewers compared to pair programming but both are held equally effective for team building and quality assurance.

---

[4]The only exception to this assessment is the work conducted by this author and his co-authors (Schmidt et al. 2012; Spohrer et al. 2013a,b). Those single conference pieces are not scrutinized here as they constitute only partial elements of the overall study described in this paper.

2.2.5   Summary

Researchers intensively investigate pair programming in the fields of IS, software engineering, as well as in education. Despite its broad adoption in industry and its central quality impact in open source communities, research on peer code review is scarce, even more so in for-profit organizations. Existing work on pair programming is primarily concerned with the evaluation of pair performance and the empirical elicitation of its antecedents. For this endeavor, scholars abundantly rely on empirical investigations but only rarely explore or test emerging patterns in the light of theory from management or the social sciences. By consequence, the empirical body of literature contains many contradicting results and explanations remain often ad-hoc and situated to very specific contexts.

Both academia and practice are aware of the significant efforts that are necessary to conduct pair programming and are looking for alternative techniques to collaboratively assure software quality in ISD teams during daily routine. Peer code review has been proposed as a potential substitute of pair programming and there are initial investigations that examine this proposition. These investigations are experimental and compare code quality of pairs of programmers to pairs of authors and reviewers. On the one hand, this may lead to a lack of external validity; on the other hand, it may lead research to overlook effects that go beyond simple defect detection.

Literature acknowledges influences of cognitive factors on the adoption of ISD techniques and states that teams rarely rely on idealized textbook stereotypes of single techniques. Instead, ISD teams do not only adopt a technique but may actually adapt it to their specific context. Nevertheless, little is known regarding how and why ISD techniques such as pair programming and peer code review are appropriated by teams to their specific needs. Literature further highlights that individual developers have the chance to learn from their team members during pair programming. It is generally assumed that such learning also translates to improved team cognition in larger groups. Surprisingly, extant research does not investigate these points in more detail and generally overlooks the necessity to examine the role of the larger ISD team in the application and the results of collaborative quality assurance techniques. As this study aims to close these gaps partially, it reviews literature on team cognition in ISD teams below.

2.3   Three Perspectives on Team Cognition in ISD

Learning and cognition on a team level constitute one decisive factor influencing the performance of work groups (Mohammed and Dumville 2001; Wilson et al. 2007). A variety of research streams across disciplines treats group level cognition and learning as its focal research area (Salas et al. 2012). Nevertheless, these streams differ in focal concepts, underlying theory, and targeted outcome variables (Edmondson et al. 2007). There are several comprehensive general overviews of team cognition research by renown scholars (Decuyper et al. 2010; Edmondson et al. 2007; Goodman and Dabbish 2011; Mohammed and Dumville 2001; Salas et al. 2012; Sessa and London 2008; Wilson et al. 2007). Consequently, this study does not aim to provide a better or more complete overview of general team cognition research. Instead, this section focuses primarily on structuring the work that addresses team cognition in research on ISD which provides an adequate overview as a basis to answer the research questions of this study. Only where research on team cognition in other disciplines diverges from research in ISD, this is highlighted. Authors of extensive recent reviews of literature on team cognition and knowledge sharing in ISD teams structure their reviews based on topics regarding activities (Davern et al. 2012) or independent variables (Ghobadi 2015) respectively. This study, by contrast, adopts the major categorization schema for team level cognitive research proposed by Edmondson et al. (2007) and picked up by Spohrer et al. (2012). Edmondson et al. (2007) differentiate three conceptualizations of team learning and cognition prevalent in literature: based on the central conceptualization of team cognition, research streams can be identified that focus on particular research questions, underlying theories, methods, and assumptions. This section shows that research on team cognition in ISD broadly follows the same paths as in management literature (Edmondson et al. 2007) but has several research areas which receive outstandingly little attention in spite of their arguably high relevance for ISD.

2.3.1 The Team Learning Curve

A first stream of research is primarily concerned with the central theme of outcome improvement through learning on a team level. Research on performance improvement is traditionally conducted with an emphasis on learning curves (Argote et al. 1990), without any deeper investigation into the underlying mechanisms of team cognition at a group level. That is, scholars of this research area traditionally acknowledge that collective cognitive activity is present and helps work groups improve in their task performances over time. However, such learning curve research does not intend to understand and explain the underlying mechanisms of team cognition. Instead, studies typically aim to find reasonable determinants of team performance, and specifically for improvements thereof. Accordingly, the concept of team cognition is one of mere outcome improvement (Edmondson et al. 2007). Based on observed improvements in productivity and logical reasoning, research assumes team learning to occur, without empirical proof, direct measurement, or theoretical explanation of underlying mechanisms (Edmondson et al. 2007).

For example, Teasley et al. (2002) reason that a performance increase they observe in settings of radically collocated ISD teams is largely caused by better opportunities for team learning. Whether and how such learning takes place, however, exceeds the boundaries of this school of research. As such, Mookerjee and Chiang (2002) study team level learning as an input factor for analytical models of coordination policies. Based on these models and an additional case study,

Mookerjee and Chiang (2002) show that tighter coordination policies are more appropriate for ISD teams which are at lower stages of the learning curve than they are for more experienced teams. Following the same school of thought, Boh et al. (2007) define learning as "the increase in productivity of developers as their experience increases" (Boh et al. 2007, p.1322). At the same time, they acknowledge that individuals' experience alone is not decisive, but relational aspects between individual team members' expertise are assumed to be similarly relevant (Boh et al. 2007). Accordingly, different types of experience are frequently examined and empirically related to teams' performance in this research area. For example, the experience of developers and project managers in their respective roles within their ISD teams is found more predictive for team outcomes than general experience in a company (Huckman et al. 2009). In accordance with this finding, other scholars highlight that experience with the software development methodology a team applies is decisive for its performance (Kang and Hahn 2009). Similarly, team productivity is found to be higher if ISD team members possess diverse experience with related tasks than if they are experienced in more unrelated systems or specialized in a single task (Boh et al. 2007). In general, findings of this stream of research also suggest that higher familiarity of team members is beneficial for ISD team performance, and improved learning is frequently argued to result from such familiarity (Boh et al. 2007; Huckman et al. 2009).

Despite its achievements, learning curve research on ISD team performance does not provide a conclusive answer to why such learning occurs or which mechanisms produce that interplay of experience and performance. In particular, there is no clear, explanatory conception of team cognition. Instead, this stream of research assumes learning effects on a team level but treats them as a black box. Accordingly, there is an absence of theories in this stream of research that might explain such effects. Only a minority of studies provides hints at concepts that might be useful for explaining these relationships (e.g., Teasley et al. 2002). Regarding used research methodology, learning curve research in ISD builds on mostly quantitative analyses of archival data (Boh et al. 2007; Huckman et al. 2009; Kang and Hahn 2009; Teasley et al. 2002), selectively combined and enriched with other instruments like analytical models (Mookerjee and Chiang 2002) or qualitative follow-up interviews (Teasley et al. 2002). Extant learning curve research in ISD does not address team level ISD techniques as a focal part of studies.

2.3.2   Team Cognition as a Group Activity in ISD

A second stream of research on team cognition research conceptualizes team cognition as a group process of different behavioral activities within the team, including discussions, knowledge sharing, and reflection on expertise (Edmondson et al. 2007). Many studies, however, reduce their conceptual focus to only a single activity, such as knowledge sharing or knowledge transfer, that is argued to represent team cognition. In ISD, this stream encompasses significant bodies of literature on knowledge sharing and knowledge management on a team level (for seminal and recent reviews see Alavi and Leidner 2001; Bjørnson and Dingsøyr 2008; Ghobadi 2015). The focus of this stream of research is on team activities from both a theoretical and methodological perspective. Scholars of this stream highlight that knowledge held in a team only becomes useful for the team when it is applied to team tasks. Consequently, actual knowledge exchange and contribution activities are what this research focuses on. Typically, studies identify factors that drive, shape, or result from team level behaviors such as knowledge sharing. Comprehensive overviews and collections of these factors addressed in prior ISD studies can be found in Ghobadi (2015) and Bjørnson and Dingsøyr (2008).

For example, Walz et al. (1993) find that software design team members engage in the acquisition, sharing, and integration of knowledge into the group. The authors further argue that managed conflict between team members stimulates a team's learning behaviors (Walz et al. 1993). Liang et al. (2010) refine this proposition by demonstrating that the quality of developed software actually increases when there is conflict that can be attributed to team members' differing backgrounds and expertise. Such task conflict does not necessarily harm productive communication within a team, but it stimulates learning behaviors (Liang et al. 2010). Notwithstanding this finding, there is also evidence that simply teaming developers with different backgrounds and expertise does not necessarily lead to more engagement in learning behaviors or more creative results (Tiwana and Mclean 2005).

Some scholars of this stream also acknowledge that learning activities such as group discussions and reflections may have a positive influence on teams' performance, but argue that a stronger and more important effect of such learning activities is the resulting increase in individual team members' satisfaction with work (Janz and Prasarnphanich 2003, 2009). Interestingly, results from this direction of research also highlight that different types of autonomy given to ISD teams may result in different learning behaviors. As such, especially ISD teams that are empowered to autonomously assign single members to tasks are found to engage more actively in group learning activities and create stronger mutual dependence (Janz and Prasarnphanich 2003, 2009).

Reflecting the breath of research questions addressed in this stream, studies on team learning behaviors in ISD are not based on a single dominant theoretical lens. They draw from a variety of theories, such as collaborative learning theory (Janz and Prasarnphanich 2003, 2009); information theory (Liang et al. 2010); and social interdependence theory (Li et al. 2009) to name but a few. Especially research on knowledge sharing is often based on organizational learning theories such as the theory of organizational knowledge creation by Nonaka (1994).

In more recent work, scholars adopt the perspective that the individual's role within ISD team learning is more multifaceted than has hitherto been acknowledged (Sarker et al. 2011; Skerlavaj et al. 2010). They conceptualize the team as a network of individuals who interact in different ways and intensities. Team cognition for them consists of interactions between these networked actors. To examine these interactions more closely, researchers choose methods and theories that account for both the individual and the team level in their analyses. As such, some address the question why individual members can become more important for overall team cognition than others. For example, Sarker et al. (2011) show that there can be "stars" in globally distributed ISD teams who comprise the central institutions for knowledge exchange activities between team members. These stars are highly trusted by the rest of the team and communicate more frequently with other team members. As a result, they can also serve as boundary spanners for different sub-groups within the team. Interestingly, the stars' own knowledge of technologies or management is not necessarily high (Sarker et al. 2011). Nevertheless, Skerlavaj et al. (2010) show that such central actors in the learning network are often found in senior positions and that the flow of knowledge between single team members is not necessarily reciprocal. Consequently, individual team members who actively share more knowledge with their team do not necessarily receive knowledge in return (Skerlavaj et al. 2010).

Research on team learning behaviors does not often focus on specific ISD techniques but rather examines factors related to team tasks and organization such as team composition and task interdependence (Ghobadi 2015). Prior studies that address ISD techniques do not focus on knowledge sharing within ISD teams but on enabling exchange with and knowledge acquisition from external stakeholders such as customers (cf. Ghobadi 2015; Sawyer et al. 2010). There is nearly no work that focuses on collaborative quality assurance techniques. And the existing work typically stops with the finding that pair programming fosters knowledge sharing between dyads of pair programmers (Bellini et al. 2005). Specific technologies that support learning behaviors are most often studied in contexts in which they are inevitably used, such as communication technology in globally distributed teams (Ghobadi 2015). Many scholars emphasize that the presence of technology, for example of knowledge management systems, does not per se support team cognition if it is not used (Bjørnson and Dingsøyr 2008). Others acknowledge that existing technologies are often used for individual and collective learning activities that are different from the ones intended (Dingsøyr et al. 2005). Extant work however does not study why technologies such as knowledge management systems are actually used in teams or how team cognition plays a role in different appropriations of systems (Bjørnson and Dingsøyr 2008; Ghobadi 2015).

Regarding research methodologies, this stream heavily builds on quantitative survey-based designs but also conducts qualitative research, mostly based on case studies. More recent studies that take a network perspective accordingly apply social network analysis. In sum, this stream emphasizes the importance of collective action for leveraging individual team members' knowledge and using it to improve team work results but there is little research on ISD techniques or their appropriation.

2.3.3   Socio-Cognitive Structures

A last stream of literature sees team cognition as a step towards task mastery and conceptualizes it as the "outcome of communication and coordination that builds shared knowledge by team members about their team, task, resources, and context" (Edmondson et al. 2007, p. 277). This stream of research holds that teams build up a stock of shared knowledge which is explicitly and implicitly used by team members for coordination and collaboration. As individuals have only limited cognitive resources, teams in which team members can access one another's cognitive resources are argued to outperform groups of isolated individuals. This stream thereby acknowledges that teams consist of individuals among whom knowledge is unevenly distributed and that the integration of individuals' knowledge on a group level is central to realizing performance gains. Scholars of this school theorize that teams develop socio-cognitive memory structures that are more than the sum of individuals' memory (Tiwana and Mclean 2005) because they help team members make better assumptions about their colleagues' expertise and ways of work and allow them to leverage these improved assumptions for coordination and task work (Mohammed and Dumville 2001; Vlaar et al. 2008). There are different conceptualizations of socio-cognitive structures in literature which include shared mental models (Cannon-Bowers and Salas 2001; Cannon-Bowers et al. 1993), distributed cognition (Hollan et al. 2000; Hutchins 1995), and transactive memory systems (Wegner 1987; Wegner et al. 1985). Particularly the latter is attentively studied in ISD and organizational research (Choi et al. 2010; Edmondson et al. 2007; Grunwald and Kieser 2007).

One central finding of this stream of research is that knowledge and meta-knowledge shared in a group memory do indeed account for the performance of ISD teams in several dimensions. Scholars find that knowledge shared in group memory improves ISD teams' effectiveness and efficiency, and enhances their ability to transfer knowledge to others, as well as their ability to integrate external knowledge creatively into software products (Chen et al. 2013; Espinosa et al. 2007; Faraj and Sproull 2000; He et al. 2007; Hsu et al. 2012; Kotlarsky and Oshri 2005; Lin et al. 2011; Maruping et al. 2009b; Nemanich et al. 2010; Oshri et al. 2008; Schmidt et al. 2014; Tiwana 2004; Tiwana and Mclean 2005; Zhang et al. 2011). Several research endeavors aim to identify antecedents of the establishment of group memory structures in early phases of ISD team work. Scholars find that especially close and frequent interactions of team members are an important one of these antecedents (He et al. 2007; Levesque et al. 2001). However, close interactions are much harder to achieve in globally distributed software development teams whose members must potentially work across spatial, temporal, and cultural boundaries. Such distribution can therefore heavily impact a team's ability to create a group memory suiting its needs (Espinosa et al. 2007; He et al. 2007; Oshri et al. 2008). While the negative influence of team distribution can be reduced by employing coordination mechanisms of a wide range, from mutual visits over standardized organizational structures to communication technologies, these must be finely tuned as the situational settings influence the mechanisms' applicability (Dibbern et al. 2008; He et al. 2007; Kotlarsky and Oshri 2005; Oshri et al. 2008; Robert et al. 2008).

Group memory systems in ISD evolve over time and can grow or shrink (He et al. 2007). One reason is that ISD team members differ in their needs for interaction depending on their roles and tasks. For example, developers perceive different pressure points in team coordination than do ISD managers (Espinosa et al. 2007). Consequently, socio-cognitive structures of ISD teams tend to shrink if their members increasingly specialize in a solitary role and only work on tasks that have low interdependency with others (Levesque et al. 2001). In line with this argument, interconnecting practices, multi-skill development, and autonomy in ISD can enhance team cognition (Vidgen and Wang 2009). However, recent findings by Nemanich et al. (2010) indicate that there are more complex relationships between team knowledge, autonomy, individual developers' capabilities, and team cognition, than have so far been assumed to exist. Interestingly, these authors find that possession of existing knowledge does not necessarily improve ISD teams' ability to learn. Quite the contrary, they find that teams with less prior knowledge are forced to learn more rapidly and receive more benefits from doing so (Nemanich et al. 2010). Moreover, there also seems to be a dynamic interplay between the socio-cognitive structure of ISD teams and their norms and values: Maruping et al. (2009b), for example, find that collective code ownership reduces the impact of the group memory system on the quality of software development, while established coding standards increase it. Schmidt et al. (2014) show that general use of agile ISD practices, including pair programming, improves shared mental models and backup behaviors within ISD teams. Focusing more on particular ISD techniques, Vidgen and Wang (2009) identify pair programming with frequent rotations as one useful interconnecting practice that fosters team level cognitive structures. Similarly, Sharp and Robinson (2006) emphasize that pair programming, although conducted in dyads, breaks common ground for mutual understanding across the entire team. From a perspective of distributed cognition, Sharp and Robinson (2008) add that material facets of ISD techniques, including physical artifacts, may play a much more important role for ISD team cognition than previously acknowledged. They suggest that physical artifacts in ISD techniques (e.g., user story boards) can not only foster awareness of other team members' activities, they are also argued to build bridges to access other team members' expertise when it is required (Sharp and Robinson 2008). This is in line with Mangalaraj et al. (2014) who study the use of design patterns as external cognitive artifacts. They find that design patterns can be used as a source of codified knowledge by inexperienced developers: weaker team members achieve comparable performance results when programming alone using design patterns as they do when pair programming with a more experienced team member (Mangalaraj et al. 2014). Finally, scholars find that the establishment of a group memory system can also be fostered by appropriate information systems for collaboration, especially if they allow for contextualizing knowledge in day-to-day tasks (Klimpke 2013; Kotlarsky et al. 2014; Zhang et al. 2011).

From a methodological perspective, two research designs are applied in extant studies on socio-cognitive structures in ISD teams: there is a clear dominance of survey-based, quantitative analyses (e.g., He et al. 2007; Faraj and Sproull 2000; Levesque et al. 2001; Maruping et al. 2009b; Nemanich et al. 2010; Schmidt et al. 2014; Tiwana and Mclean 2005; Zhang et al. 2011), but at times scholars also apply qualitative, interview-based case studies (e.g., Espinosa et al. 2007; Kotlarsky and Oshri 2005; Oshri et al. 2008; Vidgen and Wang 2009). A number of theoretical lenses are used in this stream of research, including some with peculiar features: for example, there are some adoptions of theory on expertise integration (e.g., Tiwana 2004; Tiwana and Mclean 2005) that was originally developed to explain organizational learning rather than cognition on a group level (Grant 1996); for another example, the theory of distributed cognition (e.g. applied by Sharp and Robinson 2006, 2008) regards technological artifacts as functionally equal, accessible cognitive resources in the socio-cognitive system of a team. That is, it conceptualizes artifacts as actors just the same as individual team members (Hollan et al. 2000; Hutchins 1995). While these specific theories are fruitfully applied by the respective scholars, they remain in rather small niches. The majority of studies in this area relies on two theories of socio-cognitive structures: (1) shared cognition based on the concept of shared mental models (Cannon-Bowers and Salas 2001; Cannon-Bowers et al. 1993), and (2) transactive memory systems (Wegner 1987; Wegner et al. 1985). This distribution is largely in line with literature in general management and organization research (Edmondson et al. 2007).

2.3.4 Summary

Research on team cognition in ISD teams follows roughly the same streams as team cognition research in neighboring disciplines (Edmondson et al. 2007; Goodman and Dabbish 2011; Wilson et al. 2007). Three broad schools of thought can be distinguished: first, learning curve research that treats team cognition as a black box and assumes it to exist based on improvements in team outcome over time; second, group process research that focuses on observable team learning behaviors such as discussions, reflection, and knowledge sharing; third, research on socio-cognitive structures as team level knowledge stocks about tasks, team, and context that are shared across all team members and allow them to access one another's knowledge for task completion. While all streams of research make interesting and important contributions to team cognition literature, only little research treats the intersections of team cognition and ISD techniques. In particular, there is a dearth of research on ISD techniques in the stream of team learning curve whereas some results stem from research on group processes and socio-cognitive structures. These results can inform current as much as they demand for future research in ISD techniques.

For example, results suggest that the call for less specialization and more multi-skill development that is inherent to current ISD techniques and methodologies (Poppendieck and Poppendieck 2003; Sharp and Robinson 2006), may have ambiguous effects on team cognition: less specialization may reduce the need for keeping socio-cognitive structures up-to-date to ensure that all team members know about one another's expertise (Maruping et al. 2009b; Vidgen and Wang 2009); however, this may not only reduce the heterogeneity of expertise in a team but also fruitful task conflicts which are beneficial for creativity and performance of ISD teams (Liang et al. 2010; Tiwana and Mclean 2005). Additionally, there may be some development techniques that manipulate the relative importance of team cognition for software quality in ISD (Maruping et al. 2009b). However, which mechanisms underlie such effects remains obscure so far. Revealing these underlying mechanisms would constitute a significant step in understanding the relationship between development techniques, team cognition, and team performance (Maruping et al. 2009b). Lastly, extremely little attention is paid to collaborative quality assurance techniques in these streams of research. Whereas peer code review is not addressed at all, pair programming is primarily found to foster knowledge sharing within pairs (Bellini et al. 2005) and to break common ground for the development of team-wide group memory structures (Sharp and Robinson 2006; Vidgen and Wang 2009).

It is noteworthy that the little research that exists on team cognition and ISD techniques focuses exclusively on effects of the application of one or more techniques on team cognition. While this is a legitimate perspective, it omits the question whether and how team cognition influences the use of ISD techniques in the first place. Extant literature often highlights that the decision about the application of ISD techniques is not a dichotomous decision whether to apply a textbook technique or not (Wang et al. 2012). Instead, ISD teams purposefully select specific techniques and appropriate them to their needs in different ways (Fitzgerald et al. 2006; Maruping et al. 2009a). It appears reasonable that ISD teams should leverage their collective cognitive resources to appropriate techniques in an effective way. This study aims to close this gap.

2.4   Selection of Theoretical Lenses

This study proceeds by selecting adequate theories that help to find explanatory answers to the research questions. Following Dibbern et al. (2001), this selection is made from theories of team cognition that make similar explanatory claims in prior literature on the topic. The review of literature on collaborative quality assurance techniques and on team cognition in ISD teams showed that the former research field traditionally lacks theoretical accounts whereas in the latter field three different streams struggle for prevalence. A number of theories are mentioned in Sect. 2.3, however not all of them can be applied equally well to the phenomenon of team cognition in collaborative quality assurance techniques. As has been defined in the research questions, this study treats to understand effects in two directions: first, an appropriate theoretical account for this study must help understand how team cognition affects the appropriation of collaborative quality assurance techniques on a task level; second, it must help understand how the ongoing application of collaborative quality assurance techniques yields team level effects on team cognition and software quality as a key indicator of team performance.

This dual perspective creates specific requirements to theories of team cognition that cannot be fulfilled by all the streams reviewed in Sect. 2.3. As such, the stream of learning curve research has to be discarded for its general lack of actual explanatory theory on team cognition: treating team cognition theoretically as a black box (cf. Sect. 2.3), learning curve research cannot help understand interactions of team cognition and collaborative quality assurance techniques in sufficient detail. Research in a group process view of team cognition, on the other hand, can inherently only account for one direction of causality: defining team cognition conceptually as a behavior (e.g., knowledge sharing; cf. Sect. 2.3), the use of collaborative quality assurance techniques could either be understood to affect this behavior or be affected by the behavior. However, no account of both effects could be made over time. The reason for this lies in what Archer (1995, 1998) calls a "conflation of agency and structure" that prohibits understanding that both agency and structure can have causal efficacy over time. By consequence, the streams of learning curve and group process research cannot provide appropriate theories of team cognition to examine both effects addressed in the research questions of this study.

This leaves one promising stream of research identified in Sect. 2.3 for this study: research that conceptualizes team cognition as socio-cognitive structures. Turning to the most prevalent theories of this stream, a choice between two theories remains: theories of shared mental models (Cannon-Bowers and Salas 2001; Cannon-Bowers et al. 1993) and transactive memory systems (Wegner et al. 1985; Wegner 1987). Both theories hold that there is a group level memory structure that allows team members to draw on one another's knowledge to thereby generate team performance gains. The essential differences of these theories lie in their conceptualization of what is shared in the group memory and how the team comes to benefit from its single members (Lewis and Herndon 2011; Mohammed and Dumville 2001; Peltokorpi 2008). The theory of shared mental models holds that higher overlap in team members' knowledge is generally beneficial as it facilitates communication, exchange knowledge, common direction, and backing up for one another (Salas et al. 2012). The theory of transactive memory systems holds that team members should only have overlaps in meta-knowledge of who knows what and in vocabularies for task-related communication. Beyond that, transactive memory systems theory argues that team performance is higher if single team members have specialized knowledge that other team members can retrieve by making use of the shared meta-knowledge and vocabulary (Ohtsubo 2005). Essentially, the difference lies in how the socio-cognitive structure emerges, either from similar individual contributions (shared mental models) or from specialized and qualitatively different contributions of each team member (transactive memory systems) (Kozlowski and Bell 2008). In addition, the theory of transactive memory systems clearly defines the processes with which individual team members consciously or unconsciously engage in updating and using their teams transactive memory whereas theory of shared mental models does not do so. ISD teams are traditionally argued to consist of individuals who each bring in specialized skills and knowledge that are necessary to complete the complex knowledge-based work of software development (Faraj and Sproull 2000). For the purpose of this study, a perspective based on transactive memory systems appears therefore more appropriate because it matches the emphasis on specialization in prior ISD research and provides a more detailed account how actions of team members relate to the socio-cognitive structure of the team.

The theory of transactive memory systems immanently explains team performance based on team cognition. Therefore it appears well-suited to study the performance and team cognition effects of the application of collaborative quality assurance techniques. However, it does not bring immediate theoretical elements that explain how team cognition may affect the appropriation of collaborative quality assurance techniques on a task level. Consequently, this study relies on an additional, productive theoretical lens that focuses on appropriation on a team level: namely the concept of functional affordances (Markus and Silver 2008). The theory of transactive memory system constitutes a traditional theory in the sense that it "explains and predicts" team cognition and its outcomes based on well-defined constructs and testable, causal relationships (Gregor 2006). The concept of functional affordances, by contrast, is primarily a powerful explanatory device (Volkoff and Strong 2013) that does state well-defined causal relationships which are however not immediately testable. For this study, it takes the role of a higher-level theory that helps create an explanatory and predictive mid-range theory of how team cognition impacts the task level appropriation of collaborative quality assurance techniques on the one hand and how continued application of these techniques leads to emergent effects on team cognition and performance on the other hand. In the following, both theoretical lenses are introduced in more detail.

2.4.1 Transactive Memory Systems Theory

The theory of transactive memory systems receives attention of researchers in many disciplines. By consequence, there is a large body of research on transactive memory systems. Several scholars review and structure prior research from different perspectives. There are excellent reviews of literature on transactive memory systems in organizations (Edmondson et al. 2007; Lewis and Herndon 2011; Ren and Argote 2011), specifically in work groups and teams (Hollingshead et al. 2011; Ilgen et al. 2005; Peltokorpi 2008), and of the interplay of transactive memory systems with technology (Nevo and Ophir 2012). While there are occasional inconsistencies in empirical results and several fields for future investigations, the body of knowledge on transactive memory systems is overall rather homogeneous and empirical results strongly support the theory's central assertions, also in ISD teams in particular (Lewis and Herndon 2011; Ren and Argote 2011). It constitutes therefore a solid basis for this study of team cognition and collaborative quality assurance techniques.

A transactive memory system is a form of social cognition through which groups of people distribute information to and retrieve information from single group members to achieve a group-wide coordination of individual knowledge (Wegner 1987; Wegner et al. 1985). While this is an oversimplification, many refer to transactive memory systems as a concept that describes how team members use one another's expertise based on the shared knowledge of "who knows what" (Ren and Argote 2011). Although first applied to research on dating couples, transactive memory systems are particularly relevant for team work (Hollingshead 1998a,c; Ilgen et al. 2005). The theory of transactive memory systems posits that teams develop a transactive memory system which allows them to engage in division of cognitive work, reduce cognitive load on individuals, and thus exceed the performance of groups that are not able to draw on one another's knowledge (Hollingshead 1998a; Wegner 1987). Indeed, teams with well-developed transactive memory systems are frequently found to show better recall of information as well as work performance (Hollingshead 1998a; Jarvenpaa and Majchrzak 2008; Kanawattanachai and Yoo 2007; Liang et al. 1995; Majchrzak et al. 2007; Moreland and Myaskovsky 2000). In particular, transactive memory systems are considered to be highly relevant for ISD teams as they improve team performance regarding effectiveness, efficiency, knowledge integration, and the ability to transfer knowledge to others (Espinosa et al. 2007; Faraj and Sproull 2000; Kotlarsky and Oshri 2005; Lin et al. 2011; Maruping et al. 2009b; Oshri et al. 2008). Similarly, related disciplines show that transactive memory systems increase teams' creativity as well as the success of new products they develop (Akgün et al. 2006; Gino et al. 2010).

2.4.1.1   A Bipartite System of Structure and Processes

Conceptually, transactive memory systems consist of two components: (1) a transactive memory structure, that is an organized storage of knowledge and meta-knowledge which is distributed across the single team members; and (2) a set of "knowledge-relevant transactive processes" (Wegner et al. 1985, p. 256). There are three transactive processes that allow team members to learn what others know, communicate new information to the team member whose expertise will facilitate information storage, and to retrieve information from team members based on the knowledge of their expertise (Ren and Argote 2011). These processes represent human activities to assign shared labels to pieces of knowledge and expertise of individuals (encoding), store knowledge with the appropriate team member (storage), and obtain task-relevant knowledge from team members based on their areas of expertise (retrieval) (Lewis et al. 2007; Ren and Argote 2011; Rulke and Rau 2000). Transactive processes are therefore the actions taken by team members to create, update, and leverage the transactive memory structure which is present in the memories of individual team members (Lewis and Herndon 2011).

Transactive memory structure, in turn, consists of actual task knowledge and meta-knowledge that is required to communicate about tasks and expertise in order to store, locate, and retrieve information (Wegner 1987). It provides the resources that allow single team members to coordinate knowledge contributions to task work and thereby connects the individual with the team level (Ren and Argote 2011; Yuan et al. 2010). Transactive memory structure is conceptualized as consisting of three types of knowledge and meta-knowledge that are stored in individuals' minds but are partially equal across individuals. First, teams may vary in the differentiation of their single members' expertise areas (Lewis and Herndon 2011). This study refers to *specialized knowledge* as the fully differentiated task knowledge and expertise across team members, that is, specialized knowledge exclusively held by a single expert in a team (Akgün et al. 2005; Ren et al. 2006). Second, in order to be able to engage in knowledge coordination, team members need to possess a certain level of shared language about the problem domain, required expertise, and possible solutions. Previous research refers to these terms as a shared ontology or *shared labels* (Nevo et al. 2012; Wegner 1987). Third, teams may vary in the extent to which they possess shared conceptions of the expertise areas of their single members; that is, they require shared pictures about who knows what and who can credibly contribute expertise to specific tasks (Lewis and Herndon 2011; Liang et al. 1995; Wegner 1987). This study refers to that last part of transactive memory structure as *shared meta-knowledge*.

A *transactive memory system* is therefore a system consisting of both *transactive memory structure* (alternatively called *transactive memory*) on the one hand and *transactive processes* on the other hand. It is a theoretical mechanism that explains how individuals' knowledge becomes usable for other team members (Griffith et al. 2003) as they use one another as a memory source (Oshri et al. 2008). The *theory of transactive memory systems* emphasizes on the specialization of single team members in different expertise areas that are coordinated for team work by means of the transactive memory system. It explains knowledge coordination processes in groups, including the factors influencing these processes, and predicts higher performance outcomes for teams with well-coordinated and specialized expertise (Lewis and Herndon 2011). In more detail, it holds that work groups show higher team performance if they develop both (1) a transactive memory structure with specialized expertise, shared labels, and shared meta-knowledge and (2) transactive processes for encoding, storing, and retrieving information (Lewis et al. 2007; Ren and Argote 2011).

The bipartite character of transactive memory systems can be exemplified through an imaginary ISD team: a newly constituted team of three developers receives software development tasks from its manager. Without being initially aware of it, each of the three developers has a different field of specialization where she holds much more expertise than her team members. One is, for example, a very proficient interface developer. That is, each of the developers possesses specialized knowledge in a particular area of their team's tasks, but they don't know about one another's knowledge. When a new task is given to the team, they analyze the task together against the backdrop of their knowledge and come to the conclusion that it involves primarily interface development. Agreeing on this view, they call the task an "interface task". The result is a newly developed label (interface task) that is shared between the team members and can be reused for similar tasks in the future. The activity of analyzing the task for its basic characteristics based on the group's knowledge and assigning it a label constitutes an encoding process. Finding out that one of them is particularly apt to complete interface tasks, the team members moreover create shared meta-knowledge about the interface developer. The shared label and shared meta-knowledge now allow for better information distribution in the future. When, for example, one of the other developers is notified of a change in the requirements for the interface, she is able to forward this information to her interface developer colleague who can more easily understand the change and put it into context more easily based on her extant knowledge. Thereby, the team members conduct a storage process. If they happen to be looking for details on a particular interface programming technique in the future, the other developers can lastly also turn to the interface developer in their search for expertise, thereby conducting a retrieval process. Shared labels and shared meta-knowledge therefore enable the team to benefit from the specialized expertise of the interface developer by retrieving information on interfaces from her when needed and storing new information on interfaces with her when available. Encoding processes are executed to alter the stock of shared labels and meta-knowledge (e.g., they help identify new tasks as related interface tasks). The effectiveness of encoding, storage, and retrieval processes thereby depends of the amount of specialized knowledge, shared labels, and shared meta-knowledge (i.e., on the transactive memory structure of the team). In this case, the interface developer cannot easily use the specialized expertise of her colleagues because she does not have any meta-knowledge on their expertise areas. However, transactive processes can be interrupted by external factors without changing transactive memory structure. For example, time pressure may inhibit proper retrieval of information from a colleague whereas physical separation can prevent the chance for timely interaction and thereby inhibit effective storage of new information (Ren and Argote 2011).

2.4.1.2 Transactive Memory System Development and Effects

In line with general propositions of the theory of transactive memory systems, literature finds that members of teams specialize in different parts of their teams' knowledge-intensive tasks, especially if tasks are highly interdependent, novel, and complex (e.g., Akgün et al. 2005; Brandon and Hollingshead 2004; Griffith and Sawyer 2010; Lewis 2004; Liang et al. 1995; Moreland and Myaskovsky 2000; Rulke and Rau 2000; Yuan et al. 2010). Moreover, the presence of an extensive transactive memory system generally predicts task performance in small groups such as dyads (e.g., Hollingshead 2000) as well as in large groups such as open source communities (e.g., Chen et al. 2013; Chou and He 2011). These findings are broadly supported across different disciplines and strengthen theory on transactive memory systems with extensive empirical examinations (Hollingshead et al. 2011; Lewis and Herndon 2011; Nevo and Ophir 2012; Ren and Argote 2011).

Some scholars closely examine the question how far the specialization of single team members should go. On the one hand, they find that specialized knowledge enables teams to be more effective (Hollingshead 2000; Ohtsubo 2005; Wang et al. 2008) and reduces communication and coordination effort for team tasks (Liang et al. 1995; Yoo and Kanawattanachai 2001). On the other hand, strong specialization in different roles creates knowledge boundaries (Kotlarsky et al. 2015), reduces communication possibilities (Peltokorpi 2008), and thereby increases the danger for specialists to be left out of the loop in decision and learning activities (Jones and Kelly 2013). Hollingshead et al. (2011) recommend a general balance of commonly shared conceptual knowledge for higher level concepts and specialized expert knowledge in task details to ensure the working and ongoing maintenance of transactive memories. Moreover, extant research suggests that teams with tasks for which there exist clearly right or wrong answers can benefit from redundant expertise that allows for controlling one another's work results (Ellis et al. 2003; Gupta and Hollingshead 2010; Ilgen et al. 2005). However, where tasks require creative answers and large amounts of information have to be handled, teams may benefit more from diversity and the advantages of specialization (Fægri et al. 2010; Gupta and Hollingshead 2010; Hollingshead 2000). As ISD falls arguably in the latter category (Faraj and Sproull 2000), one may expect to see more beneficial effects of specialized knowledge in ISD teams in this study.

Importantly, teams need time and the chance to interact before a transactive memory system emerges; a chance not given to all teams (Majchrzak et al. 2007). Especially task-related communication like it is common during group trainings and joint task work is beneficial for a team's transactive memory system development (e.g., Hollingshead 1998b; Kanawattanachai and Yoo 2007; Peltokorpi 2004). Based on rather superficial information about team members and their activities that can be exchanged already early on after team constitution, collocated teams can make common experiences and roughly estimate "who knows what"; assumptions that can later be refined and extended (Wegner 1987). Where teams cannot easily communicate, for example because of spatial separation, the development of a transactive memory can pertinently be impacted. This is evidenced in the results of a large number of IS studies on virtual teams (e.g., Griffith et al. 2003; Kanawattanachai and Yoo 2007; Kotlarsky and Oshri 2005; Peltokorpi 2008). Interestingly, this stream of research emphasizes that there are effects beyond a lack of communication that inhibit transactive memory system development. For example, O'Leary and Mortensen (2010) find that the creation of one comparatively small subgroup at a remote location can lead to social boundaries in virtual teams that inhibit transactive memory system development stronger than in teams where all members are located in different locations. Nevertheless, scholars argue that communication and knowledge management technology can partly bridge the spatial distribution between team members and facilitate the development of a transactive memory system (Oshri et al. 2008; Nevo et al. 2012; Su 2012). However, also after the initial establishment of a working transactive memory, a restriction to purely computer-mediated communication often does not allow for perceiving a large amount nonverbal cues and leads to less effective knowledge retrieval (Hollingshead 1998c).

Moreover, the effectiveness of a transactive memory system depends on the accuracy with which team members associate specific tasks with specific expertise requirements and the respective expertise holders (Brandon and Hollingshead 2004). Where team members leave, expertise areas disarrange, or teams face fundamentally new work contexts, also formerly accurate transactive memory systems can become corrupted (Hollingshead 1998a; Lewis et al. 2007; Lewis and Herndon 2011). Consequently, transactive memory systems not only need to become established in an initial phase of a team, but also need to be constantly maintained by explicit or implicit updates. Ellis et al. (2008) propose that this process be looked at in two stages: during an initial transactive memory development, team members establish a rough picture of expertise areas based on common experiences and explicit communication. Thereafter, team members specialize in their task areas, gain new knowledge, and draw on others' expertise where needed during every-day work routine. Based on the success or failure of these retrieval activities, the transactive memory structure is incrementally refined and updated in a second phase. Ellis et al. (2008) emphasize that this incremental refinement can only work for teams that continue working in the same composition and in the same work context. In spite of the differences acknowledged for phases of initial transactive memory system development and later maintenance, the vast majority of organizational research focuses on project teams and other short-lived groups that primarily struggle with the first phase while disregarding the second (Ren and Argote 2011). As the present study is concerned with ongoing and collocated ISD teams in a professional context, especially this second phase of transactive memory system maintenance and refinement during daily routine appears relevant to this study.

2.4.1.3   General IS Research on Transactive Memory Systems

In recent years, scholars focus more closely on the specific mechanisms how technology can support the development and the maintenance of accurate transactive memory systems. As such, research often proposes that IS which allow for codifying task knowledge and explicit expert directories may enhance the initial development of transactive memory systems by providing information that would not be accessible otherwise, even across larger distances (Choi et al. 2010; Nevo and Wand 2005; Oshri et al. 2008; Peltokorpi 2004; Su 2012; Yuan et al. 2007). These systems often intend to provide explicit knowledge to distributed or large groups where tacit knowledge would be relied on in small and collocated groups (Nevo and Wand 2005). Lewis and Herndon (2011) highlight that such technology basically aims to substitute transactive memory systems but fails in doing so: in fact, the presence of these technologies is rarely found to constitute a relevant antecedent to team performance (Lewis and Herndon 2011). The reason for this lack of performance effects is arguably that traditional knowledge management systems and expert directories only emulate structural elements of a transactive memory system but disregard transactive processes (Child and Shumate 2007; Lewis and Herndon 2011; Ryan and O'Connor 2013). Researchers therefore introduce social cues to their IS that are not only intended to facilitate but also to stimulate encoding, storage, and retrieval processes (Nevo et al. 2012). Moreover, scholars now argue for more IS that facilitate transactive processes within day-to-day work routines. These scholars reason that facilitation of transactive processes in the scope of daily work allows for more contextualization of knowledge and more direct application of retrieved information than transactive process support in separate systems that are not part of daily work (Kotlarsky et al. 2014; Zhang et al. 2011). With peer code review systems, this study looks at such a system that is applied during daily software development tasks.

For ISD teams, research on transactive memory systems finds a large number of positive outcome effects including increased effectiveness and efficiency, facilitated knowledge transfer to externals, and more creative integration of information in software products (Espinosa et al. 2007; Faraj and Sproull 2000; Hsu et al. 2012; Kotlarsky and Oshri 2005; Lin et al. 2011; Maruping et al. 2009b; Oshri et al. 2008; Ryan and O'Connor 2013). In particular, transactive memory systems facilitate communication and coordination in ISD teams (Hsu et al. 2012) as well as in open source communities (Chen et al. 2013; Chou and He 2011). Davern et al. (2012) call for research on team cognition and ISD techniques. However, to date there is only scarce research on the role of actual ISD techniques in relation to transactive memory systems theory. Maruping et al. (2009b) show that the performance impact of transactive memory systems in ISD teams can vary depending on the enactment of team norms such as shared code ownership and coding standards. Majchrzak et al. (2013b) study how individuals contribute knowledge and rework existing knowledge contributions, frequently drawing parallels to ISD techniques such as refactoring. Their findings suggest that transactive memory systems help individuals set their own expertise on a specific topic in relation to their colleagues' and helps them decide how to use their own knowledge for collaboration (Majchrzak et al. 2013b). These results may indicate that transactive memory systems possibly also influence how ISD teams are able to make use of ISD techniques. But whether and why ISD techniques might alter a team's transactive memory system remains unclear (Davern et al. 2012).

2.4.1.4 Summary

In sum, this study builds on transactive memory systems theory to study collaborative quality assurance techniques in ISD teams. Transactive memory systems theory is well established in IS research as one of the most productive theories on team cognition. However, there is only a limited number of studies in ISD research and nearly no academic work focuses on ISD techniques. Transactive memory systems theory holds that work groups such as ISD teams develop a transactive memory system which allows them to effectively coordinate specialized knowledge of their single members to achieve better team level outcomes. Transactive memory systems theory is advocated as a good choice for this study because of the clear theoretical account of a team level knowledge structure and individual level transactive processes as well as a strong empirical basis. As a theoretical lens on team cognition in ISD, it is expected to better explain how teams come to use collaborative quality assurance techniques and how ongoing application affects team cognition in turn. In line with extant research, this study conceptualizes transactive memory systems as a bipartite system of transactive memory structure and transactive memory processes. Transactive memory structure consists of (1) the specialized knowledge of single team members, (2) a body of shared labels and vocabulary to describe tasks, issues, and needs for expertise, (3) a shared body of meta-knowledge that associates specific tasks with specific expertise requirements and individual team members with the respective expertise. Transactive memory processes are the behavioral actions and interactions of team members to encode, store, and retrieve information that is relevant for the team's tasks. By consequence, transactive memory structure constitutes the basis for conducting transactive processes, but transactive processes have the potential to change transactive memory structure.

2.4.2 Concept of Functional Affordances

Peer code review originates from the distributed environment of open source communities. In such a setting, collaborative quality assurance is only possible via electronic review systems that allow community members at different locations to act as authors and reviewers. Hence, the technology that underlies peer code review can be assumed to play a key role when studying its application in collocated settings. When engaging in pair programming, developers not only create software as a technological artifact, but also use technology in order to do so. More specifically, developers jointly use the hardware and software of a workstation computer. That is, they share input and output devices as well as programming environments. Consequently, pair programming has an central technological element as well. Given that both techniques under consideration rely heavily on technology, this study requires also an analytical lens that is able to account for the different technologies that are involved in the social process of conducting collaborative quality assurance techniques. A particularly useful and increasingly popular analytical concept of the socially-embedded use of technology is the concept of functional affordances. It is especially appropriate for this study because it fulfills "the demands in the IS literature for mid-range theories that provide explanations of causality at a level of granularity that is specific with respect to the technology while also providing some generality beyond individual case examples" (Volkoff and Strong 2013, p. 10).

2.4.2.1 Historical Roots

The concept of affordances was introduced in ecological psychology to describe how animals (and man as one of them) perceive their surroundings (Gibson 1986). More specifically, the main argument is that objects in the environment provide animals with possibilities to make use of them and are also perceived with respect to their contextual usefulness rather than their physical properties. Gibson (1986) uses the term *affordance* to describe what an object provides, offers, or furnishes to an individual actor and argues that "what we perceive when we look at objects are their affordances, not their qualities" (Gibson 1986, p. 134). For instance, a man may initially perceive little of the physical properties of a stool (e.g., that the stool is wooden and knee-high, has a flat surface and three legs, and its center of gravity is in the middle of the surface) but may first recognize what that stool affords him (e.g., to sit on it). However, the possibilities that an object affords to an actor are not objective, general traits of the object and are not invariant across actors. Instead, it depends on the single actors what an object enables them to do. For instance, an adult may perceive the affordance of sitting on a knee-high stool while a small child may not perceive this possibility for the same stool, simply because the stool, knee-high to the adult, is too high for the child. Discussions, reconceptualizations, and debates ensued Gibson's original proposition[5] in eco-logical psychology (cf. Chemero 2003; Hutchby 2001; Stoffregen 2003) which eventually led to the consensus that affordances are relational; relational in the sense that affordances are neither a property of the object nor of the actor but the result of an interaction of the features of an object and the abilities of an actor (Chemero 2003).

2.4.2.2 Contemporary Conceptualization

In their seminal work, Markus and Silver (2008) transfer the concept of affordances to IS research.[6] Research on IT appropriation (i.e., how users make sense of IT and use it to achieve their goals) acknowledges that the explanation of IT effects is not possible based on IT properties exclusively, as users apply IT in their own ways that do not necessarily conform to the intentions of an IT artifact's designers (DeSanctis and Poole 1994). In particular, Markus and Silver (2008) line out how studies on the appropriation of IT can benefit from a more realist view on both technology as well as sociality while accepting individuals' limited views on and interpretations of the real world. The authors thereby take a critical realist perspective and rely on the concept of affordances to rework existing theory on technology appropriation proposed by DeSanctis and Poole (1994). They coin the terms of *functional affordances*, *material properties*, and *symbolic expressions* to describe the relational aspects between IT artifacts and users who appropriate these artifacts. In line with Markus and Silver (2008) and slight later refinements (Strong et al. 2014; Volkoff and Strong 2013), this study defines functional affordances as *the possibilities for goal-oriented action toward an immediate concrete outcome that are afforded by*

---

[5]This research aims to fruitfully apply and extend the concept of functional affordances in the context of ISD techniques and team cognition. For this purpose, this research primarily relies on the concepts established and discussed in IS research. While an interesting debate about ontological and epistemological aspects of functional affordances has been going on in the field of ecological psychology, that debate is not in the focus of this study and is therefore not elaborated on. Interested readers find a comprehensive summary and discussion of the debate in Robey and Anderson (2013).

[6]A different perspective on affordances is used in the field of human-computer-interaction. Pozzi et al. (2014) provide a good starting point to recapitulate research in that area.

technical objects to a specified user or user group.[7] Symbolic expressions, on the other hand, are defined as *the communicative possibilities of technical objects toward a specified user group* (Markus and Silver 2008, p. 625). In essence, Markus and Silver (2008) posit that an IT artifact is a real entity with specific immutable and material properties that influence but do not determine how human actors perceive and use the artifact. In this perspective, artifacts are developed to be used in specific ways intended by designers who thereby create the artifact's material properties. However, individual actors look at these material properties from their personal, biased perspectives and find that an IT artifact enables or constrains them in their actions of pursuing their numerous goals. Consequently, these actors do not dichotomously choose between using the artifact in the ways intended by its designers on the one hand and not-using it at all on the other hand; they may also perceive the artifact as particularly useful to create outcomes that the designers did not have in mind. The artifact can thereby afford additional possibilities for goal-oriented action based on its material properties. However, the specific ways in which users make use of the artifact are not at random; many users typically use the same artifact in very similar ways although their personal contexts do differ. Markus and Silver (2008) explain this based on their concept of symbolic expressions: the artifact's material properties may also transport elements that allow users to discern values and intentions embedded in the material properties of the artifact, these are called symbolic expressions. Symbolic expressions communicate values and intended ways of use that are interpreted by the users. They thereby guide the users' perceptions of the artifact toward specific affordances but are not deterministic causes of actual use as they depend on users' interpretations (Goh et al. 2011).

For example, a simple calculator software with a graphical user interface (consisting of a display area and buttons for digits and operators) may have the capability to store the calculations visible in the interface to text files. The material properties of this software include the source code that calculates results, displays the interface, and stores the data. They are implemented by its designers to allow for calculating and storing calculations; and to most users, the calculator will thereby afford executing and storing calculations. At the same time, the calculator may be able to store text that is displayed in the interface, even if it is not a calculation; this is a material property, although it may be one that the calculator's designers did not intend to provide to users. Nevertheless, this property may afford the creation and editing of text files to some users. But most would probably rather use the calculator software for calculations and rely on a dedicated text editor for changing text files. That is because the presence of digits and operators (and absence of letters) in the graphical interface is interpreted by most users in the way that operations with numbers may be "better" to conduct with this piece of software than operations with text. The material properties of the calculator thereby

---

[7]In the following, this study adopts Markus and Silver's conceptualization of functional affordances and refers to this conceptualization, even if the prefix "functional" is omitted at times.

signal the value of calculations over text editing; this is what Markus and Silver (2008) refer to as symbolic expressions that constitute communicative possibilities. Importantly, both symbolic expressions and functional affordances are subject to the interpretations of the user, may therefore differ across users, and are not the same as the actual behavior of using an object (Markus and Silver 2008; Volkoff and Strong 2013).

More precisely, the concept of functional affordances holds that material properties of an IT artifact cause functional affordances in that they objectively *enable and constrain what can be achieved with the artifact* (Leonardi and Barley 2010). Material properties therefore constitute necessary but non-sufficient conditions for the existence of specific functional affordances. However, the possibilities of using an artifact do not depend on the material properties of an artifact only; there are also other factors that may play key roles such as "[c]onditions other than technology— users' characteristics and goals, their interpretations of technology, their work practices, and institutional contexts" (Markus and Silver 2008, p. 627). The concept of functional affordances posits that the interplay of two real forces has the generative power to create functional affordances of an object: the object's material properties and the context of the actor who is to make use of the object (Volkoff and Strong 2013). Independent from any interpretations, these two elements create the entire *space of possibilities for an actor to achieve immediate, concrete outcomes* from using the object. Based on his or her own interpretations, the actor then perceives a subset of these affordances and enacts, consciously or unconsciously, some of these affordances. That is, the actor *actualizes* affordances based on the affordances he or she *perceives*. Only actualized affordances may ultimately be conceived as what is commonly referred to as the effects of IT use (Bernhard et al. 2013). In sum, the concept of functional affordances explains in a non-deterministic and context-variant but generalizable way why and how the properties of IT artifacts influence the appropriation of these artifacts by specific users or user groups (Markus and Silver 2008; Volkoff and Strong 2013).

Renown scholars advocate the concept of functional affordances as a foundation for technology-related behavioral research in IS in various research streams and premier outlets (Faraj and Azad 2012; Majchrzak and Markus 2012; Robey and Anderson 2013; Volkoff and Strong 2013; Zammuto et al. 2007). A major reason for this broad support may be that it builds on a critical realist base that overcomes several ontological and epistemological issues of both positivist and social constructivist perspectives (Markus and Silver 2008; Volkoff and Strong 2013). As such, the concept of functional affordances as a foundation for IS research moves away from a purely "feature-centric" view that assumes the presence of objective, general functionality of IS that is invariant for all users and therefore leads to deterministic effects in user behavior (Faraj and Azad 2012). But it also rejects a purely social constructivist view (i.e., that technology has essentially different meanings for each individual) by acknowledging that (1) there are real properties of technological artifacts which exist independent of a user's interpretation and that (2) these properties do exert causal influence on how users perceive and use the technology (Markus and Silver 2008). Functional affordances thereby provide a relational view of technical functionality which is argued to develop in the relation between an actor and a physical object (Robey and Anderson 2013).

2.4.2.3 Broad Application in IS Research

Broadly-spread and fruitful applications of the concept help understand how specific types of IS afford functions that support organizational change (Goh et al. 2011; Leonardi 2011; Volkoff and Strong 2013; Zammuto et al. 2007), for example toward more environmentally sustainable business practices (Seidel et al. 2013) or toward higher service quality (Strong et al. 2014); how different technologies support communication, social interaction, and information exchange within organizational groups (Leonardi 2012; Malhotra and Majchrzak 2012) and on social media platforms (Majchrzak et al. 2013a; Sutcliffe et al. 2011); how different contexts such as organizational roles (Rosenkranz 2011) or membership in a group (Balci et al. 2014; Leonardi 2012) shape individuals' perceptions of affordances; and how technology itself is modified over time in organizations (Goh et al. 2011; Leonardi 2011). Because the majority of these contributions is concerned with organizational level phenomena, this stream of research significantly impacts our understanding of how functional affordances yield emergent effects on an organizational level. Extant research emphasizes that there are several conditions which determine whether IS have emergent effect on levels beyond the individual or not: first, only the actualization of affordances has the potential to create higher level outcomes (Bernhard et al. 2013; Goh et al. 2011; Volkoff and Strong 2013). That is, only if individuals make use of a technology, this technology may create effects, whereas the mere presence of affordances does not create any impact. Second, only if groups of individuals consistently actualize the same affordances, they produce outcomes that add up to a higher level effects (Leonardi 2012; Strong et al. 2014; Sutcliffe et al. 2011). Although single individuals may not necessarily share the same motivations for making use of a function of an IS, they can nevertheless actualize the same affordance and achieve the same immediate outcomes (Leonardi and Barley 2010). For example in a hospital, a medical doctor may have motivations to record patient data electronically in an IS that are different from the motivations of a nurse and of administration staff (e.g., doctors may be motivated by ease of recording while nurses may strive to ensure good care for the patient and administration staff may aim to comply with regulatory rules). But nevertheless the immediate outcome of all three actors' recording activities can be a structured data entry for a patient. If these actors consistently record patient data in the same structured way, the emergent result of a database with structured patient data becomes independent of the actors' motivations in the first place and constitutes the basis for organizational level impacts (Strong et al. 2014). Third, actualized affordances may result in emergent effects even if neither the affordances nor their effects are consciously recognized by the individual actors (Bernhard et al. 2013; Leonardi 2012; Strong et al. 2014; Van Osch and Mendelson 2011). For example, in settings of computer-mediated or technology-based communication, individuals may communicate different content and in a different manner, even without being aware of it (Van Osch and Mendelson 2011). Emergent changes in an organization's resources may similarly result from individual actions without the actors' awareness of such change (Strong et al. 2014). Lastly, affordances can interact and build on each other, eventually producing higher level outcomes (Leonardi 2011; Strong et al. 2014; Volkoff and Strong 2013). As the actualization of affordances creates immediate, concrete outcomes, these outcomes may constitute the basis for further affordances but may also conflict with previously existing affordances. Thereby, affordances can interfere with and foster one another (Goh et al. 2011; Leonardi 2011). In particular, recent research proposes that basic affordances can create advanced affordances through the outcomes of their consistent and frequent actualization (Strong et al. 2014; Volkoff and Strong 2013).

2.4.2.4   Application in Group Cognition Research

Few but notable studies apply the concept of functional affordances to research on group cognition. As such, Leonardi (2012) studies advice networks and how new simulation technologies change advice networks in highly interdependent engineering work groups. He finds that technology appropriation needs to converge to group-wide, shared patterns of feature use for group level improvements in advice networks to occur. Where individuals make use of the same affordances, they are found to create possibilities for mutual exchange of advice that do not exist without technology support. In particular, only where sets of "shared affordances" are actualized by all group members, higher level affordances emerge which allow an entire work group to draw and give advice more effectively (Leonardi 2012). Majchrzak et al. (2013a) study knowledge sharing through social media between employees in organizations. They find that social media afford a set of four particular functions to employees who engage in communal knowledge sharing. The authors show how these four individual level affordances of social media yield ambivalent effects on the effectiveness of knowledge sharing on a group level. The investigated technology helps individuals achieve their goals in specific ways (e.g., by providing the possibility to draw on networks of close colleagues when looking for information). However, the individuals' actual actions have positive as well as negative effects on the quality of knowledge sharing in their group (Majchrzak et al. 2013a). Lastly, Malhotra and Majchrzak (2012) study knowledge coordination through virtual workspace technologies in distributed teams. In particular, the authors focus on technological features for direct, synchronous communication (e.g., instant messaging, screen sharing) and written, asynchronous communication that clearly identifies the participants (e.g., annotations in shared files with author names, revision histories with team members' contributions). They find that team members' satisfaction with knowledge coordination in virtual teams increases if teams make use of two specific affordances of virtual workspace technologies: knowledge evolution monitoring (i.e., the possibilities to gather and understand how team members' expertise changes compared to one's own expertise), and virtual co-presence (i.e., showing activity at the same time with other team members). Virtual co-presence is found to be afforded by synchronous communication tools, whereas the asynchronous communication technologies are found to foster knowledge evolution monitoring (Malhotra and Majchrzak 2012).

2.4.2.5 Application in ISD Research

Although some scholars argue that the concept of functional affordances is particularly promising for research on the design of IT artifacts (Davern et al. 2012; Markus and Silver 2008), only few studies use the concept for ISD research: Cao et al. (2013) study the adoption of agile processes in ISD firms based on functional affordances and its theoretical predecessor, adaptive structuration theory by DeSanctis and Poole (1994). In particular, the authors look at how the appropriation of agile IT funding processes is influenced by contextual factors such as the adoption of agile ISD techniques. Interestingly, they argue that by studying a process of IT funding rather than the use of a technology "the notion of restrictiveness, which refers to the degree of freedom a user has in applying technology, is not as critical in our context due to the inherent flexibilities of processes enacted by individuals when compared with what is afforded by information technologies that implement processes" (Cao et al. 2013, p. 202). The authors find that the adoption of a new, agile IT funding process creates structural conflicts with surrounding contexts such as more or less agile ISD techniques in use and the remains of the old funding process. Organizational actors are found to react on these conflicts which eventually leads to the appropriation or the abandonment of the new process (Cao et al. 2013). Rosenkranz (2011) takes a functional affordances perspective to conceptually analyze a generalized ISD process in which users and designers iteratively interact and a software artifact is created incrementally. He aims to find a conceptualization of an ISD process that aids in hypothesizing about the social workings in ISD between users and designers while acknowledging the role of the IS under development. The author proposes an extension of the concepts of Markus and Silver (2008) by two types of actors (users and designers), three types of activities (design, communicate, use), and the concept of design affordances which refers to affordances of an IS as conceived and intended by its designers as opposed to its users (Rosenkranz 2011).[8]

2.4.2.6 Critical Assessment of Extant Work

In sum, the concept of functional affordances is applied successfully in research on team cognition in a number of cases, whereas little research uses it in studies on ISD.

---

[8]The idea of distinctive design affordances perceived and intended by an artifact's designers has come up before (Van Osch and Mendelson 2011).

Studies on team cognition outline that the concept can serve as a productive basis to understand knowledge coordination in teams, but theory on transactive memory systems currently does not play a role in that area of research. Extant work on ISD does, to the best of this author's knowledge, not address specific team level ISD techniques from a perspective of functional affordances. Scholars who study processes in ISD highlight that there are important differences between the appropriation of a technology and the appropriation of ISD procedures that encompass the use of technology (Cao et al. 2013; Rosenkranz 2011). These differences warrant a careful reinterpretation of the concepts proposed by Markus and Silver (2008) and refined during the last years (e.g., Strong et al. 2014; Volkoff and Strong 2013). This conclusion is in line with the evaluation of scholars in organizational change who highlight the enormous potential of functional affordances for the study of routines but also ask for appropriate reconceptualizations (Robey and Anderson 2013). The valuable work of researchers who advanced into this topic, however, has not yet completed this task. A large part of studies in routines and processes based on the concept of functional affordances theorizes in a versatile manner how routines and technology affordances interact to co-evolve (e.g., Goh et al. 2011; Leonardi 2011). However, these studies conceptualize technology as a force *influential* on but *external* to inherently social routines or processes. That is, they partly neglect that technology plays actually a constituting role in some routines (D'Adderio 2011; Mutch 2010; Volkoff et al. 2007). For example, ISD techniques such as pair programming would not exist without a workstation computer and programming environment in which two developers can program together. Such an over-emphasis on the social and the partial neglect of material aspects which traditionally guides studies in organizational routines (D'Adderio 2011; Mutch 2010; Volkoff et al. 2007) also dominates the little research on functional affordances in routinized ISD processes. For example, Cao et al. (2013) explicitly downplay the role of technology in the IT funding process they study to emphasize exclusively on its social aspects (see above). This is slightly paradoxical, as renown scholars convincingly propose functional affordances as a potential remedy of exactly this insufficient consideration of technology in processes and routines (Robey and Anderson 2013). At the same time, the only extant reconceptualization trying to account for the constitutional role of technology in an ISD process, provided by Rosenkranz (2011), is still in an early stage of development, introduces a number of concepts that are highly specific to the interaction of users and designers, and can therefore not be easily transferred to another context. To sum up, the study of ISD techniques and team cognition with the concept of functional affordances is highly promising (Davern et al. 2012) but requires reinterpretations of the major concepts (Robey and Anderson 2013). Prior studies do not deliver acceptable reinterpretations for this research on group level ISD techniques. Consequently, this study proceeds by adapting the concepts of functional affordances, material properties, and symbolic expressions to the context of collaborative quality assurance techniques.

2.4.3   Adaptation of Functional Affordances to ISD Techniques

In a recent review of IS literature, Davern et al. (2012) call for research on ISD techniques and their socio-cognitive implications. More specifically, the authors call for research on the affordances of ISD techniques with respect to group cognition in teams of software developers (Davern et al. 2012, p. 300). While this study strongly supports the idea that a functional affordances perspective on ISD techniques may be particularly valuable, it also agrees with scholars who demand a careful examination of the relevant concepts for including IT as a central part of routines (Robey and Anderson 2013). Consequently, this study builds on prior conceptualizations of functional affordances, material properties, and symbolic expressions to partially extend and adapt these conceptualizations for the analysis of team level ISD techniques, in particular of collaborative quality assurance techniques.

The concept of functional affordances is traditionally used to understand the use of physical objects or information technologies. By focusing on the functional affordances of ISD *techniques* this study breaks new ground. In line with the definition provided in the previous section, affordances of an ISD technique refer to the possibilities for goal-oriented action toward an immediate concrete outcome that are afforded by a technique to specified actors. However, collaborative ISD techniques are immanently different from other pieces of IT in that they incorporate not only technology but also prescriptions for actions and interactions of individual actors; they are socio-technical. In this regard, the question arises what constitutes the material properties of an ISD technique. Markus and Silver (2008) describe the characteristics of an IT artifact as "material and immaterial real things, the properties of which are potentially causal, that is, necessary conditions for people to perceive them and use them in particular ways with particular consequences" (Markus and Silver 2008, p. 625). That is, material properties of an artifact can be seen as the real, immutable elements of the artifact that actually cause possibilities for use. While these elements are interpreted by individuals when assessing the artifact's affordances, the elements *exist* independently from any interpretations in their own right (Volkoff and Strong 2013). Whereas individuals' interpretations of an element may differ, it is objectively the same single element (Bernhard et al. 2013). Transferred to ISD techniques, this means that material properties must refer to the constitutive elements of a technique that are real, immutable, and exist relatively independent of interpretations, but their properties are potentially causal for people to perceive them and conduct them in particular ways with particular consequences. That is, they are ontologically not dependent on human beings' perceptions, but they epistemologically influence human beings' perspectives.

Based on this slight reconceptualization, material properties of an ISD technique can be argued to consist of the *technology that is applied to conduct the technique on the one hand and the most elementary prescriptions of actors' actions and interactions including their physical and temporal properties on the other hand*. For example, the simultaneous presence of exactly two developers at a workstation

computer is one material property of pair programming.[9] While developers may
have different perceptions which immediate, concrete outcomes can be achieved in
this setting (i.e., what the setting affords), the basic, constraining factors of this
setting are objectively clear: The moment that one of two developers leaves or
a third developer joins the activities, they clearly abandon the technique of pair
programming.

Extant research focuses less on the concept of symbolic expressions than on
material properties and resulting affordances (for exceptions see Balci et al. 2014;
Bernhard et al. 2013; Goh et al. 2011; Pozzi et al. 2014; Rosenkranz 2011). In
their seminal work, Markus and Silver (2008) refer to symbolic expressions as
the communicative possibilities of an artifact that transport values and implicit
recommendations how a user may want to behave. For example, specific graphical
user interfaces are material properties of an artifact but can transport symbolic
expressions that aim to communicate values and recommendations. As such, red
color is often used to indicate warnings. Importantly, the perception of red color as a
warning is entirely subject to the user's interpretations; nevertheless, it steers many
users, specifically the ones in whose cultural background red signifies a warning,
toward being cautious (Markus and Silver 2008). Symbolic expression therefore
result from material properties but are relational between an artifact and a specified
group of users. Sticking to the example, only those users who know that red is
sometimes used as a warning sign will be able to understand that the graphical user
interface issues a symbolic warning.

Users who understand the symbolic expressions embedded in an artifact thereby
gain a more precise picture of what the artifact affords to them (Balci et al.
2014; Bernhard et al. 2013; Goh et al. 2011; Rosenkranz 2011). Transferred to
collaborative quality assurance techniques, not only the technology that is applied
in the scope of an ISD technique may carry symbolic expressions but also the
other material aspects of the technique. For example, the physical properties and
elementary prescriptions of interaction may hold symbolic expressions. As such,
two pair programming developers who sit at the same computer and program the
same piece of source code may or may not perceive the symbolic expression that
criticism of their programming partner's ideas and code is desirable. Whether they
perceive such a valuation of criticism then arguably impacts what the developers
perceive they can achieve with pair programming. Consequently, this study adapts
the concept of symbolic expressions to the context of ISD techniques and sees them
as the *communicative possibilities of a technique for a specified group of developers*.

Previous work highlights that actors' knowledge of an artifact influences their
perception of affordances (Markus and Silver 2008; Strong et al. 2014; Volkoff and
Strong 2013) as well as symbolic expressions (Balci et al. 2014; Goh et al. 2011).
Arguably, this also holds true for ISD techniques. Where developers are provided
with information and opinions on an ISD technique or where they receive training,

---

[9] A full assessment of material properties and symbolic expressions of pair programming and peer
code review follows in Sect. 4.1.3.

they gain additional background information about the technique and can more easily perceive its embedded symbolic expressions and, by consequence, receive hints how and toward which ends the technique can be helpful for them. It appears therefore very worthwhile for this study to gain an understanding of symbolic expression of collaborative quality assurance techniques when ultimately aiming to find their affordances and effects.

In sum, this study argues that only slight adaptations to the concepts of material properties and symbolic expressions are necessary when relying on a perspective of functional affordances for research on collaborative quality assurance techniques. Overall, the examination of ISD techniques from this perspective of functional affordances has several advantages over positivist views that search for deterministic effects of IT and over constructivist views that only focus on social interaction and see technology as an external influence on this behavior. As such, it acknowledges that (1) ISD techniques such as pair programming and peer code review can be appropriated differently by different ISD teams, but there is rational ground why specific appropriations are more reasonable in a particular context; (2) technology constitutes an invariable and central element of ISD techniques that exerts generalizable causal influences on the existence of affordances (i.e., to what ends a technique *can* be applied) but does not *determine* how techniques are ultimately applied; (3) ISD techniques have immutable, constitutive elements that go beyond technology and cannot be changed without abandoning the techniques; and (4) team members' perception of an ISD technique's affordances is not solely based on symbolic expressions internal to the technique but can also be established and reinforced by external sources, for example by trainings.

2.5 Summary and Preliminary Research Framework

Despite its central meaning for ISD, extant ISD research does not pay much attention to team cognition . In particular, research on team cognition and ISD techniques, let alone collaborative quality assurance techniques, is extremely scarce (Davern et al. 2012). This study aims to partially overcome this dearth of research. It seeks to create a mid-range theory that explains (1) how team cognition affects the appropriation of collaborative quality assurance techniques in collocated ISD teams; and (2) how emergent effects on team cognition and performance result from the application of these techniques. Based on a review of extant literature, theory on transactive memory systems and the concept of functional affordances were selected as a theoretical foundations of this study. These two lenses have both proven their utility in impressive amounts of prior research and were shown to appropriately address the central elements of this study. Transactive memory systems constitute a central factor influencing ISD team coordination and performance in extant work. Extant research on affordances seeks to understand the basic mechanisms of affordances creation, perception, actualization, and effect emergence in the appropriation of IT artifacts (Bernhard et al. 2013; Strong et al. 2014; Volkoff and

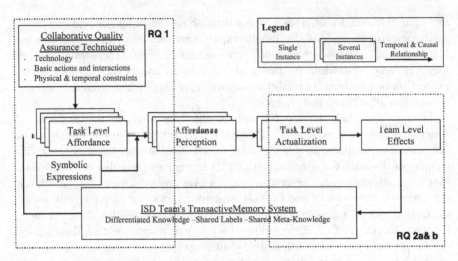

Fig. 2.1 Initial research framework (based on Bernhard et al. 2013)

Strong 2013). This study considers ISD techniques and thereby extends research on these mechanisms to a new field. The concepts of material properties and symbolic expressions were adapted for studying collaborative quality assurance techniques.

Based on prior work of Bernhard et al. (2013), Fig. 2.1 depicts an initial framework that delineates the content of this study. Extant research shows that functional affordances result from material properties of an artifact on the one hand and the specific context of a user on the other hand (Markus and Silver 2008; Volkoff and Strong 2013). The collaborative quality assurance techniques of pair programming and peer code review are collaboratively applied in ISD teams. Therefore, a dominant contextual influence is argued to stem from a team's distributed cognitive structure, namely its transactive memory. Answering Research Question 1, this study aims to explain how team cognition influences the task level application of collaborative quality assurance techniques. Based on the mentioned theoretical foundations, this study initially suggests that there is an interplay of ISD techniques' material properties and an ISD team's transactive memory that causes opportunities for developers to apply the techniques in order to achieve specific, immediate, and concrete goals on a task level (i.e., this interplay causes task level functional affordances). However, due to limited human perception, not all existent affordances are necessarily perceived by the developers. This study further suggests that symbolic expressions that are embedded in the techniques can, if detected, increase the perception of functional affordances by developers. Depending on their concrete goals, developers arguably draw from the affordances they perceive to put them into action on specific tasks. Only if members of an ISD team consistently and frequently make use of the same task level affordances, this can be expected to result in emergent effects on team level aspects such as performance or team cognition. Answering Research Questions 2a and 2b, this study aims to explain why and how such ongoing application of collaborative quality assurance techniques results in impacts on teams' transactive memory system and software quality (cf. Fig. 2.1).

The first research question of this study consequently focuses primarily on the causal mechanisms that create functional affordances of collaborative quality assurance techniques in the light of team cognition. As functional affordances are constructs in the "domain of the real" (cf. Mingers 2004, p. 94) they cannot be observed directly (Markus and Silver 2008; Volkoff and Strong 2013). Consequently, this study refers to perceptions of functional affordances by single developers for deducing the existence of particular affordances (cf. Fig. 2.1). The remaining two research questions of this study focus on the identification and explanation of emergent effects of collaborative quality assurance techniques on software quality as a key indicator of team performance and on transactive memory as a key form of team cognition. To find such effects, if they exist, this study focuses on consistent and frequent applications of collaborative quality assurance techniques within single ISD teams across the teams' individual tasks. By consequence, the individual level cognitive processes of selecting perceived affordances for actualization are not in the scope of this study and remain open for future investigations (cf. Fig. 2.1).

Chapter 3
Research Design

This chapter outlines and discusses the research strategy underlying this study. First, critical realism is introduced and put forward as the central epistemological and ontological stance of this study. Subsequently, this study's sequential mixed-methods research strategy is delineated from traditional positivist quantitative and interpretive qualitative approaches. This strategy encompasses a sequence of research activities ranging from an initial exploration followed by four in-depth case studies in ISD teams to a questionnaire-based survey of more than 600 participants. In their sequence, these distinct activities mesh to provide answers to this study's research questions: (1) the phase of initial exploration first serves to elicit the functional affordances of collaborative quality assurance techniques. It shows that there is a bounded set of functional affordances of these techniques, but not all teams perceive the same subset of affordances. In fact, this phase finds hints toward the influence of team cognition on the perception of functional affordances of collaborative quality assurance techniques in teams. (2) The phase of in-depth case studies serves to provide an explanation why teams differ in the subsets of affordances they perceive. It finds that their transactive memory restricts them in the application of collaborative quality assurance techniques. Moreover, this phase serves to find and explain the emergent effects of collaborative quality assurance techniques on a team's transactive memory. (3) The questionnaire-based survey serves to corroborate this explanation and tests the economically relevant consequences implied by the explanation. In the following, the single research steps are discussed with respect to their internal consistency, rigor, and validity. Lastly, this section also examines the validity of the integrated research design.

© Springer International Publishing Switzerland 2016   59
K. Spohrer, *Collaborative Quality Assurance in Information Systems Development*,
Progress in IS, DOI 10.1007/978-3-319-25163-9_3

3.1 Ontological and Epistemological Stance: Critical Realism

Traditionally, empirical and theoretical research in the information systems discipline relied on one of two major stances regarding the philosophy of science: positivism on the one and interpretivism on the other hand (Lee 1991; Lee and Baskerville 2003; Mingers 2004; Orlikowski and Baroudi 1991; Tsang 2014).

The positivist tradition provides a strongly realist view of ontology, i.e. of what constitutes reality and if there actually exists one objective reality (Fleetwood 2005; Orlikowski and Baroudi 1991). Originating from natural sciences, positivism posits that reality consists of observable entities following universal, law-like rules that *determine* how single entities behave within the world. Human beings are argued to be able to observe this behavior and to infer the laws of reality from their unbiased observations. In this perspective, the ontological criterion for accepting the existence of something is its observability (Mingers 2004). Empirical positivist research then aims to create theories that fully describe the universal rules by reasoning on prior observations, predicting how entities should behave if a theory described the rules correctly, and verifying[1] or refuting the theory by comparing predictions to observed behaviors.

The interpretive research tradition has heavily criticized positivist philosophy for a number of underlying assumptions: positivist research requires unbiased, objective observations of reality to be carried out by human actors, and the law-like rules to be discovered are seen as deterministic for phenomena. Scholars have argued that these assumptions, even if partially acceptable for natural sciences, may definitely not be transferred to the social sciences that investigate social phenomena. According to this reasoning, social phenomena deal with at least partially intentional human actions and interactions that are rooted in single individuals' perceptions, motives, and capabilities (Foucault 1980; Schütz 1970). Consequently, these human actors are not seen to follow deterministic, law-like rules but to make decisions about the actions they take based on their own biased and subjective reasoning (Giddens 1984). Ontologically, there is consequently not one reality of a social phenomenon but a multitude of realities, each dependent on a single actor's interpretation. From this perspective, the best social science can do is to *understand the interpretations* of social phenomena as perceived by their decisive actors, to explicate conflicts, and to support their resolution (Schütz 1970). This tradition thereby conceptualizes social phenomena as ontologically distinct from natural phenomena, but it does so based on its epistemological conceptualization, i.e. based on an idea of what constitutes knowledge and how human beings generate it.

---

[1]Although early positivist work had strong inductive elements, substantial philosophical critique on objective and preconception-free inductive reasoning (Kuhn 1970; Popper 1959) led to a dominance of positivist research based on deduction and falsification. The latter is what is commonly referred to as *positivist* in the information systems discipline (Lee 1991). Nevertheless, there have been notable intents to reintroduce inductive methods into the positivist tradition that are frequently referred to in IS (Eisenhardt 1989).

Researchers from both philosophical traditions have contributed enormously to the body of knowledge in the IS discipline and interpretive work has become one accepted foundational pillar of IS research (Klein and Myers 1999; Myers and Klein 2011; Walsham 1995b). Both streams of research come with a set of research methods that are accepted by the respective stream's scholars and in line with their philosophical stance. As such, positivist research is predominantly deductive, quantitative, and testing in nature (Venkatesh et al. 2013) with qualitative research being acceptable in the process of theory development regarding phenomena that are hard to operationalize in quantitative research (Dibbern et al. 2008; Eisenhardt 1989). This quantitative dominance originates from the aim of generalizing theory across different settings to come closer to discovering the universal laws. Additional settings in which a theory provides correct predictions are thereby seen as a sign of its validity and generalizability (Lee and Baskerville 2003). Interpretive research, on the other hand, is primarily qualitative in nature (Orlikowski and Baroudi 1991) and quantitative analyses are heavily criticized as oversimplifications that do not allow for appropriate analyses of interpretations necessary to understand each specific setting (Klein and Myers 1999). The interpretive researcher's goal is not to generalize theory to as many other settings as possible but to understand each setting as thoroughly as possible (Lee and Baskerville 2003). Some researchers have tried to bridge at least methodological differences between these dominant philosophical schools in IS (Lee 1991), but the essential differences have remained unresolved (Walsham 1995b). And so the IS research community has long felt a divide between "qualitative empirical researchers" and "quantitative empirical researchers" who typically pertained to the interpretive and positivist schools respectively (Lee and Baskerville 2003; Venkatesh et al. 2013). Consequently, there has been a dearth of research that relies on both qualitative and quantitative methods in pari passu, conducting investigation in both areas equally rigorously and gaining substantive findings from investigations that combine methods (Ågerfalk 2013; Mingers 2001, 2003; Venkatesh et al. 2013; Zachariadis et al. 2013).

However, in the late twentieth century, scholars developed a new philosophical stance, *critical realism*, that convincingly resolves philosophical issues with both the positivist as well as the interpretive perspective and strongly argues for the application of research methods from both research streams (for key contributions see Ackroyd and Fleetwood 2000; Archer et al. 1998; Bhaskar 1998a; Fleetwood 2005; Fleetwood and Ackroyd 2004; Sayer 2000). During recent years, critical realism has gained much acceptance within the IS discipline as can be seen from recent special issues (Mingers et al. 2013), numerous insightful studies conducted in this stance (e.g. Aaltonen and Tempini 2014; Bygstad 2010; Mutch 2010; Volkoff et al. 2007), and an emergent set of methodological guidelines for this stream (Bygstad and Munkvold 2011; Mingers 2001, 2003; Tsang 2014; Wynn and Williams 2012; Zachariadis et al. 2013).

This study takes the epistemological and ontological stance of critical realism (Archer et al. 1998; Archer 1995; Bhaskar 1998a; Mingers 2004). Critical realism incorporates a realist ontology that overcomes the drawbacks of the ontological perspectives of both the positivist and the interpretive stance: neither does it conceptualize social structures and mechanisms as deterministic and universal laws nor does it deny the existence of causal powers in social phenomena that are more than the results of an individual's perception (Mingers 2004). Critical realism acknowledges a stratified ontology by accepting that there is a *reality of structures and generative mechanisms with enduring properties that exist relatively independent of human perceptions* but cannot necessarily be observed; while these mechanisms have *causal powers* and tendencies to create actual events, they are *not deterministic and several mechanisms can interact* at a time to produce a phenomenon (Bhaskar 1998a; Mingers 2004). That is, generative mechanisms set the enabling and constraining boundaries for actual events to happen. For example, technological aspects enable and constrain actions a user can take in an information system (Strong et al. 2014). And differences in technology create non-deterministic but nevertheless frequently-found tendencies how users tend to behave in spite of their own authority to actively decide about their behavior (Markus and Silver 2008; Volkoff et al. 2007). In fact, functional affordances of information systems can be seen as one prominent type of generative mechanism in the focus of contemporary critical realist research (Markus and Silver 2008; Volkoff and Strong 2013).

Critical realism further acknowledges that *human perceptions are constrained* by individual capabilities and preconceptions and that only a limited subset of actual events can be observed empirically (Bhaskar 1998a; Fleetwood 2005; Mingers 2004). At the same time, human knowledge is seen as relational within the open and dynamic structures of social systems, dependent on individuals' interpretations, and inherently fallible (Archer et al. 1998). From an epistemic perspective, critical realism parallels interpretive research by accepting that knowledge is always local and historical and many views exist on the same phenomenon. However, in contrast to interpretive research, critical realism does not hold that each view is equally valid; based on a realist ontology, there is rational ground for choosing between more and less appropriate views (Mingers et al. 2013). Taking these aspects into account, the goal of critical realist research is then to find theories that best describe the generative mechanisms and their interplay that causes a phenomenon, i.e. to provide causal explanations of partially observable events (Tsang 2014; Wynn and Williams 2012).

In more detail, this study follows Archer's approach of analytical dualism which, as opposed to other scholars (Giddens 1984), posits that social structure and human action can be separated analytically (Archer et al. 1998; Archer 1995, 1998, 2010). This approach holds that social structure has generative powers and, through these powers, generates the structural conditions in which human agency unfolds. In following their own projects, individual actors then act subject to but also in reaction to these conditions. Through such individual agency and human reflection, social structures can be reinforced or altered over time (Archer 1995, 2010). This perspective helps separate the effects of behaviors, such as developers' interactions during collaborative quality assurance, from effects of social structures, such as teams' distributed knowledge structure, in which actions are embedded (Archer 1995). Analytical dualism, consequently, gives this research not only its ontological and epistemological foundation, but also provides the meta-theoretical basis to study behavior and socio-cognitive structures in ISD teams.

Moreover, critical realism and analytical dualism appear particularly compatible with the theory of transactive memory systems presented in Sect. 2.4.1. Based on the assumptions of critical realism, transactive memory structure is seen as a team-level structure that is part of the domain of the real. Therefore, transactive memory structure is seen as not immediately observable, but has generative power to influence actual, observable behavior of human actors. Transactive processes for encoding, storing, and retrieving information in a group are observable behaviors that are strongly influenced by transactive memory structure but also have the potential to alter this structure.

The ontological and epistemological assumptions of critical realism also impact the research process following this philosophical stance. As opposed to inductive or deductive inference, critical realist research applies *retroduction* (Bhaskar 1998b; Mingers 2004; Tsang 2014; Wynn and Williams 2012). In retroduction "we take some unexplained phenomenon and propose hypothetical mechanisms that, *if they existed*, would generate or cause that which is to be explained" (Mingers et al. 2013, p. 797).[2] In contrast to induction, retroduction takes existing theory into account but is, contrary to deduction, not bound to inferential logic stemming only from existing theory (Mingers 2001). Tsang (2014) describes different classes of retroduction based on Eco (1983) that differ in the proportions of explanations taken from existing theory and creative explanations devised by a researcher: essentially all types of explanations, including explanations fully deductible from extant theory and explanations purely based on creative reasoning, are acceptable if they show high explanatory power (Tsang 2014). Retroduction is then an iterative approach where theoretical explanations are taken from extant theory or devised on the basis of observed events, contrasted with alternative explanations, applied to additional data, and finally selected if possessing the highest explanatory power (Bhaskar 1998b).[3] Iterations of data collection, analysis, and retroduction are therefore desirable to gain a broad picture of the researched phenomenon and to rule out explanations inferior to the final one (Mingers 2001).

3.2   Mixed Methods Research Strategy

Assuming a stratified ontology and the situatedness of human knowledge, it is commonly held that critical realist research should not rely only on a single, isolated research method because this would increase the probability of missing

---

[2]Emphasis in the original.

[3]Some scholars have argued that retroduction is essentially the same as "abduction" coined by Charles Pierce (Mingers et al. 2013; Tsang 2014). In line with current critical realist work in IS (Volkoff et al. 2007; Wynn and Williams 2012; Zachariadis et al. 2013), this paper only refers to the term "retroduction".

or misinterpreting actually observable events (Ågerfalk 2013; Mingers and Brock-lesby 1997; Tsang 2014; Zachariadis et al. 2013). Especially a sole reliance on survey-based statistical analyses must be deemed inappropriate for research that wants to establish causal explanations (Mingers 2004). Instead, a mix of research methods is recommended where different methods compensate for shortcomings of others (Mingers 2001): intensive, qualitative investigations may be seen as most appropriate to create a detailed understanding of observable events and to infer the underlying generative mechanisms of a phenomenon (Mingers 2001; Tsang 2014; Wynn and Williams 2012), whereas quantitative analyses may serve better to elicit demi-regularities of a phenomenon that can be used either as a starting point for further exploration or for subsequent triangulation and corroboration of proposed mechanisms (Miles and Huberman 1994; Mingers 2004; Wynn and Williams 2012; Zachariadis et al. 2013).

This study follows a sequential mixed methods approach where qualitative examinations are followed by a phase of quantitative corroboration. It consists of three phases of data collection and analysis (cf. Table 3.1) in which results of the earlier inform the later, while the later complement the earlier and help corroborate and even reinterpret findings based on additional insights (Mingers 2001; Venkatesh et al. 2013). The three phases correspond to this study's research questions so that each later phase helps refine the answers to the questions gained before (Zachariadis et al. 2013). In more detail, a first phase explores the effects of team cognition in ISD teams on their collaborative quality assurance activities on a task level based on immersion in a case company and semi-structured interviews with key informants from nine teams. The second phase consists of in-depth case studies of four ISD teams based on a large variety of data sources. It examines the detailed mechanisms underlying the effects of team cognition on task level collaborative quality assurance identified in Phase 1 (i.e., Research Question 1) as well as the emergent effects of team-wide collaborative quality assurance activities on team cognition (i.e., Research Question 2a). Two generative mechanisms are proposed that explain why and how collaborative quality assurance on a team level affects a team's transactive memory. The third phase consists of a questionnaire-based survey with a multitude of ISD team members, team leaders, and team managers. It examines teams in different contexts for demi-regularities that should result from the generative mechanisms proposed in the second phase and links these emergent effects to performance impacts in ISD teams. All phases are conducted within a major international software development company, more specifically in its German locations.

This research strategy seems appropriate and promising for a number of reasons:

1. As discussed before, a mixed methods design is recommended based on the ontological and epistemological underpinning of critical realism (Miles and Huberman 1994; Mingers 2001; Venkatesh et al. 2013; Zachariadis et al. 2013).
2. Chapter 2 showed there is no extensive established body of knowledge applicable to answer the research questions. For streams of research in such a premature or

Table 3.1 Research design overview

	Initial exploration	Critical realist case studies on four ISD teams		Questionnaire-based survey
Time	Summer 2012	October 2012–July 2013		November 2013–January 2014
Goal	*Find* functional affordances, material properties, and symbolic expressions of techniques	*Explain* how team cognition affects functional affordances and how team cognition is affected by the techniques		*Corroborate* explanation and *extend* it to quality impacts
Activities	• Review of literature • Attendance of trainings in peer code review and pair programming • Exploration of functional affordances of techniques	• Participatory observations of full working days • Interviews after sessions of collaborative quality assurance • Interviews with team leaders, managers, and stakeholders	• Analysis of peer code review systems • Workshop with participating teams	• Questionnaire-based survey with diverse ISD teams of the case company • Gain responses from product managers, team leaders, and members of the teams
Collected data	• Informal talks with trainers and participants of trainings • Ten semi-structured interviews with agile method trainers, scrum masters, senior developers • Three interviews with developers of an open-source peer code review platform used in the case company • Training materials • Open-source tool documentation, incl. recommended review procedures	• Semi-structured field notes of 12 observation days (incl. meetings, interactions, work procedures, lunch breaks, context) • Semi-structured observation field notes of 30 sessions of pair programming and peer code review • Semi-structured post-session interviews (10–40 min) for observed events of collaborative quality assurance • Four semi-structured interviews with team leaders (35–60 min)	• Informal interviews with two product owners and two managers • More than 700 code changes from peer code review systems of three teams from August 2012 to January 2013, including the code changes created and reviewed during observed peer code review sessions	• Data from 81 ISD teams (452 team members, 79 team leaders, 38 product managers) • Team level use of collaborative quality assurance, transactive memory, quality of results, as well as team, task, and product characteristics

(continued)

Table 3.1 (continued)

	Initial exploration	Critical realist case studies on four ISD teams		Questionnaire-based survey
Time	Summer 2012	October 2012–July 2013		November 2013–January 2014
Data analysis	• Recording, transcription and coding of interviews • Examination of training materials and tool documentation • Reflection on attended trainings	• Aggregation of data to episodes representing observable, abstract events • Coding of data regarding structure and explanations of events	• Coding of team and task characteristics • Team level interaction analysis of review systems • Within-case and cross-case analyses	• Variance-based structural equation modeling
Insights	• Understanding of organizational structure and culture • Teams differ in perceived functional affordances of collaborative quality assurance	• Teams' transactive memory structure and techniques' properties cause functional affordances • Techniques afford less to teams with restricted transactive memory	• Pair programming causes homogenization and peer code review transparency of teams' transactive memory	• Peer code review improves quality and provides an alternative to transactive memory structure for knowledge-coordination • Pair programming homogenizes knowledge is beneficial for personally distant but harmful for close teams

intermediary state, mixed methods with a strong reliance on qualitative elements have been highly recommended in the past (Edmondson and McManus 2007; Venkatesh ct al. 2013).

3. Due to the variegated backgrounds, capabilities, and motives of individuals, social systems are inherently open and influenced by many forces that, in their combination, result in specific social actions (Wynn and Williams 2012). ISD teams' work and behavior may for example not only be influenced by their tasks, development practices, and cognition but may also depend on aspects proprietary to the company and the culture they are embedded in. Especially quantitative research approaches, however, assume a high level of closure and the elimination of external forces. Closure becomes less feasible the broader the context of a study gets (Mingers 2004; Zachariadis et al. 2013). Consequently, this study follows a research design where all empirical research, including the questionnaire-based survey, is conducted within the limits of a single company. This allows for quasi-closure and for a reduction of external influences impacting the research setting (Zachariadis et al. 2013).

4. A broader qualitative inquiry at the beginning allows researchers to familiarize with the research context and to reduce its impact on later research steps by explicitly accounting for known and relevant context factors. On the one hand increased numbers of cases in such an exploratory state limit the researcher's resources that can be devoted to each case; on the other hand a higher number of cases increases the chance to observe relevant events (Yin 2009). The first phase of this study therefore explores a larger number of cases albeit less intensively. Deeper investigations of few cases in a second phase are then more appropriate for creating a detailed understanding of the phenomenon of interest (Eisenhardt 1989; Lee and Baskerville 2003). In the scope of this study, four such in-depth investigations of ISD teams are conducted. Finally, the third phase quantitatively discovers regularities in line with the theoretical results of the previous two phases. This shows that findings are not idiosyncratic to the conducted case studies but exist also outside these boundaries. That is, a subsequent quantitative phase adds generalizability to the existing findings of qualitative work (Eisenhardt 1989; Miles and Huberman 1994; Venkatesh et al. 2013).

3.3 Case Company

The selected case company is one of the world's largest enterprise software companies with more than 60,000 employees worldwide, locations in more than 130 countries, and a yearly revenue of over e 15 billion in 2013. It provides a broad range of enterprise software products such as for enterprise resource planning, supply chain management, customer relationship management, and business intelligence to large, mid-sized, and small client enterprises. While its traditional products are typically run on premise, that is at its client's facilities, its market share in software provided as a service (Stuckenberg 2014; Stuckenberg et al. 2014) is rapidly increasing. Consequently, information systems development teams of this company serve a huge variety of products and target markets with diverse technologies.

This study was conducted with ISD teams located at the company's headquarters and two further company sites nearby where large parts of the company's core products are developed. This setting was deemed appropriate as it provided a trade-off between closure and representativeness: while it allowed for eliminating many important external influences such as national and organizational cultures (Levina and Vaast 2008), the company's teams still show a strong degree of heterogeneity with regard to their tasks, internal constitutions, and individual characteristics which allows to still draw conclusions of significant external validity. This trade-off is known to both qualitative and quantitative research (Miles and Huberman 1994; Yin 2009), and it is well accepted in ISD literature (e.g., Dibbern et al. 2008; Kotlarsky and Oshri 2005; Maruping et al. 2009a,b). Especially critical realist research tends to consciously focus on units and structures within the boundaries of single firms (Wynn and Williams 2012).

The chosen company is particularly interesting for research on collaborative quality assurance as its ISD teams work based on the agile ISD method Scrum (Schwaber and Beedle 2002) and are free to choose whether and how to apply specific ISD techniques. Consequently, teams and individual members may tend to reflect more on their application of practices (Janz and Prasarnphanich 2009) and individual opinions may be of high value during the investigations. Most of the company's teams furthermore received centralized trainings in agile ISD techniques, including collaborative quality assurance, within the scope of an organizational transformation toward agile software development in 2011/2012. They have thereby been provided with the same information about and instructions on how to conduct collaborative quality assurance. This helps to reduce confounding influences that may result from different initial understandings of the practices. In addition, it is the company's policy to minimize the number of virtual collaborations within single teams. That is, ISD teams at the European sites of this company are typically collocated in the same office space. Prior research has shown that physical distribution of ISD teams heavily impacts their socio-cognitive abilities (Kotlarsky et al. 2014; Oshri et al. 2008). As this study focuses on the interaction of collaborative quality assurance and team cognition, a setting of collocation arguably allows for more precise examination of relevant effects because there are no interferences caused by distributed collaboration.

3.4   Initial Exploration

In a first phase of this study, the primary goal was to explore the effects of team cognition on the execution of collaborative quality assurance on a task level. In the case company, ISD teams were trained in collaborative quality assurance techniques but free in their decisions whether and how to apply them. In order to gain an initial understanding of the techniques that exceeded extant literature, these trainings for collaborative quality assurance were attended and teaching materials were analyzed. In addition, documentation was retrieved and analyzed for the peer code review systems used in the case company. Intensive contacts and the immersion in a case constitute important steps of qualitative research in social systems and help researchers gain a profound understanding of research context (Miles and Huberman 1994; Yin 2009). Consequently, the author of this study engaged in a multitude of informal talks to training participants as well as trainers who provided personal opinions and helped establish a first overview of anecdotal experiences with collaborative quality assurance techniques in the case company.

Together with extant literature, these first steps served as a basis to conceptualize the material properties of the collaborative quality assurance techniques as well as the symbolic expressions embedded in trainings, documentations, and technological artifacts. That is, the data helped conceptualize pair programming and peer code review as techniques relying on a number of immutable characteristics (material properties as per Markus and Silver 2008) and symbolic expressions as a set of mutable properties that constitute "the communicative possibilities" (Markus and Silver 2008, p. 623) of a technique for a specified user group (cf. Sect. 2.4.3).

With the techniques' material properties and symbolic expressions, a series of key informant interviews was conducted to explore the different ways in which pair programming and peer code review were executed in different teams and to which ends they were perceived as useful under varying conditions. The central outcome of this broader exploration of collaborative quality assurance in different teams was a concise set of the functional affordances of pair programming and peer code review on a task level. Moreover, findings indicated that teams with more sophisticated transactive memory systems perceive collaborative quality assurance techniques as useful for more and different tasks than teams with less advanced transactive memory systems.

3.4.1   Data Selection

For the purpose of exploration and theory building, Eisenhardt (1989) recommends a sample of four to ten cases. At the same time, Yin (2009) holds that the number of cases depends on the purpose of the investigation but that more cases are usually perceived as better because additional cases allow for corroboration of developed theory in different contexts and thereby for stronger generalization. Clearly, a pure "the more the better"-sampling is based on a rather naive positivist understanding; and followers of other epistemic schools have proposed to prefer the depth of a single case study over the breath of several (Lee and Baskerville 2003; Wynn and Williams 2012). This study values arguments of both perspectives and applies two different sampling strategies in its two qualitative phases. While the first phase of exploration relies on a broader scope with nine teams working in diverse contexts, the second phase concentrates on four very detailed studies of ISD teams.

Regarding the effects of team cognition on collaborative quality assurance tasks, the breadth of the first phase provides more possibilities to elicit rare effects while the intensity of the second phase provides more detailed insights into the mechanics of these effects.

Data collection for the initial exploration comprising the attendance of trainings, archiving of training materials, and execution of case study interviews took place in summer 2012. Nine ISD teams were examined based on 13 semi-structured face to face interviews with key informants of approximately 1 h on average. Key informants can make more detailed statements on a phenomenon than their colleagues if their organizational roles are explicitly or implicitly concerned with that phenomenon (Houston and Sudman 1975). Thus, interview partners were acquired based on their roles and their involvement with collaborative quality assurance techniques in their teams. Aiming at a broad and rich set of opinions, four categories of informants were interviewed that provided diverse insights from their perspectives (cf. Table 3.2):

- *Senior developers* who had experience in developing with pair programming and/or peer code review but had also developed software without these techniques before;
- *Scrum Masters* (i.e., team leaders in the Scrum method Schwaber and Beedle 2002) whose role forced them to reflect on techniques and practices their teams applied;
- *Agile method trainers* who were actively engaged in promoting agile development techniques such as collaborative quality assurance techniques;
- *Senior peer code review developers* who actively contributed to an open-source project that develops the peer code review system most frequently applied within the case company.

Table 3.2 Overview of exploratory interviews

ID	Role	Development context
A	Agile method trainer and scrum master	User interface for software
B	Agile method trainer and scrum master	Process modeling software
C	Senior developer	Code correction maintenance
D	Senior developer	Client installation suite
E	Senior developer	Installation framework
F	Senior developer	Process modeling software
G	Senior developer	Web portal
H	Senior developer	Version verification for products
I	Senior developer	Installation framework
J	Scrum master	Custom language compiler
K, L, M	Scrum master and two senior developers[a]	Open source peer code review system

[a]Not distinguished in order to ensure anonymity

A purposive case sampling method was applied (Yin 2009) to ensure that (1) all nine teams had experience with at least one of the two collaborative quality assurance techniques of pair programming or peer code review and that (2) their work contexts and joint experiences varied significantly. Eight of the teams applied one or both techniques while one team used but also actively developed an open-source peer code review platform. An interview guideline for semi-structured interviews was developed that elicited extensive details about the key informants' teams and how pair programming and peer code review were actually applied there for single tasks. The guideline can be found in Sect. B.1 of the appendix. Informants had to describe single events of collaborative quality assurance as well as the general use of the techniques within their entire team. In particular, information about structure, context, and events of collaborative quality assurance was elicited (Wynn and Williams 2012). Data analysis was conducted in an ongoing manner and influenced further selections of teams for case studies. Data collection was driven on until a comprehensive set of patterns emerged that described what the single techniques afforded to ISD teams in different contexts and no additional functional affordances could be identified in several interviews.

3.4.2 Data Analysis

The initial exploration phase served to elicit and understand the material properties, symbolic expressions, and functional affordances of collaborative quality assurance techniques. A tentative understanding resulted from the numerous visits at the case site, the attendance of trainings on pair programming and peer code review and the analysis of training materials, as well as the interviews with key informants of the nine ISD teams.

First, the collected data and academic literature were analyzed for relevant material properties that constituted real and immutable characteristics of the techniques. This is a reasonable starting point for data analysis when dealing with the concept of functional affordances: it allows for gaining insight into obvious but important properties of the technique or technology at hand; these properties are central enablers and constraints to any potential functional affordances (Markus and Silver 2008). While current literature often starts directly by examining perceived affordances (e.g., Strong et al. 2014; Volkoff and Strong 2013), this study's approach arguably reduces the risk of focusing too much on pure perceptions and interpretation while missing the strong realist elements that underly this concept (Markus and Silver 2008). The second step of analysis then aimed at finding relevant symbolic expressions, that is embedded values of designers or trainers of the techniques which signal a desirable behavior to potential users. In order to do so, training materials, manuals, and interview transcripts were examined and coded but also subjective impressions from the trainings were taken into account when interpreting the data. This resulted in a comprehensive set of material properties and symbolic expressions of the techniques which were later on verified in the key informant interviews (cf. Sect. 4.1.3).

Third, all semi-structured interviews with key informants were tape-recorded, transcribed, and coded using the qualitative research software NVivo. In accordance with prior critical realist literature (Strong and Volkoff 2010; Strong et al. 2014; Volkoff and Strong 2013), the guidelines for open, axial, and selective coding provided by Strauss and Corbin (1998) were followed roughly, but it was ensured to remain sufficiently flexible to have codes arise from the data rather than from external frameworks. Thus, this study actually followed qualitative guidelines more in a critical realist tradition than pure grounded theory (Miles and Huberman 1994) but borrowed the methodological devices that helped structure the data meaningfully. As exemplified in Table B.1 of the appendix, open codes were attached to different emphasized aspects as well as repeating patterns in the data (open coding). Subsequently, interrelations of these open codes were carved out while constantly updating and refining the aggregations. In particular, this process aimed at eliciting conditions, actions/interactions, and consequences (Strauss and Corbin 1998) of the application of pair programming and peer code review, but it also remained open for ideas that could not be forced into this framework. This resulted in a multitude of situations, ways, and goals that were identified and described with labels such as "complex tasks" (condition), "intensive discussion" (interaction), "code intelligibility", or "share knowledge" (consequences). Consequences thereby described the specific goals the teams aimed at when applying collaborative quality assurance techniques to certain tasks, that is they described functional affordances of the techniques. Selective coding then meant moving away from explicit statements towards causal themes that explained why the techniques were perceived as particularly useful for specific tasks and why teams differed in the affordances of collaborative quality assurance techniques they perceived. In line with prior research (Strong and Volkoff 2010; Strong et al. 2014), selective codes were not actually attached to text explicitly. Instead, the focus was on understanding the emerging themes of the techniques' functional affordances, also taking knowledge gained during the immersion phase into account. Section 4.1.2 provides a set of exemplary codes that serve to outline this approach. In sum, this exploratory phase resulted in tentative functional affordances of collaborative quality assurance that emerged from a variety of data as well as a broad understanding of the context in the case company. While there was overlap regarding the sensible use of pair programming and peer code review for basic quality assurance tasks, both techniques also provided idiosyncratic affordances to some teams. It appeared that collaborative quality assurance could be used to more and very different ends by teams with a more sophisticated transactive memory.

3.5 Critical Realist Case Studies

Equipped with the insights from the initial exploration, four in-depth critical realist case studies were conducted with selected ISD teams (Bygstad and Munkvold 2011; Tsang 2014; Wynn and Williams 2012). These case studies served two major purposes: (1) gaining a detailed understanding on a task level how and why a team's transactive memory enables or restricts the application of collaborative quality assurance techniques towards very different ends; and (2) aiding the development of a mid-range theory that describes how and why the ongoing application of · collaborative quality assurance techniques in turn has an emergent effect on a team's transactive memory. Detailed analyses were therefore necessary both on a task level and on a team level. In order to enable such analyses, several work days were spent with the case teams observing their interactions and knowledge exchange before, during, and after sessions of collaborative quality assurance, their written conversations in code review systems were analyzed, and numerous formal and informal interviews with team members and external team stakeholders were conducted.

3.5.1 Case Sampling

The four ISD teams were purposefully selected for the in-depth case studies based on what Yin (2009) calls a *theoretical replication logic*. That is, assuming that the same causal mechanisms exert their influences in all cases, albeit to varying degrees, cases should be sampled so that the intensity of the central effect of interest varies across the cases (Yin 2009). An appropriate resulting theory should then be able to explain these variations in each case very well (Miles and Huberman 1994). Moreover, it is central to any critical realist study to collect rich data on events of the phenomenon of interest in order to develop adequate explanations how these events were caused in a specific context (Wynn and Williams 2012). In the scope of this study, it was consequently adequate to examine cases of teams that strongly relied on different collaborative quality assurance techniques and frequently conducted pair programming or peer code review.

Cases were selected so that two of the teams used both pair programming and peer code review, whereas the others heavily relied on either pair programming or peer code review. The teams' transactive memory systems were assessed in the course of the case studies but were no sampling criterion. This was because the validity of an a-priori assessment of such complex socio-cognitive structures based on the little data available before actually entering a team appears highly questionable from a critical realist perspective. Regarding other criteria, cases were sampled so as not to be equal but easily comparable: all teams were of medium size with seven to ten members because extreme variations in team size can strongly influence transactive memory development (Lewis and Herndon 2011); all teams had been using pair programming and/or peer code review at least for half a year, so that the significant hurdles of newly introducing and adopting a technique (Dybå and Dingsøyr 2008) had passed and all teams had established ways of applying collaborative quality assurance techniques; all teams were collocated, all were working based on the same ISD method Scrum, and none of them had lost members during the last 6 months which would potentially have caused unobserved disruptions of their transactive memory (Lewis et al. 2007).

3.5.2   Data Collection

The selected teams were approached during autumn 2012 and the case studies were conducted between October 2012 and July 2013. In initial meetings, the leaders of the teams were introduced to the goals of the research endeavor and the desired data collection. These team leaders then communicated with their team members to see if they were all willing and interested to participate in the study. This was intended to reduce social desirability bias by ensuring that team members were intrinsically motivated, willing to openly interact during the data collection, and did not have reservations that might have been introduced by approaching their managers rather than the teams themselves (Nederhof 1985). In a first interview of 35–60 min, the team leads provided background information on their teams and the team history that allowed for familiarization with each team's context. These interviews also yielded first hints towards the teams' transactive memory and helped validate that they actually applied the techniques as frequently as desired for an adequate sampling of the cases. The interview guidelines that these meetings followed can be found in Appendix C. After the team leads had signaled the team members' agreement, briefing sessions were held with each team that introduced them to the researchers involved and served to inspire confidence (Schöne 2003). All team members agreed to openly participate in the study and were looking forward to hearing its results.

In order to obtain a detailed picture of single sessions of collaborative quality assurance and their consequences, rich data was subsequently collected and analyzed by the author of this dissertation in close collaboration with two further researchers. Several full days of participatory observations of the teams' daily routine were conducted. This included observing and documenting the teams' meetings, daily work, and more than 30 sessions of collaborative quality assurance through pair programming or peer code review, formal interviews, as well as a multitude of informal talks with team members and stakeholders during various occasions such as common coffee breaks and lunches.

Participatory observations are a recommended tool for intensive case research that allows for much deeper understanding and better interpretation of a case than relying exclusively on opinions of important actors (Schöne 2003; Walsham 2006). The observations were conducted by two researchers at a time in order to provide different viewpoints on the same sessions and to be able to follow all collaborative and coordinative activities in the teams (Walsham 1995a). During the observation of the single sessions of collaborative quality assurance, semi-structured observation report sheets were filled out by the researchers (Schöne 2003) who focused on the developers' actions and interactions, the contribution of expertise and meta-knowledge by single members, and how this was acknowledged and incorporated into task completion. The observation report sheets can be found in Appendix C.

Immediately after they had completed their task or closed the session for other reasons, the involved developers were interviewed in a semi-structured format, together after pair programming and separately after code reviews. In line with recommendations for case studies of all schools (Eisenhardt 1989; Walsham 1995a; Wynn and Williams 2012; Yin 2009), this served to elicit subjective perceptions on what expertise had been required for a task, who contributed how to the result, and what knowledge had been transferred. Moreover, the developers were asked how and why they were involved in a particular task, why they had decided to apply the chosen collaborative quality assurance technique, and how they evaluated the result of applying the technique. These interviews provided insights into both explicit and implicit rationals behind using the techniques as well as much richer background of the task at hand (Walsham 2006; Wynn and Williams 2012).

Close attention was also paid during daily routine, including meetings and informal talks, in order to record when team members referred to activities, expertise, or challenges that were related to the collaborative quality assurance sessions. For example, multiple times developers informed other members of their team about task-related issues they had been struggling with during pair programming sessions the day before, and sketched out how they had resolved these issues. In addition, semi-structured formal and free informal interviews were conducted with team members and stakeholders such as product owners and managers. This helped elicit detailed information about the teams, their work contexts, as well as patterns of collaboration, specialization, and knowledge coordination within the teams but also about their performance. Due to explicit requests, only selected interviews with stakeholders and team members were audio-taped and transcribed. Instead, documentation of the observations and interviews heavily relied on field notes. Field notes and impressions were discussed by all present researchers at the end of the same day, and summaries were written and archived together with the notes (Walsham 1995a).

With full access to the peer code review systems of the three teams that applied peer code review, it was also possible to extract their written code reviews. In February 2013, these archival data were extracted for a time span from August 2012 to January 2013. In total, there were more than 700 code changes that had been submitted to the code review systems during this period. By recording the identifiers of code changes that developers worked on during the participatory observations, it became possible to later match the single observations with archival data of reviews and revisions in the code review systems. The system data allowed not only for re-interpreting the statements regarding who contributed which knowledge that were gathered from interviews and impressions during observations but could also provide information that the team members would not mention because they used it implicitly. This additional data source thereby generated a better understanding of the actual events and allowed for effective triangulation (Volkoff et al. 2007; Wynn and Williams 2012).

Finally, a workshop was conducted with the teams in July 2013 that communicated preliminary results of the case studies and encouraged feedback on these results as well as an exchange of opinions across the teams. During this workshop, the teams expressed consent and appreciation of the results, but they also provided additional data to validate the assessments of the teams' transactive memories that had resulted from observations, archive analyses, and interview data. The concept of transactive memory was introduced to them and they discussed in their teams how they would assess themselves. The assessments of their own teams' transactive memory were archived on posters that each team created, feedback on the preliminary results was collected on extensive field notes, and a summary document of the workshop was written down on the same day (Walsham 1995a).

In sum, a large variety of data was collected that allowed for both analyses of single events of collaborative quality assurance on a task level as well as analyses of emergent effects resulting from ongoing application of the techniques. Importantly and in contrast to previous studies on pair programming and peer code review, the gathered data allowed not only for analyzing the execution of collaborative quality assurance sessions but also the related activities before, during, after the sessions.

3.5.3   Data Analysis

The analysis of the collected data aimed at two goals: (1) creating a detailed understanding how a team's transactive memory constrained or enabled the team in applying collaborative quality assurance techniques; and (2) understanding and conceptualizing the generative mechanisms through which continued application of collaborative quality assurance affected the teams' transactive memory. Naturally, this had to be done based on empirically observed events which necessarily constitute only a partial picture of what actually happens (Mingers 2004). In order to gain a more holistic view on the application of collaborative quality assurance techniques on a task level, the single data sources pertaining to the sessions of pair programming and peer code review were integrated into *event episodes*. These event episodes leveraged the information gathered from all available data sources to describe the developers' behavior, the tasks at hand, the contribution and exchange of knowledge, as well as the evaluations of these sessions from the participants' perspectives. The relevant events became thereby more easily observable than they would have been based on a single data source such as the participatory observations only (Mingers 2001; Walsham 2006).

Table 3.3 Exemplary integration of data to event episode, abbreviated episode

	Exemplary data gathered	Resulting event episode
Observation	• December 3: Developer M mentions in daily meeting that he is going to revise a code change at the component "indexer" that had been under review • M is only going to implement parts of the critique, the rest should be done in separate work package • M addresses some minor change requests like renaming methods and using better-performing data types, splits off major part	BPM: Developer M changes a component "indexer" that is deeply integrated in the BPM software and interdependent with many other parts. M is equally familiar with the indexer as other team members, but has to delve deep into its functions to change it. M broadcasts review requests to team and one external expert. Two team members review the code, one pointing to minor issues (e.g., performance), the other relating this code change to some other classes that should be changed together with the "indexer". The external expert, however, raises concerns about problems that demand much more work for solution. In reaction, the involved team members discuss R's concerns and M pairs with reviewer B two days later to further investigate the issue. Together they decide to create two different work packages: one taking only the minor review remarks into account and providing a quick fix, the other to do as soon as possible for fixing the underlying problem. The next day, M implements the minor changes and broadcasts another review request, pointing out the separation of the two tasks. R reviews once more, criticizes only a method name and accepts the change
Code review system data	• M had sent out a review request for a code change in the component "indexer" on November 29 to his entire team and external developer R • R and team members B and A reviewed on the same day • A pointed to minor issues regarding performance, ambiguous names, and potential ambiguities with data provided by another component • B commented he had found issues in other code the day before that were related to this change. Proposes to look into that together later • R raised fundamental concerns with the solution provided, showed that this code change can lead to database problems in several places. Knows that old code did not handle the issue either, R proposed to get in touch to discuss an appropriate way of approaching this problem • After inactivity for several days, M addressed the minor change comments and linked these changes to a future work package that should handle the underlying major issues. Labels this change "For documentation purposes only" • R approved the small change 1 day after observation	
Interviews	• M did pair programming with B the day before the observation. They went through major issues mentioned by R and realized revising would be a major effort. They created two work packages, one with minor changes addressed immediately, one for fixing the underlying issue • R is a team-external developer formerly responsible for the "indexer" • M has similar expertise in this component as any other team member. Indexer is at the core of the product and changes can create issues in many other parts of the BPM software	

One exemplary event episode from the case study of team BPM is provided in Table 3.3. During this event, a core component of the team's product called "indexer" was to be changed. Collaborative quality assurance was conducted in order to create a high-quality solution: developer M created a solution that was reviewed by fellow team members and one subject matter expert. However, the event did not end there, and collaborative quality assurance was not limited to this peer code review process: when the review process brought up complicated problems based on insights of one reviewer with specialized expertise, developer M went on to pair program with one senior colleague to jointly develop a solution, split off unresolvable issues, and conduct another round of code review aiming at both broad and expert feedback. During several work days, multiple actors contributed differently to the final result of the task by bringing in expertise in multiple, directly connected collaborative quality assurance sessions.

Analyzing only isolated single sources of data would have provided a much more limited view on what was going on during this event (cf. Table 3.3). As such, participatory observations yielded only a snapshot view on the event, but helped observe the interactions of M and his team during the daily meetings after the first round of code review. Archival data from the code review systems did not show any signs of the pair programming and informal talks that developers B and M had, but allowed for qualitatively assessing review requests in terms of required knowledge for revision and provided a traceable history of 6 days (four before the observation and one after). Interviews during daily work did not allow going into every single review comment, but helped outline the complexity of the task, the perceived distribution of expertise in the team, and the perceived usefulness of collaborative quality assurance techniques for this task. In sum, the integration into an event episode helped gain a more detailed understanding of the event starting on November 29th and ending on December 4th, accounting for the task, the expertise provided before, during, and after different collaborative quality assurance sessions, the members' involvement, and the perceived usefulness of the techniques. Thereby, this data integration constitutes a central tool to comply with requirements of in-depth case studies such as thick descriptions of events, actors, and structures involved in these events (Eisenhardt 1989; Wynn and Williams 2012).

The integrated event episodes as well as the constituting data elements were analyzed in the scope of within- and cross-case analyses of the single teams (Miles and Huberman 1994). Using the qualitative research software NVivo, the data was coded along different aspects. The tentative functional affordances of pair programming and peer code review gained from the initial exploration were taken as conceptual inputs for the coding. The explicated goals of each of the collaborative quality assurance sessions were compared to the tentative affordances which were refined iteratively until they formed a coherent picture. In the end of the coding process, all sessions of pair programming and peer code review could be associated with one or even two functional affordances that the respective developers wanted to make use of. Not in all instances did the developers perceive they achieved their goals. Beyond the association with functional affordances, event episodes were coded along the knowledge contributions of the single actors. Especially when multiple sessions of collaborative quality assurance were conducted to complete a single task, it was analyzed where different contributions came from in each step.

Taking a critical realist view on transactive memory systems, transactive memory structure constitutes the distributed knowledge and meta-knowledge in a team and must be seen as an entity or structural condition that is part of the domain of the real. Therefore, a team's transactive memory structure is not necessarily observable. In fact, knowledge specializations and meta-knowledge are often implicit in nature, and even team members themselves may not be able to make all their knowledge explicit (Nonaka 1994). In line with this conception, the existence of shared labels, distributed specialized knowledge, and shared meta-knowledge within the four ISD teams was derived from observations as well as formal and informal interviews. Particularly, interviews with team-level stakeholders such as team leads, product owners, and managers who provided information about how the teams distributed and shared knowledge to coordinate their work served as data sources. This allowed for a description of each team in terms of overlaps and differences in shared labels, domain expertise, and meta-knowledge. In an iterative process of coding and recoding, consulting literature and re-interpreting data (Eisenhardt 1989; Wynn and Williams 2012), themes emerged that showed for each case how the distributed knowledge of the team members was accessed before, during, and in the aftermath of collaborative quality assurance sessions. Within the scope of each case, this allowed for gaining a detailed understanding why the single teams applied collaborative assurance techniques in their particular ways.

Abstracting and comparing findings across cases (Miles and Huberman 1994), again iteratively refining emergent themes (Wynn and Williams 2012), led to an understanding of the ways in which all teams were restricted and enabled to successfully conduct collaborative quality assurance in different ways. Their differently sophisticated transactive memory systems allowed only particular applications of collaborative quality assurance to be successful. When trying to leverage affordances that were not in line with the structural distribution of knowledge and meta-knowledge in the teams, collaborative quality assurance sessions were not perceived to be useful for the team or for task completion.

Several measures were taken to answer the question why and how the continued application of collaborative quality assurance techniques impacts the transactive memory of ISD teams: first, knowledge transfer and application was coded for the observed sessions of pair programming and for the code review comments. As changes in actual knowledge distribution on a team level emerge from multiple events rather than being directly observable (Kozlowski and Bell 2008; Kozlowski and Klein 2000), this approach provided a possibility to assess the *incremental alteration* of knowledge distribution between participants in the collaborative quality assurance sessions. Second, for three teams that relied on peer code review, a large number of review comments was examined. These comments were first analyzed for the connections they represented in the teams, that is which team members gave each other feedback on their code and how often. Based on reviews and revisions from August 2012 to January 2013, this allowed to draw a map of feedback relations via peer code review for these teams. Third, for pair programming, observations and interviews served to elicit how often pairs rotated within the teams, if there were stable pairs or team-wide exchange relations. In addition, the teams reported how they were using and had adapted their use of collaborative assurance techniques in the scope of the workshop in July 2013. Fourth, the assessments of the teams' transactive memory were compared over time: on the one hand, team members reported on their specializations and knowledge distribution at the beginning of the case studies in late 2012. Together with observation and interview data, this resulted in qualitative assessments for shared labels, specialized expertise, and shared meta-knowledge in each team. These assessments were cross-validated by two researchers. On the other hand, team members discussed and assessed their transactive memory during the final workshop in summer 2013 in the presence of three researchers who jointly interpreted and recorded these assessments. Consequently, it became possible to evaluate the changes in teams' transactive memory and their ongoing use of collaborative quality assurance techniques over a period from August 2012 to July 2013.

In line with recommendations for critical realist case studies (Bygstad and Munkvold 2011; Tsang 2014; Wynn and Williams 2012), these time-dependent changes were used to hypothesize on the causal mechanisms that created alterations in the teams' transactive memory. In many sequences of probing different potential explanations to the data (Wynn and Williams 2012), two generative mechanisms resulted as the best explanations of what happened in the cases: (1) through intensive social interactions between many individual team members over time, pair programming leads to strong homogenization of meta-knowledge and redundancy of expertise. This may lead to situations where teams with tense personal relationships gain access to hitherto hidden expertise of single members. At the same time, redundant expertise may reduce team level advantages of the specialization of single members. (2) Through connecting many team members in a review system and directly querying their personal knowledge for a specific task, peer code reviews inherently help executing team-wide knowledge retrieval processes. Using peer code review systems to conduct collaborative quality assurance may therefore constitute an alternative mechanism to transactive memory systems for knowledge retrieval and application.

In sum, the in-depth case studies of four teams helped to clearly explain why ISD teams are afforded different functions by collaborative quality assurance techniques based on their transactive memory system. At the same time, two generative mechanisms were identified that explain how and why the continued application of collaborative quality assurance techniques influences the transactive memory system of ISD teams. In line with current guidelines, several measures were taken in order to ensure high internal as well as external validity of the insights gained from the four case studies (cf. Table 3.4). Following a mixed-methods research design, this study then proceeded by translating the effects of the two proposed generative

Table 3.4 Quality criteria of case studies based on Wynn and Williams (2012)

Principle	Evaluation criteria	Approach taken in this study
Explication of events	• Thick description • Abstracted events	• Abstracted events from observable experiences to event episodes • Analysis provides excerpts and exemplary events • Detailed information about the four teams gathered and reported
Explication of structure and context	• Description of structural entities, constituent parts, relationships of entities • Explication of changes to structure	• Assessments of teams' transactive memory over time, substantiated with exemplary data • Analyses of material properties, symbolic expressions, and functional affordances of collaborative quality assurance techniques • Analytical differentiation of three structural components of transactive memory: shared labels, specialized knowledge, and meta-knowledge • Explication of transactive processes executed by individual actors during pair programming and peer code review
Retroduction	• Identification of causal mechanisms • Logical and analytical support	• Retroduction of events to (1) functional affordances of peer code review and pair programming rooted in interplay of techniques' properties and teams' transactive memory; and (2) generative mechanisms of homogenization and transparency • Logical and analytical support based on various data sources, perspectives, and extant literature • Retroduction of changes in transactive memory to task context and collaborative quality assurance on team level
Empirical corroboration	• Analytical validation • Assessment of explanatory power • Selection of best explanation	• Applied established qualitative methods ranging from initial exploration to within- and cross-case analysis • Feedback session with case teams discussing preliminary results of the study • Deduction of testable hypotheses based on proposed generative mechanisms • Subsequent questionnaire survey in broad variety of teams • Neither techniques and task context, nor transactive memory and task context alone could provide explanations for events, only combined analysis showed that structures interact to produce different functional affordances
Triangulation and multimethods	• Multiple perspectives • Multiple techniques • Various data sources and types • Multiple investigators	• Broad variety of data and analysis methods (see Table 3.1) • Many perspectives gathered from different stakeholders of teams • Multiple researchers engaged in data collection, analysis, and retroduction • Mixed-methods research design leading from initial exploration over case studies to questionnaire-based survey

mechanisms into hypotheses based on theory of transactive memory systems and the mid-range theory under development.

3.6   Questionnaire Survey Study

Based on the preliminary theory that resulted from the in-depth case studies and extant theory on transactive memory systems, a coherent set of hypotheses was formulated. The hypotheses described the effects on individual developers' perceptions that could be expected if the proposed causal mechanisms were indeed present in ISD teams that rely on collaborative quality assurance. A questionnaire-based survey was developed that had two major goals: (1) corroborating the preliminary theory on the emergent effects of ongoing collaborative quality assurance in ISD teams with respect to their transactive memory system; and (2) explaining and predicting the quality impact of these effects. That is, this third phase aimed at complementing (cf. Venkatesh et al. 2013; Zachariadis et al. 2013) the results of the qualitative parts of the study by challenging and enriching the theory developed so far and extending its scope to quality impacts in teams of heterogeneous backgrounds. Nevertheless, also the survey study was conducted within the boundaries of the same case company as explained in Sect. 3.2.

3.6.1   Instrument Development and Pretest

A questionnaire was designed that measured the constructs involved in the theory by eliciting individual perceptions of the group level phenomena. More specifically, individual respondents in different roles provided assessments of the extent to which collaborative quality assurance techniques were applied, of personal relationships and transactive memory in their team, characteristics of their software development tasks, and the quality of software resulting from their work (cf. Sect. 4.3.2 for details). Individuals provided the primary data, their actions and perceptions the subject of theoretical interest. Both the *unit of analysis* as well as the *level of theory* of the survey phase were thus on the individual level. Nevertheless, this theorizing was based on the causal team level mechanisms proposed in the previous research phases and thereby served to provide corroborating evidence for the existence of these mechanisms.

Validated measurements from extant literature were reused or slightly adapted wherever possible. Stronger adaptations were necessary especially regarding the measures of collaborative quality assurance on a team level and the quality of software provided by the team. Such adaptations are common in questionnaire-based IS research and are usually not addressed in much detail even in high-ranking journals. Nevertheless, it was deemed appropriate to rigorously validate all adaptations in the scope of this study. Items were consequently created and pretested roughly following the process proposed by MacKenzie et al. (2011). After conceptualizing and describing the theoretical constructs that were to be measured in detail, items were developed modifying items of prior studies based on the theoretical conceptualizations and findings from this study's qualitative phases. To assess content validity and to ensure convergent as well as discriminant validity, a construct sorting exercise according to MacKenzie et al. (2011) was conducted. Eight IS researchers and subsequently 156 students in IS and business with a specialization in IS participated in the sorting exercise. Items were rephrased or ultimately deleted if they were not understood well, if their ratings did not converge to the respective construct, or if they had high cross-correlations with other constructs. In addition, a pretest was conducted with five teams of the case company where respondents not only filled out the questionnaires but also provided qualitative feedback on any ambiguous or unclear items. This process did not allow for a full, statistically valid assessment of the psychometric properties of all scales as would be necessary for measurement items developed from scratch. Nevertheless, it was arguably appropriate for this study in which all items had been created based on extant ones published in renown IS journals.

3.6.2   Survey Design and Method

Three distinct questionnaires were designed for three groups of survey participants: ISD team members, team leaders, and product managers. This way, different stakeholders of the teams could be queried about aspects they could arguably answer best. Such a tripartite design arguably increases accuracy of the collected information and at the same time reduces common method bias (Podsakoff et al. 2003).

Product managers were primarily asked to describe and rate characteristics of the software product that was developed. Such characteristics included the modularity of its design as well as its internal and external quality of the software developed by a team. Product managers are arguably better sources for describing these characteristics than single team members as they can compare several teams and see the resulting software more holistically in terms of a product. Team leaders were asked details about descriptive characteristics of their team, existing team-wide norms, and the overall development process. This included questions about the continuous integration of work of their teams' single members and norms of code ownership; aspects regarded as highly relevant for the quality of software a team provides (Maruping et al. 2009a). In addition, they provided supplemental details on the use of collaborative quality assurance techniques in their teams such as the type of review system applied. Team leaders could thereby give information that did not need to be gathered redundantly per team member for example on the overall development processes. Moreover, team leaders are responsible for ensuring effective collaboration within their teams and directing them towards team goals. They may consequently reflect more on the collaboration and norms of interaction within their teams than single team members who are primarily responsible for executing development tasks. It appears thus appropriate to gather especially information on these topics from team leaders. Finally, single team members provided information on the use of collaborative quality assurance techniques, the personal relationships within, and the transactive memory system of their teams. While team members may arguably give more accurate information on their immediate actions than any third person, they also provided ratings for their team's transactive memory and inter-personal relationships. This was deemed appropriate as both a team's relationship as well as its transactive memory emerge from actions and interactions of single team members (Kozlowski and Klein 2000). Further details on the research model tested in the survey and on the operationalization of involved variables can be found in Sect. 4.3.

3.6.3 Data Collection and Sample Characteristics

Between fall 2013 and spring 2014, a questionnaire-based field study was conducted with 81 collocated ISD teams in the same large European enterprise software company as the qualitative studies. As most of the teams in the target company work according to the project management method Scrum (Larman and Vodde 2010; Schwaber and Beedle 2002), the product manager and team leader roles of the questionnaires were completed by roles specific to a Scrum context: "area product owners" (Larman and Vodde 2010) completed the product manager questionnaires about one to three teams that worked on their product and about the software they developed. While Scrum also defines the role of a "product owner", which might have been an alternative surrogate for the product manager role, this role is typically responsible for only one team and its interface to the customer (Schwaber and Beedle 2002). It thereby lacks the external perspective that is typical for a product manager responsible for the outcome of a development endeavor. Consequently, the role of an area product owner was deemed to more appropriately resemble the one of a product manager. Only in special cases where there was no area product owner, the product owner completed the product manager questionnaire. "Scrum masters" (Schwaber and Beedle 2002) completed the team leader questionnaires for their team. This role is well compatible with the idea of a team leader as it is a Scrum master's defined role responsibility to ensure smooth collaboration within the team and to shield it from external forces that may interfere with team goals (Schwaber and Beedle 2002). Finally, single software developers answered the team member questionnaires. Questionnaires were printed on paper and filled in by all respondents: product managers received and returned the questionnaires by mail, team leaders and team members answered the questionnaires individually during physical team meetings with one of the involved researchers.[4]

On the one hand, a truly representative sample for software development teams in general can arguably not be drawn from a single company. On the other hand, prior research conducted in the ontological and epistemological stance of this study has even questioned the existence of true representativeness (Mingers 2004). Rather than claiming to draw a fully representative sample of ISD teams, the design of this study aimed at sampling teams and team members of different backgrounds, using different technologies, and developing different products while at the same time keeping some control over central aspects such as a roughly comparable understanding of collaborative quality assurance and a cultural background accessible to the researcher (cf. Sect. 3.2). Consequently, teams of the case company located at three major locations in Germany were approached to gain their interest and have them participate in the study. In total, 81 ISD teams with responses from 492 team members, 79 team leaders, and 90 managers participated in the study. Where "area product owners" were available, only their answers were used as product manager responses for the respective teams. For single teams where this was not the case, either the team's product owner or a responsible line manager provided the answers. In total, responses from 38 product managers or surrogates were used to provide the respective data for 81 teams. While responses of team leaders and product managers were without apparent issues, 40 questionnaires of team members were dropped after data screening because of low response quality (e.g., crossed out, all answers the same value, or left blank except for the first page). This resulted in a total of 452 usable responses from team members, 79 from team leaders, and 38 from product managers or surrogates.

Individual developers in the sample were rather experienced in professional software development (cf. Fig. 3.1); only 36 % had less than 10 years of experience in professional software development while 30 % had even more than 15 years of experience. Sixteen percent of the developers had been affiliated with their team

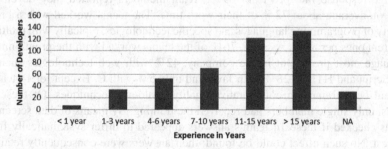

Fig. 3.1 Experience of individual developers

---

[4]For one visually impaired developer, a research assistant read out the questionnaire and filled in the answers in a separate room.

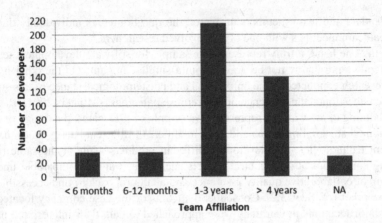

Fig. 3.2 Team affiliation of developers

Table 3.5 Team level sample characteristics

	Team size	Average development time[a]	Member attrition (6 months)[b]
Mean	9.00921	71.8	14.5
SD	2.264595	12.3	17.5
Min	4	27.5	0
Max	14	90	87.5

Note: All values on team level
SD standard deviation, *Min* minimum value, *Max* maximum value
[a]Percentage of working hours
[b]Percentage of current team members

for less than 1 year, 31 % had been with their team even for more than 4 years
(cf. Fig. 3.2). Average team size in the sample teams was nine team members,
average response rate per team 69 %. Team members reported they developed
code on average about 72 % of their work time. The teams worked with a broad
variety of programming languages and specific technologies, typically with multiple
different ones per team. As such, 76 % of the teams worked with the programming
language most prominent in the company, 42 % with web technologies such as
JavaScript and HTML, 28 % with Java, and only 5 % with C. Except for 14 teams,
all had been trained in collaborative quality assurance techniques. Of these 14
teams, only single members had received the training. By means of data screening
it was checked if these 14 team's answers appeared to differ systematically from
the rest. No such effect could be found; their answers were consequently retained
in the final sample. Table 3.5 depicts team level characteristics of the cleaned
sample.

In sum, the sample drawn from the case company represents a broad variety of
teams in different contexts and an even broader variety of individual backgrounds.
Despite the fact that the sample appears somewhat biased towards more experienced

developers, investigating the emergent effects of collaborative quality assurance in these teams appears therefore very worthwhile.

3.6.4 Variance-Based Structural Equation Modeling: PLS

A variance-based approach to structural equation modeling with partial least squares (PLS) was employed to estimate the measurement and structural models of this study (Chin 1998; Kock and Lynn 2012). Compared to traditional multivariate regression analyses like ordinary least squares (OLS) regression, structural equation modeling provides several advantages for this study: (1) traditional multivariate regression approaches such as OLS assume that there is no measurement error in the data collected. In a questionnaire-based survey this means that each respondent must assess the real value of each variable with absolute accuracy. This study, however, deals with latent concepts such as transactive memory systems that cannot be measured directly. Measurement error gets thereby more probable and must be accounted for (Gefen et al. 2011). In addition, a critical realist perspective suggests that individuals' perceptions are often inaccurate and their knowledge is inherently fallible (Mingers 2004). The assumption of error-free measurement must therefore not be made in this study.

Structural equation modeling takes measurement error into account: covariance-based approaches can control for measurement error, whereas variance-based approaches such as PLS can reduce the effect of measurement error (Gefen et al. 2011). While the latter reduction is not necessarily given under all circumstances (Rönkkö and Evermann 2013), it is present and a strong argument for PLS if indicators vary in reliability and variables are embedded in their nomological net. Therefore, both approaches to structural equation modeling, covariance-based as well as variance-based, provide strong advantages over multivariate linear regression when dealing with latent variables, especially if there are latent endogenous variables (Gefen et al. 2011). PLS was preferred to covariance-based structural equation modeling in this study because it preserves more information regarding the endogenous constructs than covariance-based structural equation modeling (Chin 1998). In addition, transactive memory is a major endogenous construct in this study and it is conceptualized as a formative second order construct (Majchrzak et al. 2013b). Covariance-based structural equation modeling can only deal with endogenous formative variables if there are also at least two reflective global measures of these variables. That is, at least two reflective indicators of the global variable must be provided in addition to the formative specification (Cenfetelli and Bassellier 2009). While there exist reflective indicators for the single dimensions of transactive memory, there are no reflective indicators for the latent second order construct and it is questionable whether it is possible to develop valid reflective global measures for this latent construct. Covariance-based approaches to structural equation modeling would therefore not allow for the formative estimation of a team's transactive memory. Moreover, a critical realist lens renders the assumption of fully normal distributed data questionable (Mingers 2004), and PLS is particularly useful for data that does not fully comply with normality assumptions (Kock 2013). Based on both the requirements of this study and a critical realist perspective, structural equation modeling based on PLS appears consequently the more appropriate choice.

In more detail, WarpPLS 4.0[5] (Kock 2013) with *PLS regression* and linear path estimation was used to calculate the outer (measurement) and inner (structural) models respectively. The chosen algorithm for calculating the measurement model, namely *PLS regression*, does not allow the structural model to influence the measurement model (Kock 2013). This is different from the traditional PLS modes A, B, and M which iterate between estimating measurement model and structural model with the goal to maximize the explained variance in the dependent variable (Chin 1998). PLS modes A, B, and M thereby increase, and often overestimate, absolute path coefficients as well as significance levels (Rönkkö and Evermann 2013). For these and other reasons, they have recently received strong critique which argued they are not appropriate for hypothesis testing (Aguirre-Urreta and Marakas 2013; Goodhue et al. 2012; Ringle et al. 2012; Rönkkö and Evermann 2013). PLS regression, by contrast, is a more conservative approach than PLS modes A, B, and M (Kock 2013), and has explicitly been excluded from fundamental critique by renown scholars in this area (Goodhue et al. 2013). Consequently, significance levels and explained variance calculated with the chosen PLS regression algorithm can be expected to be lower but less inflated (i.e., more accurate) than with traditional PLS modes (Kock 2013). This makes the selected approach more appropriate for hypothesis testing (Kock 2013). In line with established recommendations, all indicators were standardized and a bootstrap calculation with 999 resamples was conducted for path analysis (Gefen et al. 2011). The reporting of survey results in Sect. 4.3 adheres to the guidelines for evaluating PLS models set by Ringle et al. (2012) and Gefen et al. (2011).

3.7   Summary

Based on the ontological and epistemological foundations of critical realism, this study follows a mixed-methods research strategy. Qualitative and quantitative approaches have been integrated into a sequential design of qualitative exploration, in-depth case study, and quantitative complementing. The methods used in the different phases aim at sequentially answering the posited research questions and subsequently refining proposed explanations. As such, the initial exploration serves to elicit the functional affordances of collaborative quality assurance techniques and finds hints toward the influence of teams' knowledge distribution on the affordances they perceive. Subsequently, four in-depth case studies help provide an explanation of this phenomenon based on the causal influence of a team's transactive memory

---

[5]http://www.scriptwarp.com/warppls/.

on functional affordances of the techniques. Moreover, the case studies serve to conceptualize two mechanisms that explain why the continued application of pair programming or peer code review causes emergent changes in a team's transactive memory system. Lastly, a questionnaire-based survey corroborates this explanation and tests for the economically relevant quality impact of these mechanisms. As demanded by Venkatesh et al. (2013), the validity of the individual research designs of each phase have been discussed as well as the validity of the overall integrated research strategy. The following chapter presents the results of executing the single phases and the overall research endeavor.

Chapter 4
Findings

This chapter presents the findings from the three empirical investigations conducted in this study. An initial exploration yields insights into the structure of collaborative quality assurance techniques and shows that different teams use the same techniques for distinct tasks and towards various ends. That is, on a task level, the techniques provide distinct functional affordances to different teams. Subsequently, an in-depth analysis of four ISD teams and their collaborative quality assurance practices provides a detailed understanding why different teams perceive distinct functional affordances. Qualitative differences in teams' transactive memory systems can be seen as a major driver of these perceptions. The in-depth case studies also yield insights into the emergent effects of continuously applying collaborative quality assurance techniques on a team level. While pair programming fosters knowledge transfer and creates redundant knowledge in a team, peer code review fosters the task-based retrieval and application of specialist knowledge by supporting transactive memory processes. A questionnaire-based survey of 81 ISD teams with more than 600 individual respondents corroborates these findings and relates them to software quality as an outcome variable. Results show that frequent and team-wide peer code review can partially substitute for extensive transactive memory structures in producing high-quality software. In teams with distant personal relationships, pair programming can help team members build the common ground to access one another's expertise while teams with already close relationships can harm their transactive memory with too much pair programming. Peer code review helps directly improve software quality and reduces the dependence of software quality on existing transactive memory structures.

© Springer International Publishing Switzerland 2016
K. Spohrer, *Collaborative Quality Assurance in Information Systems Development*,
Progress in IS, DOI 10.1007/978-3-319-25163-9_4

4.1   Empirical Exploration of Collaborative Quality Assurance

As a first empirical step of this study, the application of quality assurance techniques was explored in different contexts in the case company. This exploration resulted in:

- A set of one basic and six advanced functional affordances of pair programming and peer code review on a task level. These affordances constitute the different goals that developers aim at when applying the techniques for specific tasks. While both techniques share a basic affordance for error correction, they also provide potential for idiosyncratic applications towards different ends. Advanced affordances are not perceived and used in all ISD teams in the same way.
- An understanding of the specific material properties and symbolic expressions of each technique. The immutable, material properties of the techniques are found decisive for the goals that can reasonably be achieved with their application. Symbolic expressions communicate values and suggest particular behaviors to developers but are not perceived by all individuals. Where symbolic expressions are missed or ignored, only basic error correction can reasonably be achieved with collaborative quality assurance techniques.
- Indications of the influence of team cognition on task level applications of collaborative quality assurance techniques. While the initial exploration cannot provide a comprehensive picture how team cognition affects the task level application, it certainly finds initial evidence for an interaction of team cognition and material properties of the techniques in creating potential applications.

In the following, these results are presented together with supporting evidence gathered from interviews in nine ISD teams, trainings in collaborative quality assurance, and documentation of peer code review systems during the initial exploration. First, this section provides background data about the ISD teams of the interviewed key informants. Thereafter, the encountered ways of appropriating pair programming and peer code review are presented by elaborating on the different functional affordances of the techniques. Subsequently these different appropriations are set into relation with the material properties and symbolic expressions of the techniques. Lastly, initial evidence is presented for the influence of team cognition on the way how teams can appropriate the techniques for different tasks.

4.1.1   Application of the Techniques in Nine Teams

In order to explore the effects of team cognition on task level collaborative quality assurance, 13 semi-structured interviews were conducted with key informants from nine ISD teams of the case company. Table 4.1 provides information about the teams

Table 4.1 Overview of exploratory interviews during summer 2012

	INSTALL3	UI	CORRECT	BPM1	INSTALL1
PP use	High	High	High	High	High
PCR use	No	Low	Moderate	High	High
Product	Version verification for products	User interface for software	Code correction maintenance	Process modeling software	Installation framework
Team size	3	10	5	10	10
Interviews	SD	SM/TR	SD	SM/TR, SD	SD,SD

	INSTALL2	PORTAL	REVIEW	COMPILE	
PP use	Moderate	Low	Low	No	
PCR use	Moderate	High	High	High	
Product	Client installation suite	Web portal	Open source PCR tool	Custom language compiler	
Team size	4	4	8	8	
Interviews	SD	SD	SM, SD, SD	SM	

SM scrum master, *TR* agile technique trainer, *SD* senior developer, /: informant with multiple roles

and interviewees ordered by their use of the single collaborative quality assurance techniques. Teams with high values applied the techniques to nearly all their tasks, teams with low values applied the techniques only rarely. Each team consisted of team members whose work places were physically close together, at least on the same floor. Teams were further sampled so that they differed strongly in size and in the software products they developed. As such, several teams (INSTALL1–INSTALL3) were concerned with different steps of providing an installation program for the case company's complex products. Such products include a business process modeling software which was partially developed by team BPM1 as well as a large database solution for enterprise resource planning software. This software was based on a custom language for which another team (COMPILE) created a compiler. In addition to these teams developing business logic, teams UI and PORTAL developed graphical user interfaces for stand-alone (UI) and web clients (PORTAL) of different products. Finally, two teams were concerned with developing complex tools to improve internal software development processes at the case company: while CORRECT's software allowed for automatically transferring bug fixes from one version of a product to many older but still maintained versions, REVIEW developed a peer code review platform that was based on an open-source project.

The initial exploration led to an understanding that the teams had different perspectives on the usefulness of the techniques for different tasks. That is, their perceptions differed with regard to the goals that could be reasonably pursued and achieved by applying the techniques. The concept of functional affordances helped (1) to categorize these perceived potentials for goal-directed behaviors into a comprehensive set of seven functional affordances of pair programming and peer code review and to (2) understand how these affordances were rooted in the material properties of the techniques on the one hand and influenced by the symbolic expressions of the techniques on the other hand.

4.1.2 Distinct Functional Affordances of Pair Programming and Peer Code Review

Figure 4.1 outlines the seven distinct functional affordances that were identified on a task level across all interviews. In several but not in all teams, pair programming as well as peer code review were perceived to be useful in achieving goals beyond ensuring the functional correctness of developed code. In line with prior literature on functional affordances (Volkoff and Strong 2013), the affordances of collaborative quality assurance techniques can therefore be separated into basic affordances for error correction and advanced affordances that go beyond this most elementary task of quality assurance. Importantly, pair programming was perceived to afford other reasonable ways of use than peer code review. That is, when deciding to conduct peer code review for a task, teams did so in order to achieve different goals than when deciding for pair programming. The techniques therefore provided identical basic affordances but distinct advanced affordances.

Pair Programming		Peer Code Review
	Correction of Errors • partners correct programming errors • ensure adherence to quality guidelines • achieve formal correctness	
Shared Task Understanding • partners exchange fundamental domain knowledge • explain their actions and rationales • achieve shared understanding of task		**Code Intelligibility** • reviewers provide critique from their diverse perspectives • ensure clarity and comprehensiveness • achieve code that is easy to understand for team members
Joint Solution Satisficing • two arbitrary members work jointly • combine skills and knowledge to solve problem together • achieve more probably an acceptable solution		**Broad Feedback Integration** • authors publishes code change, reviewers volunteer to criticize code • author consolidates broad feedback • achieve satisfactory solution and keep team up to date about changes
Optimized Expert Solution • targeted selection of most knowledgeable pairing partners • two experts pair program elaborating problem and developing a solution • achieve optimal achievable solution		**Expert-Approved Solution** • targeted invitation of one or more renown expert reviewers • author includes targeted feedback • achieve solution that conforms with expert requirements

Fig. 4.1 Functional affordances of PP and PCR

All key informants agreed that collaborative quality assurance constituted a significant investment of resources for the team. Developers had to invest time and effort during pair programming or during reviews and revisions. Consequently, the teams had all reflected on their application of collaborative quality assurance techniques in order to align these investments with their team goals. All interviewees could report on explicit or implicit agreements in their team how and for which tasks they conducted collaborative quality assurance. As such, there was a general consensus across all teams that a development task had to exceed a certain size and complexity for collaborative quality assurance to be worthwhile. It was mentioned several times that substituting a word or renaming a method was not error-prone and therefore not worth the effort of pair programming or peer code review. That is, where team members perceived no danger that errors might occur they completed the task without any collaborative quality assurance. Unsurprisingly, both collaborative quality assurance techniques were perceived as useful for *correcting one another's errors* and ensuring compliance with official quality guidelines of the case company (e.g., providing required unit tests and documentation). That is, the techniques both afforded the developers mutual error correction during development tasks.

> "If someone double-checked it [i.e., the code], that gives you a bit of confidence: someone else also thinks you can solve it this way and you have not really screwed up." (Senior Developer INSTALL2)

> "[Without pair programming and peer code review] I would miss that someone else calls my attention to the small mistakes [...]. I would miss that a lot! Actually, that was what I wished for before there were pair programming and code review." (Scrum Master UI)

The interviewees held that both techniques constituted equally viable ways for their teams to resolve such programming errors or careless mistakes. In line with this, several teams used both collaborative quality assurance techniques interchangeably when it came to error correction: they agreed that each development task had to involve two developers, either during pair programming or during peer code review and that either one was sufficient with regard to error correction.

> "We have this [team internal] guideline that everything [...] must pass a code review. However, we have agreed that if we conduct pair programming, it is sufficient to have the pairing partner review and approve the code, no third person has to look at it." (Senior Developer INSTALL1)

While both techniques afforded the prevention of programming errors for single tasks, several informants nevertheless argued that each technique also provided idiosyncratic benefits for different tasks. As such, pair programming was also frequently applied in order to *share task understanding* between different developers. Rather than aiming to complete a single task as good as possible, developers would pair program with the goal to create a shared understanding of an entire task area. This affordance of pair programming was perceived as especially important when dealing with new team members who were not yet used to the team tasks or did not have the domain knowledge required to perform these tasks effectively.

"Especially the new colleagues in the team; you always try to have them pair program with someone who has a bit more experience because that makes it easier to get into the code. [...] Pair programming has helped a lot to get these three new colleagues quickly into the topic. Of course, they also read a lot but it is better to see the code and how it works and have someone who explains it to you [...]." (Senior Developer BPM1)

"Pair programming is ideally suited for that [i.e., integrating new team members]. Starting with small and manageable backlog items [i.e., tasks], going through the code, and looking at the different classes you quickly develop an understanding how they are connected, how the tests work and so on." (Senior Developer INSTALL2)

At the same time, pair programming was also frequently used for *joint solution satisficing* for tasks that did not have obvious solutions, when teams were not sure about desired outcomes, or when they did not know which knowledge would be required to achieve outcomes. Arbitrary team members would then pair program, focus on the problem, and try to develop a creative solution by pooling their knowledge and skills. Importantly, this problem solving strategy did not aim at creating an optimal solution to the problem. Instead, pairing team members were typically not familiar with the problem. They assumed they could reach an acceptable solution to the problem more easily when pair programming with another team member.

"[We decided to pair program] because we wanted to try out something new and we both did not have much of a clue of it. I had looked at other projects, how they realized the technological principles. [...] Together we created a good solution. I am more of an 'experimental physicist' who quickly wants to see whether and how it works. The other one is more of an 'architect', he thinks in structures and wants to understand why it works in the first place. [...] That is quite complementary." (SM REVIEW)

Lastly, pair programming was also perceived as particularly useful for complex tasks that required expertise from two different domains, knowledge about interdependencies in the existing product, or adjoining business logic. Two team members who held expert knowledge from the appropriate areas would then pair program aiming to create and optimal solution, an *optimized expert solution*, that accounted for all existing dependencies and embedded the bundled expertise of the team members most prolific in these domains.

"If we have got a task where we need to change the content of a framework, we try to have two [developers] work together where one knows about the framework and the other knows about the content. They can see better if a change in the framework impacts the content. You may not even see that if you are an expert in the framework but not in the content area." (Senior Developer INSTALL1)

It's the "most productive if both know the domain and work hard. I used to have a colleague [...]. When the two of us worked on the UI you could really see we changed a lot. We touched many things, we rectified things we would not have dared touching alone!" (Senior Developer CORRECT)

At the same time, also peer code review afforded the teams task-level activities that went beyond simple error correction. As such, one central goal of conducting collaborative quality assurance through peer code review was to ensure *code intelligibility*—making sure that code developed by one team member could be understood by others intuitively. In order to do so, developed code was reviewed by team members not only for its functional correctness but also for comprehensibility, conciseness, clarity, and formatting. For several teams, code intelligibility was even the reason why they also put code to peer code review that had been developed in pair programming.

> "I mean, our architect also looks at the changes but he is more interested in comments. I am more interested in readable code. One must be able to read code also without comments." (Senior Developer CORRECT)

> "In my view, the biggest advantage [of peer code review] is that every single code change gets trimmed for comprehensibility, [because] you can't just 'quickly explain it' [to the reviewers]. In pair programming you discuss a lot and develop a common understanding over time. And in the end, both understand it, but it might be so complex that nobody else can understand it anymore. [... If you want a piece of code peer reviewed,] you have to refine it so that it is understandable. The advantage is that it can still be understood in one year." (SM REVIEW)

In addition, peer code review afforded several teams a *broad integration of feedback* and information. That is, during peer code review, a number of team members were involved in the review process who provided feedback and helped improving the code change. At the same time, these team members were keeping up with new developments in different areas of the product they were interested in. Technically, an author would submit a piece of code to the review system and team members would be notified of a code change pending for peer code review. Each team member would then decide if the code change was of interest to him/her and whether his/her expertise could be helpful in creating a better solution. If so, the team member would read the code and write down review comments accessible to the author and all other team members. The author could thereby receive feedback from other team members based on their expertise although the author may actually have been unaware of the expertise of the colleagues before the review. By consequence, a variety of different opinions about a solution could be solicited along with potential improvements while all team members could stay informed about the newest developments in code areas of their interest.

> "I think we really live that. Each one [i.e., reviewer] gives a lot of feedback. By no means are review requests answered by only a single one but from several [reviewers]. And then we comment a lot [on the code change], also with possible ways how to improve it or how to do it differently." (Senior Developer BPM1)

> In the end, I "set my focus on clean code. [...] Others watched for typos, my soft spot, others said formatting is important. [...] And of course, there are the functional things you are interested in. You really want to understand them." (Senior Developer PORTAL)

Lastly, peer code review was also conducted in order to create *expert-approved solutions*. Teams made use of this affordances of peer code review when tasks fell fully or partially in the area of expertise associated with a specific developer but were not completed by this developer. When a task for which an expert existed was completed by a non-expert (e.g., due to time constraints of the expert), the resulting code was uploaded to the peer code review system. The expert was then kindly invited to review the developed solution and evaluate it from his or her expert perspective. Invitations were issued via invitation functions of the peer code review system, via email, or even verbally. Feedback from the expert would then ensure the quality of the solution but would be less time-consuming for the expert than pair programming or completing the task alone.

"[...] some people have expertise in particular areas of the product and it is important if [a] change touches that area to be reviewed by particular persons. In that case the developer has the chance to explicitly invite someone to review the change." (Senior Developer REVIEW)

"If we know there is one who knows much about it, we invite him as a reviewer. In the framework area or if someone has changed something in the user interface [...] he comes to me or to the other colleague." (Senior Developer INSTALL1)

All in all, this suggests that there is a common basic affordance of both collaborative quality assurance techniques. Both techniques help conducting simple error correction and enforcing compliance to rules. In addition, three idiosyncratic affordances per technique were identified that were used in some of the teams. Pair programming was used as a tool for sharing domain knowledge and task understanding, for joint satisficing with a solution, and as a tool to create optimized solutions by combining all available expertise. Peer code review was used to ensure that code was easily intelligible, to broadly integrate feedback from many team members while keeping them informed, and as a lean way of gaining feedback from experts.

This does not mean, however, that peer code review *cannot be used* for sharing knowledge and understanding or that pair programming cannot increase the intelligibility of code. Instead, the techniques do only not *afford* these activities in the context of the participating teams. That is, peer code review was not perceived as a particularly useful way for sharing domain knowledge and task understanding given the available alternatives: because team members could freely meet, talk, and pair program, they preferred these actions to text-based, asynchronous conversations in peer code review systems for sharing knowledge and task understanding. Similarly, pair programming was not perceived as particularly useful for ensuring code intelligibility because pair programming developers develop the code together and become more absorbed in it; it becomes harder for them to recognize issues an external developer may face who only looks at the final piece of code. The collected functional affordances thereby constitute the goals for which the techniques were seen as particularly well-suited to achieve them.

However, not all of these affordances were perceived in all nine teams of this exploration. Indeed, several advanced affordances of the techniques were not perceived by all teams (Table 4.3 in the next section depicts this distribution). Two questions come automatically to mind: (1) why did not all teams make use of all seven functional affordances of the techniques; and (2) what are the causes that make each of the two collaborative quality assurance techniques afford idiosyncratic uses? The next section elaborates on the material and relational elements of the techniques that help understand these phenomena.

4.1.3 Material Properties and Symbolic Expressions of Collaborative Quality Assurance Techniques

In order to understand the origins of the variegated functional affordances of collaborative quality assurance techniques, it is indispensable to examine both the material properties of the techniques and the symbolic expressions that they encompass. Material properties are the immutable characteristics of a technique, that define what the technique actually is and include elementary prescriptions of participants' interactions regarding their physical and temporal characteristics (cf. Sect. 2.4.3). Material properties are therefore a structure in the domain of the real that enables or restricts actors in making use of a technology or a technique (Markus and Silver 2008; Mingers 2004). That is, these properties exist immutably and independent of human interpretations. Symbolic expressions, by contrast, are relational in the sense that they do not exist without interpretation by the acting persons (Markus and Silver 2008). They represent the communicative possibilities and values (Goh et al. 2011; Markus and Silver 2008) embedded in a technique or technology that may or may not be accepted by the human beings who apply it. Symbolic expressions are thereby rooted in and transported by material properties of a technique but they depend on human interpretation and are not necessarily accepted by someone who appropriates the technique. Nevertheless, symbolic expressions tend to be interpreted in similar ways by individuals of similar backgrounds. By consequence, symbolic expressions can be used by designers to communicate specific values and desirable behaviors to users (Markus and Silver 2008). Despite differences in individual interpretations, the general tendencies implied in symbolic expressions for individuals with similar backgrounds allow to capture symbolic expressions in an intersubjectively accepted form (Goh et al. 2011). This study therefore reports on the symbolic expressions that were frequently reported by informants and also perceived by the researcher.

An analysis of the material properties and symbolic expressions of the two techniques led to a better understanding why they afforded not only error correction as a form of collaborative quality assurance but also advanced and idiosyncratic ways of use. Table 4.2 provides a brief overview of the material properties and symbolic expressions of pair programming and peer code review.

Pair programming invariably consists of two programmers who develop code at a single workstation. Doing so, they utilize a single set of hardware and software such as a programming environment present on the chosen computer. Typically, this is the workstation of one of the developers and the paring partner joins him or her at that workstation. The two developers take turns in being the one who actively uses the workstation to write source code and being the one who continuously observes his partner, questions ideas, criticizes taken approaches, and recommends improvements. In peer code review, by contrast, an author invariably fully develops a piece of code, submits it to the peer code review system, and thereby requests code reviews from other team members. Peer code review systems provide functionality for both broadcasting review requests to all team members as well as inviting single team members manually as reviewers. Although a peer code review process requires

Table 4.2 Material properties and symbolic expressions

Pair programming	Peer code review
Material properties	
• Exactly two developers • Developers at same computer • Shared hardware and programming environment • Role changes with one coding and one navigating • Spoken, synchronous communication • Jointly developing code	• Author and reviewer(s) • Developers at own computers • Examination on own computer, review online in peer code review system • Fixed role: author develops, reviewer criticizes and recommends alternatives • Text-based, asynchronous communication • Review comments displayed alongside code • Buttons labeled "looks good to me but someone else should approve" • Broadcast/invitation functions for review requests
Symbolic expressions	
• Critical discourse is necessary (navigator thinking 'out of the box') • Intensive interaction is desirable • Frequently taking each other's positions is good, understand each other's perspectives	• Broad variety of opinions is valuable • Stick to the proposed code (in-line comments), give concise feedback (no code editor) • Create code that is 'easy to review' (quickly), iteratively refine it through feedback

at least one reviewer, technically all team members can review a single piece of code. Doing so, each reviewer uses his or her own workstation to examine the code and to comment on all encountered issues in the peer code review system. That is, the author's existing solution is the basis for all reviews so that a reviewer does not develop an own solution but criticizes the existing code and potentially makes conceptual recommendations how to improve it. In the peer code review systems, comments made by reviewers are graphically embedded in the source code they refer to. That is, there is no separate review document, but comments are presented as small in-line comments on the web pages presenting the code. In contrast to pair programming, reviewers moreover do not necessarily give feedback immediately: while communication during pair programming is face to face and synchronous, peer code reviews are conducted asynchronously and based on written text. Having completed all of his or her review comments, a peer code reviewer then recommends how to further proceed with the reviewed piece of code: obviously, it can be accepted or rejected, but peer code review systems also provide several recommendations that emphasize on the need for further review.

Embedded in these immutable characteristics of the collaborative quality assurance techniques come symbolic expressions that carry values and beliefs about the techniques and their application to the actual team members who apply the techniques. Symbolic expressions can also be found in trainings, training materials, manuals, and process documentations (Goh et al. 2011). They signal to individuals how a technique should be applied and lead to a perception of what is seen as faithful application of a technique. As such, symbolic expressions of pair programming were transported to the interviewees of the initial exploration by material properties of pair programming on the one hand and by trainings and guidelines on the other hand (cf. Table 4.2). Pair programming carries a symbolic expression that critical discourse is necessary and desirable in order to achieve creative solutions. The major mechanism that pair programming values in fostering this critical discourse is intensive face to face interaction. This is reflected in the training materials of the case company which describe the role of the navigator as an observer of his or her pairing partner who is "not actively developing code but thinking out of the box". This suggests to a potential pair programmer that more creative solutions can and should be achieved by having one developer challenge not only superficial particularities of the generated code but even the assumptions that underlie it. In order to achieve such discourse, pair programming clearly values intensive interaction of both programming partners which is not only enabled by their physical collocation at the same computer but also by forcing them to work simultaneously at the same problem. Also the company's trainings transported the desirability of intensive interaction and discourse in pair programming:

> "Pair programming is intense. Plan for breaks (at least 5 min each hour).[. . .] If pairings cause emotional stress, ease off. There is no need to force anything." (Training materials for pair programming)

At the same time, pair programming emphasizes the value of mutual understanding by forcing both developers into the same programming environment. They inherently have to observe how their counterpart uses hardware and more importantly different pieces of software such as advanced source code editors. Moreover, pair programming incorporates the switching of roles between driver and navigator so that pair programmers automatically have to take each other's positions from time to time. Indeed, also trainers for pair programming in the case company recommended to switch roles very frequently and to be responsive to a partner's critique and ideas. They thereby suggested to trainees that taking the viewpoint of a pair programming partner is actually desirable.

In contrast to pair programming, symbolic expressions embedded in peer code review and the accompanying peer code review systems focus less on the personal interaction of developers and more on the actual code being developed. Reading and commenting already developed code, reviewers focus on the code at hand rather than on the person that developed it. Indeed, symbolic expressions of peer code review hint towards valuing iterative improvement of the code at hand over radically new alternative pieces of code for the same problem. This can be inferred from existing peer code review systems as well as from peer code review trainings. As such, reviewers criticize issues with the piece under review by inserting comments, doubts, and recommendations into the code. Those are graphically highlighted at the respective positions in the source code rather than compiling one condensed review document with all comments. Moreover, none of the observed peer code review systems contain any support for inserting source code as part of a review comment. For example, there is no specific formatting or highlighting for source code within a review comment. Only plain text is available and presented as a reviewer's comment. The display of longer review comments or source code contained in comments can quickly become confusing due to this arrangement. Peer code review thereby incorporates disincentives to writing very long review comments and to providing full-fledged alternative solutions as part of review comments.

Peer code review moreover carries symbolic expressions that clearly value the variety of opinions provided by multiple reviewers. For instance, even though requesting a review from a single person is possible, sending review requests to the entire team and displaying them to all team members is the default configuration of the tools used in the case organization. In line with this, the user interface of the most popular peer code review system provides reviewers with four potential decisions about the code at the end of their review; only one of these decisions accepts the change while all others emphasize the need for further reviews and revision. Decision buttons with labels like "Looks good to me but someone else should approve" signal the additional value of others' perspectives. Lastly, peer code review embeds symbolic expressions that emphasize on the need for source code to be "easy to review". As team members voluntarily decide to review an author's code they are discouraged by enormously large and cluttered pieces of code. Expecting that colleagues will read and hopefully review their code soon, authors perceive the need to structure, format, and comment their code in a way so that it becomes accessible for potential reviewers. Only if colleagues provide feedback on their code, authors have the possibility to iteratively improve it. This is also in line with the recommendations given by trainers and developers of peer code review systems:

> "Sure, there are many things you can do [as an author to motivate reviewers]. The most important one is the granularity of the code change. You should focus on a single thing and not mix a new feature with some bug fixes and a little refactoring. [...] And then there are some styling conventions, if you comply to them you can save a round-trip [i.e., a round of review and revision]." (Senior Developer REVIEW)

Material properties such as a peer code review system's graphical user interface or the shared use of hardware and software in pair programming are immutable, fixed parts of the techniques. They constrain and enable all actions that individual developers may take when they perform collaborative quality assurance. For example, pair programming enables developers to jointly develop acceptable solutions (satisficing) and to share knowledge through face to face discussions by forcing them to work at the same computer. At the same time, it prevents them from collecting feedback from many other team members during the pair programming session as those are not part of the pair. Peer code review, by contrast, physically constrains developers in their interactions by forcing them to write down their review comments and responses in plain text and along the existing lines of code while it enables many team members to participate in the same review process. Material properties are therefore causal to the identified functional affordances of the techniques in the sense that they enable and constrain actions. Thereby, they make different techniques more or less appropriate for achieving different goals; that is, they lead to distinct functional affordances of the techniques.

In contrast to the unchangeable material properties, symbolic expressions are not immutable; they depend on interpretations made by individuals and may or may not influence developers' behavior. As such, pair programming embeds symbolic expressions that signal positive valuations of intensive, critical discussions and participating developers tend to follow these symbolic expressions. However, some individuals may interpret these symbolic expressions differently or they may deliberately decide not to follow them. The initial exploration of this study showed that the perceived usefulness of the collaborative quality assurance techniques for purposes other than error correction was diminished when individuals (intentionally or unintentionally) did not follow the commonly perceived symbolic expressions. For example, pair programming with little interaction of the partners was perceived as merely one way of checking the functional correctness of developed code without much additional value:

"[...] it is cumbersome if the other one does not develop own ideas. Sometimes, I have conflicts with my colleague who does ask good questions but never comes around with own ideas how to solve it. It is quite tiring if you permanently have to come to a solution on your own." (Senior Developer INSTALL3)

"He really took out his i-phone and acted indifferent! [...] If I do something I expect feedback from the one sitting next to me. Taking out an i-phone may also be a kind of feedback but not the one I expect." (Senior Developer REVIEW)

Similarly, peer code review was perceived as too slow and too cumbersome in situations when authors did not adhere to the symbolic expression that emphasizes the need for creating source code intuitively accessible to the reviewers. These situations discouraged reviewers from performing a quick and concise review, they led to a high number of unanswered review requests and ultimately to code that was submitted to the teams' shared code base without having received any review. Moreover, some informants did not perceive the symbolic expression of valuing a broad variety of opinions in peer code review. Their teams did not rely on multiple reviewers per code change but typically only on a single one. By consequence, these informants saw only very little value of peer code review beyond error correction. In particular, when code had been developed in pair programming, they did not see additional benefit in peer reviewing this code because the pairing partners had already controlled for functional correctness. Teams that perceived this symbolic expression by contrast argued for peer code review also after pair programming.

[After "pair programming,] we see therefore a lot of code changes [in the peer code review system] where the one proposing the change is also the one submitting it [without engaging any reviewers]. Sometimes the commit message says who was the other member of the pair, sometimes not. But that is OK." (Senior Developer UI)

"[...] if a team uses pair programming, there is nothing against this change being reviewed after that. Pair programming is done with two people, but maybe a third one has another opinion!" (Senior Developer REVIEW)

Table 4.3 Advanced functional affordances as perceived in the teams

	INSTALL3	UI	CORRECT	BPM1	INSTALL1
PP use	High	High	High	High	High
– Share understanding	(x)	x	x	x	x
– Solution satisficing		x	x	x	x
– Optimized solutions		x	x	x	x
PCR use	No	Low	Moderate	High	High
– Intelligibility		(x)	(x)	x	x
– Broad integration				x	x
– Expert approval				x	x
Missing perception of symbolic expression	PP	PCR	PCR		

	INSTALL2	PORTAL	REVIEW	COMPILE	
PP use	Moderate	Low	Low	No	
– Share understanding	x	x	x		
– Solution satisficing	x	x	x		
– Optimized solutions					
PCR use	Moderate	High	High	High	
– Intelligibility		x	x	x	
– Broad integration		x	x	x	
– Expert approval				x	
Missing perception of symbolic expression	PCR			PP	

PP pair programming, *PCR* peer code review
x: affordance perceived, (x): affordance perceived but rarely actualized or often with problems
Note: Only advanced affordances contained in table; all teams used error correction affordances

Table 4.3 outlines the perceived advanced affordances of the techniques for each team. In addition, the table depicts for which technique team members of a team did not perceive the symbolic expressions or deliberately ignored them. In teams where team members did not perceive and follow the respective symbolic expressions, there was only rudimentary perception of advanced affordances. Symbolic expressions of collaborative quality assurance techniques must therefore be argued to interact with functional affordances that are perceived by different teams. Only if the symbolic expressions of pair programming are perceived and followed, the technique provides advanced affordances beyond error correction. That is, pair programming becomes useful for more than correcting errors only if the pair programmers are willing to engage in intensive interactions, discussing issues, questioning each others' assumptions, and contributing their own skills and knowledge to generate a solution. If partners refrain from speaking up, asking questions, and criticizing ideas mutually, the technique is not perceived as particularly helpful for sharing task understanding, acceptably solving problems, or creating optimized solutions. In the same way, peer code review only affords achieving goals beyond error correction if team members perceive and follow the symbolic expressions that emphasize the value of multiple opinions and perspectives on the same piece of code for iterative refinement. If there exists an implicit assumption, or even an accepted norm, that no more than a second team member should look at and understand the code, authors lose incentives to generate particularly intelligible code, the code does not reach a broad distribution in the team, and reviewers' duty burns down to ensuring there are no functional errors contained. Figure 4.2 depicts this interaction of functional affordances and symbolic expressions of pair programming and peer code review. For reasons of conciseness, the set of symbolic expressions embedded in pair programming is labeled *intensive discourse*, the set of symbolic expressions embedded in peer code review is labeled *diverse opinions*.

This more detailed conceptualization of the material and relational properties of pair programming and peer code review helps to understand why they provide distinct advanced functional affordances. In several teams, team members did not perceive or follow the techniques' embedded symbolic expressions. By consequence, the respective techniques afforded them only error correction but no advanced use. However, these explanations were not enough to understand all variations in the perceived affordances across the different teams. Some teams perceived and followed the symbolic expressions embedded in the techniques but

Pair Programming		Peer Code Review
intensive discourse		diverse opinions
	Correction of Errors • partners correct programming errors • ensure adherence to quality guidelines • achieve formal correctness	
Shared Task Understanding • partners exchange fundamental domain knowledge • explain their actions and rationales • achieve shared understanding of task		**Code Intelligibility** • reviewers provide critique from their diverse perspectives • ensure clarity and comprehensiveness • achieve code that is easy to understand for team members
Joint Solution Satisficing • two arbitrary members work jointly • combine skills and knowledge to solve problem together • achieve more probably an acceptable solution		**Broad Feedback Integration** • authors publishes code change, reviewers volunteer to criticize code • author consolidates broad feedback • achieve better solution and keep team up to date about changes
Optimized Expert Solution • targeted selection of most knowledgeable pairing partners • two experts pair program elaborating problem and developing a solution • achieve optimal achievable solution		**Expert-Approved Solution** • targeted invitation of one or more renown expert reviewers • author includes targeted feedback • achieve solution that conforms with expert requirements

Fig. 4.2 Functional affordances of PP and PCR with symbolic expressions

still did not perceive all affordances. In fact, further analysis showed that the distribution of expertise within the teams appeared to be a key aspect that decided about how they applied the techniques.

4.1.4 Unclear Effect of Transactive Memory on Functional Affordances

Taking ignored symbolic expressions into account, it was possible to explain why in teams UI, CORRECT, and INSTALL2 there was only a very limited use of peer code review beyond pure error correction. The same holds true for teams COMPILE and INSTALL3 who perceived only basic error correction affordances for pair programming (cf. Table 4.3). Their members did not see any value in intensive, critical discourse during programming or deliberately did not engage in it. In consequence, pair programming was perceived to provide little benefit beyond error correction. Teams BPM1 and INSTALL1 made use of all affordances. For the remaining cases, however, it was unclear why the techniques were not perceived to have all affordances.

Analysis showed that distributed expertise, and the lack thereof, was a central reason that did not allow teams REVIEW and PORTAL to engage in pair program-ming with the goal to create optimized expert solutions. At the same time, they also did not perceive peer code review particularly useful for creating expert-approved solutions. This was illustrated by a comment from team PORTAL:

> "I mean [...], I could imagine if you created a totally new part [of the software] and you said 'OK, I know an expert in that [area]', you would ask him whether he got time to review it. But so far, this has never happened. We have never had anyone [with expert knowledge] because it has always been too new." (Senior Developer PORTAL)

Evidently, the distributed knowledge structure in team PORTAL influenced how the team was able to apply peer code review. More precisely, deficiencies in specialized expertise and its coordination prevented the team from relying on peer code review for the creation of expert-approved solutions: either none of the team members had knowledge that would qualify them as an expert reviewer because their expertise did not match the new tasks the team worked on, or team members did not know about their colleagues' expertise, so they could not rely on it. Team INSTALL2 similarly did not perceive pair programming particularly useful for creating optimized solutions although the team members valued intensive and critical discourse. The reason was found in the distribution of expertise in the team. INSTALL2 consisted only of three members: two who worked in completely distinct areas of their software and a third new member who had not yet acquired basic knowledge about the software to produce. While the new team member could not contribute any expertise for creating optimized solutions, the expertise areas of the two remaining members were unrelated and they did not see reasonable combinations that would create optimized solutions. In sum, deficiencies in specialized expertise and its coordination in these teams (i.e., their transactive memory) appeared to constrain the affordances of collaborative quality assurance techniques. How these constraints worked, however, could not directly be understood in the scope of the initial exploration: on the one hand, it was a lack of specialized expertise in case PORTAL that appeared to reduce the affordances of collaborative quality assurance techniques for this team. On the other hand, there was very much specialized expertise in team INSTALL2 distributed between the two experienced members. However this setting also reduced the number of affordances of pair programming in team INSTALL2. These constraints merited therefore further investigation in the scope of subsequent steps of this study.

4.1.5 Summary and Critical Assessment

The initial exploration lent insights into the genesis of functional affordances of collaborative quality assurance techniques. Material properties of peer code review and pair programming physically enabled and constrained their use in idiosyncratic ways. The exploration yielded one basic and three advanced functional affordances per technique that resulted from these constraints. The perception of advanced affordances was found to depend on the enactment of symbolic expressions embedded in the techniques: where teams did not value intensive, critical discussions and a broad diversity of opinions, they perceived the techniques merely as alternative ways of error correction. Moreover, deficiencies in transactive memory appeared to have constraining effects on the affordances of collaborative quality assurance techniques for different teams. However, the initial exploration was not able to provide an exact picture of these effects. In fact, questions about the constraining effects of transactive memory systems were even reinforced by the findings of the initial exploration. Consequently, it was one central goal of this study's subsequent steps to more clearly identify the nature and mechanism how ISD teams' transactive memory affected task-level affordances of collaborative quality assurance techniques.

Limitations of Exploration

This exploration was to a substantial extent based on broadly collected evidence from key informant interviews in nine ISD teams within a single company. For the purpose of identifying the various functional affordances of pair programming and peer code review, it was deemed necessary to value breath over depth of evidence in the exploratory phase. As such, only one to three key informant interviews were the primary data sources for the perception and use of functional affordances in each team. While the collected data allowed to identify a coherent set of functional affordances and to understand their origin in material properties and symbolic expressions of pair programming and peer code review, the choice of data also limited the possible insights into the specific context of each ISD team. In particular, the exploratory phase only yielded initial evidence that a team's transactive memory system may constrain the functional affordances of ISD techniques that team members perceive. The exact nature of this relationship could, however, not be understood based on the partial pictures of each team provided by key informants. Specifically, the assessment of a team's transactive memory requires more information beyond verbal assessments made by single members. In order to address these shortcomings, four critical realist case studies were conducted next that helped to understand the connection of teams' transactive memory and the application of collaborative quality assurance techniques. Findings from these case studies are reported in the following sections.

Lastly, this exploration was conducted only with team members that were willing to participate in interviews for this study and whose teams applied at least one of the techniques: pair programming, peer code review, or both. While the interviewees were by no means all overly enthusiastic with regard to collaborative quality assurance techniques, this sampling may still have caused a selection bias. Informants of this exploration may have had more experience with and willingness to apply collaborative quality assurance techniques than many other software developers in industry. On the one hand, this provided a fruitful basis for identifying functional affordances of these techniques. On the other hand, it may have reduced the chance to identify even frequent obstacles for the adoption and use of collaborative quality assurance techniques. Future research may therefore want to look at ISD teams that refuse applying collaborative quality assurance techniques altogether in order to better understand not only drivers of but also impediments to the application of pair programming and peer code review.

4.2 Critical Realist Case Studies

Four in-depth case studies of ISD teams were conducted that allowed to account for both the use of collaborative quality assurance techniques as well as these teams' transactive memory systems. The goals and outcomes of these case studies were twofold. On the one hand, a precise picture could be developed of the effects of extant transactive memory systems on the functional affordances of pair programming and peer code review on a task level. The techniques' different advanced affordances require specific elements of transactive memory structures. Where elementary parts of these structures are not fully developed, this constrains the advanced affordances of collaborative quality assurance techniques and teams cannot leverage their full potential. On the other hand, continued application of collaborative quality assurance techniques yields emergent effects on a team's transactive memory system. Pair programming affects a team's transactive memory system by homogenizing shared labels and meta-knowledge as well as expertise, whereas peer code review fosters the execution of transactive processes without necessarily relying on an existing transactive memory structure. After introducing the four case teams, this section first presents findings on the detailed effects of transactive memory on affordances of collaborative quality assurance techniques. Subsequently it outlines the generative mechanisms of homogenization and transparency that cause the emergent effects of collaborative quality assurance on transactive memory. It concludes with an integrative summary of the findings from the four case studies.

4.2.1   Case Descriptions

The four teams constituting the in-depth case studies all relied strongly on one or both of the collaborative quality assurance techniques. Two of them applied both techniques while two teams only applied either peer code review or pair programming respectively. All teams were of moderate size between seven and ten team members, and members of each team were located in the same office space, separated by a single door if anything. None of the teams had membership fluctuation during the last 6 months before the beginning of the case studies. Consequently, all teams had been working together long enough to have developed a working transactive memory system and were comparable in size. Nonetheless, there were major differences in their actual transactive memory systems and in their deliberate decisions how and why to apply collaborative quality assurance techniques.

4.2.1.1   Team COMPILE

Team COMPILE consisted of eight team members that had been working together for roughly 1 year. For this time, COMPILE had been responsible for newly developing a custom language compiler for the case company's most innovative software product that brought together leading database technology and successful enterprise application software. Applications would specify parts of their required database operations in the custom language which would be compiled to byte code before being executed by the database. The compiler developed by the case study team was therefore a central part of this innovative product, residing at its core and directly impacting the overall product's runtime performance. Several dozens of other ISD teams in the case company were working on this product and relied on the functionality of the compiler. Driven by rapidly expanding business demands, these internal customers frequently requested new features of the compiler that had to be developed quickly. At the same time, the team had to preserve a stringent architecture and ensure conciseness of code for the sake of high runtime performance.

COMPILE's members consequently emphasized the need to quickly create high-performance source code that was at the same time extremely reliable. In addition to extensive automated test suits, team members applied peer code review to nearly all of the code they developed or modified. Within 2 h, multiple reviewers would typically provide feedback on code submitted to the review system so that the author could often revise the code on the same day. Coping with the rapid pace of business demands, different developers had gained specialized expertise in different components of the compiler as well as in different underlying technologies. Typically, there were two developers with special expertise for each of the four architectural components of the compiler. If tasks touched these areas of expertise, one of the specialists would typically complete them. If none of the experts were free to work on an urgent task, they served as reviewers in peer code review while another team member completed the required source code development. When the team had been newly put together, team members had actively engaged in learning about one another's expertise by drawing and discussing an expertise matrix of the team. By the time of the case studies, team members were well aware of each others' focal areas of knowledge and work.

Generally, team COMPILE relied on fast feedback from multiple team members in peer code review, aiming at a rapid completion of revision cycles and quick integration of revised code into the common code base. Closer analysis of the team's peer code review system showed that roughly 85 % of their code changes completed their revisions cycles within 30 h, 45 % even within the first 2 h. Moreover, reviews were conducted broadly and across specialist boundaries. All team members frequently exchanged review comments with all the others; there was no pair of developers who did not review each other's code frequently. By contrast, most team members despised pair programming as too inefficient and cumbersome. In fact, one of the developers perceived it a "silly" idea to have a navigator who observes the programming partner: "[It is really not] as if you lose sight of your goal because your speed of programming is so incredibly high." Consequently, pair programming was not applied in the team. Over the time of the case studies, COMPILE stuck to its established ways of using peer code review and its rejection of pair programming. Team members extended their specialized expertise in their different areas of competence and picked the respective programming tasks or contributed their knowledge in peer code reviews. By the end of the case studies, management articulated that COMPILE was perceived to be the ISD team in the department that kept the fastest pace while providing top quality software.

4.2.1.2 Team BPM

Team BPM consisted of nine team members who had been working together for 1 year. Together with one other team, team BPM was a central contributor to one of the case company's successful products for business process management. The product had been on the market for several years and had gained broad acceptance in industry. Due to the product's broad customer base and the heterogeneous speed with which customers installed updates for the software, the case company had to maintain numerous different versions of this product by the time of the case studies. Most of this maintenance work was conducted by several teams in India, two teams in Germany were mostly concerned with the development of new code. Team BPM's duties consisted of minor maintenance tasks for existing code, including the correction of errors deep in the software's innermost parts and contributions to updates for customers, as well as major tasks of new development and extension of extant business logic.

In the past, the team had to face major quality issues of the business process management software. Indeed, complaints by customers and management had been frequent, and for a long time several teams had to focus on maintenance and correction work only. During this time, product management as well as the single teams had been quite unsatisfied with the situation and membership fluctuation in team BPM was high. As the team had consisted of experts from different areas, team member attrition had led to big losses of unique knowledge and new team members struggled enormously to gather some of the expertise that had left with the old team members. In fact, there had been many sections in the legacy code that nobody willingly touched because their original developer, who was at the same time the only person who understood the code's complex interrelations with other parts of the product, had left the team.

By the time of the case studies, these quality issues had been largely solved and team BPM could invest most of its resources in extending extant functionality of the product and developing new features. However, both the product's as well as the team's history strongly influenced their activities during the time of the case studies. As such, quality assurance for all new code and all changes to existing code were perceived to be of utmost importance. This included not only ensuring that code was free of errors and integrated flawlessly into the rest of the product, it was also seen as a major target to make the code easily maintainable. In addition, the team perceived that specialized expertise had done it no good in the past. Consequently, team members actively tried to distribute existing knowledge and intentionally prevented the specialization of single team members in different components of the product. All team members tried to work in all areas and the team made sure that newly developed solutions were understood by multiple developers. Nevertheless there were still several areas in the legacy code that only single team members were able to understand at the beginning of the case studies. The personally close relationship in the team had led to a situation where all team members were well aware of these remaining expert areas and the respective knowledgeable team members could always be approached if anyone was facing issues in such an area.

Team BPM relied heavily on both pair programming and peer code review. There was nearly no source code development conducted by only a single developer. Pair programming was the usual setting for all development tasks that were not perceived as trivial. Team members would meet in the morning and say which tasks they were going to address that day. Pairs would then form quickly as one team member would state interest in another's task and they would join for pair programming. The constitution of pairs varied strongly in team BPM and practically all team members were pair programming with each other over time. Single pairs always had lively discussions, willingly exchanged opinions, and brought in their expertise where possible. Team BPM further used its peer code review system intensively, on the one hand for reviews, on the other hand for documentation purposes. Developed code was always submitted to the peer code review system in team BPM. By default, all team members would be invited to review the code before it was passed on to the common code base. However, their peer code review system showed that not all developers participated equally in the reviews. While there were five developers who provided each other feedback on their code frequently and nearly equally, four other team members were less frequently engaged in reviews. Each of the latter four developers only had review connections to one or two other members of the team. When conducting peer code reviews, both authors and reviewers would usually write rather long texts to make their reasoning and arguments very explicit. Evolving discussions and intensive revisions thereby often led to longer revision cycles in team BPM. As such, revision cycles took longer than 1 day for 44 % of their code changes and even longer than 1 week for 23 %. However, not all code submitted to the peer code review system in BPM was intended to be reviewed intensively. In fact, pair programming partners sometimes accepted the commonly developed code changes as functionally correct and submitted them to the common code base. In these few cases, submissions to the peer code review system served the team primarily as a means of documentation. When other developers were later investigating the meaning of a particular piece of code, they would use the peer code review system to find out who developed or changed this piece in the past and what had been the rational.

In the course of the case studies, team BPM developed an even closer relationship than they had already had. When team members realized that there was little exchange of knowledge between particular team members, these team members actively engaged more often in pair programming with each other. While there had been several areas in which single team members possessed specialized expertise at the start of the case studies, the team perceived itself as very homogeneous with regard to knowledge distribution at the end of the case studies. Only two topic areas remained where single members still had much more expertise than the rest but the team wanted to distribute this knowledge, too. BPM's management regarded the team as a very effective and internally cohesive group. In fact, BPM was seen as a very good example how agile software development practices could be employed to focus more on the strengths of a team rather than the strengths of its individuals only.

4.2.1.3   Team DELIVER

Team DELIVER consisted of nine developers who had been working together slightly more than half a year at the beginning of the case studies. The team created and operated a software service infrastructure that allowed other development teams to host, build, and maintain their own ISD projects. Using DELIVER's infrastructure, globally distributed developers inside the case company could easily and reliably manage project documents, project member rights, and source code repositories based on a variety of different underlying system landscapes. In creating this software service infrastructure, DELIVER employed a number of open-source software solutions that they configured and extended in custom-development according to the needs of their internal customers.

Team DELIVER had been put together about 7 months before the case studies by merging two smaller teams. While not all team members of the old teams had become part of DELIVER, all tasks of the old teams had become the new team's responsibility. The two old teams had both created parts of the current software service infrastructure by using different existing software packages and developing extensions based on different technologies. Consequently, the team members that originated different teams held expertise in distinct parts of the joint infrastructure, were experienced with different technologies, and knew specifics of the custom-developed solutions from their old teams that their new team members had never seen. In order to ensure reliable service provision, many operative tasks still rested with the same developers that had fulfilled them before the merger. This allowed experts in the team to bring in their expertise on their traditional tasks, but it also hampered integration with the expertise of their new colleagues. While interpersonal relationships in the team appeared to be quite positive, there seemed to be functional boundaries along the task areas of the different members. In fact, the situation appeared as if DELIVER still consisted of two sub-teams along the traditional lines of the old teams.

DELIVER applied both collaborative quality assurance techniques, pair programming as well as peer code review. The majority of tasks that involved development of source code or reconfigurations of existing infrastructure elements were conducted in pair programming. DELIVER's team lead actively tried to foster as much pair programming as possible, especially with pairs consisting of members from both sub-teams. However, this was not always accepted by the single team members, and pair programming was still often conducted within the sub-team boundaries if developers felt these combinations were more aligned to the tasks' goals. During pair programming, developers tended to discuss intensively and to positively challenge each other. Single pairs with members of different sub-teams often consisted of one team member experienced in the task at hand and one team member practically new to this task area. Noticeably, such a pair's experienced developer would usually explain the architecture of software and relevant extant solutions before and during the completion of the task while the unexperienced would often ask questions and bring in technical experience in general software development.

DELIVER also conducted peer code review, albeit to a lesser extent than pair programming. Peer code reviews were nearly always initiated if a team member developed code alone because no pair programming partner was available and review requests were typically broadcasted to the entire team. If code was developed in pair programming, it was often also submitted to the peer code review system. Review comments were most often provided within 2 h by a single other team member and the code was then submitted to the code base after a quick revision. Teams DELIVER and COMPILE were therefore quite similar in the speed of completing peer code reviews. However, review requests in team DELIVER remained unanswered in nearly 50 % of the cases. On the one hand, this was because code developed in pair programming was submitted to the system even though the pair typically did not expect further feedback from any third developer but wanted to provide the possibility to check the code if desired. On the other hand, team members less frequently volunteered to review code after broadcasted requests, while the number of reviewers who responded to a personal invitation was much higher. Consequently, authors were forced to select one or more appropriate reviewers for the code if they wanted to be sure to receive feedback. If the author did not want or was not able to make an appropriate selection, the code often did not receive a review but was submitted to the common code base after roughly 2 days.

In the course of the case studies, DELIVER increased the amount of pair programming they conducted and applied less peer code review. Team members actually reported at the end of the case studies to conduct nearly always pair programming but only seldom peer code review. At the same time, the knowledge boundaries between the sub-teams in DELIVER were strongly reduced. Describing their team at the end of the case studies, team members stated that there were large areas of knowledge overlap between all team members, especially with respect to the central technologies and software solutions they made use of. Nevertheless, each team member still had a big amount of specialized knowledge that made each developer an expert in specific task areas. In fact, team members saw pair programming as a tool to distribute this expertise so that it would become redundant in the team and all tasks could be conducted without having to rely on any particular developer:

> "You know, I also pair program so that I can go on vacation from time to time!" (Team Lead DELIVER)

4.2.1.4   Team SELL

Team SELL consisted of ten team members who had been working together for more than half a year. In close cooperation with two other teams, SELL developed an online store with interfaces to other products of the case company. The sales proposition for this online store was that business customers who were already running the case company's customer relationship management or enterprise resource planning systems could easily install and run the web store as an additional sales channel without big integration efforts. Consequently, SELL built the online store atop of these other systems and according to their interfaces. Most of the team's development tasks were concerned with the graphical user interfaces of the product for web shop operators as well as for their customers. Several versions of the product had already been released, and SELL provided maintenance and support services for all versions. That is, SELL created bug fixes not only for the latest version of the product but also transferred these fixes to all older versions and included them in software patches that the case company's customers could install. Back end development was only in very rare cases part of SELL's tasks.

Three new members had joined SELL roughly 7 months before the case studies, but the majority of developers had been working on the team for more than 3 years while some were working part-time. Team members stated that the team had been much more homogeneous in the past than it was at the beginning of the case studies. SELL's team lead perceived that the single members had developed very strong focal work areas during the year before the case studies and that team members tended to work in their own niches in their own ways. Different team members even had distinct coding styles to the degree that the team lead ventured a guess who had authored different pieces of the software just by looking at the source code. Interpersonal relationships in the team appeared tense and communication in the common office space was very restricted. Extremely little exchange of knowledge, opinions, or even gossip could be observed during daily routine or team meetings. Team members had built up mentionable expertise in their focal areas but intentionally or unintentionally kept it separate from others'.

Nevertheless, SELL conducted pair programming with moderate frequency and no peer code review. A major reason was SELL's team lead who actually tried to foster pair programming very strongly. However, team members did not necessarily accept the ideas proposed. In fact, usually the same developers came together to pair program and there was little exchange with other team members than the traditional pair programming partners while the team lead strove to stimulate exactly such irregular combinations. When it came to these sporadic interactions, pair programming partners noticeably required some time before discussions became more active, collaboration and exchange more intensive. These pairs spent much time on resolving different views on how to approach even uncomplicated problems. Nevertheless, programming partners always reached agreement on appropriate solutions and appreciated each other's input at the end of the discussions. At the end of the case studies, the team perceived to still have multiple distinct areas of expertise and interpersonal relationships still seemed tense. However, some of the distributed expertise had become accessible for and partially shared with other team members as they had learned about and worked with personally distant team members more intensively. While management had been unsatisfied with the quality delivered by SELL in the past, they saw it on a path of ongoing improvement by the end of the case studies.

4.2.2 The Effect of Transactive Memory on Task Level Affordances

In the initial exploratory phase before the case studies there appeared to be effects of teams' transactive memory systems on the task level affordances of collaborative quality assurance techniques. However, the nature and mechanism of this effect remained unclear in the exploratory phase. The four teams of the following in-depth case studies had strong qualitative differences in their transactive memory systems as well as in the affordances of pair programming and peer code review they perceived and made use of. Detailed single and cross-case analyses showed that the teams' differently developed transactive memory systems determined to a large part why they could apply the same techniques to different ends. While all four teams valued the symbolic expressions embedded in the respective techniques, their different transactive memory systems enabled and constrained them in their sensible use of collaborative quality assurance techniques for single tasks. Transactive memory systems are found to be causal for the presence or the absence of advanced functional affordances of collaborative quality assurance techniques. This section first gives a brief overview of the findings on the effect of transactive memory on task level affordances which are then substantiated subsequently with event episodes from the case studies.

4.2.2.1 Overview of Findings

This study finds that only teams with well-developed transactive memory systems perceive and make use of all advanced functional affordances of the collaborative quality assurance techniques identified during the initial exploration. The transactive memory structure of these teams is characterized by (1) specialized expertise of single team members who are relied on by other team members for fitting tasks as the team has developed (2) shared views on and common language to describe their tasks and required knowledge while it is (3) clear who holds expertise in each area. That is, these teams hold specialized expertise, shared labels, and shared meta-knowledge for their various tasks (cf. Sect. 2.4.1).

If a team has no transactive memory whatsoever, both collaborative quality assurance techniques afford it only basic correction of errors. With qualitative improvements of a team's transactive memory for single tasks, the techniques gain additional affordances for this team (cf. Fig. 4.3): if single team members possess differentiated, specialized knowledge relevant to a task and the team reflects on this fact, the techniques afford sharing task understanding and ensuring code intelligibility, respectively. Although such teams may not necessarily know whose specific expertise is most relevant for the tasks and may not yet have developed shared labels to describe the knowledge requirements of that task, they discover the value of connecting knowledgeable software developers with each other through collaborative quality assurance techniques: pair programming becomes useful for creating a shared understanding of the task based on the distinct perspectives of developers; peer code review then allows to ensure that code is easily understandable also to developers other than the author who have distinct background knowledge. Differentiated expertise regarding a specific task at hand is thereby a necessary but not sufficient condition for the existence of the advanced affordances of sharing task understanding and ensuring code intelligibility for this task.

If a team not only consists of developers with differentiated expertise but has also established a shared vocabulary to articulate task characteristics and resulting knowledge requirements, the collaborative quality assurance techniques afford them additional ways of use: pair programming becomes useful for jointly creating

		Pair Programming		Peer Code Review
		intensive discourse		diverse opinions
LOW			**Correction of Errors** • partners correct programming errors • ensure adherence to quality guidelines • achieve formal correctness *Additional TMS structure leveraged:* • -	
Required Sophistication of TMS Strucutre / Differentiated expertise		**Shared Task Understanding** • partners exchange fundamental domain knowledge • explain their actions and rationales • achieve shared understanding of task *Additional TMS structure leveraged:* • differentiated expertise		**Code Intelligibility** • reviewers provide critique from their diverse perspectives • ensure clarity and comprehensiveness • achieve code that is easy to understand for team members *Additional TMS structure leveraged:* • differentiated expertise
Differentiated expertise + shared labels		**Joint Solution Satisficing** • two arbitrary members work jointly • combine skills and knowledge to solve problem together • achieve more probably an acceptable solution *Additional TMS structure leveraged:* • shared vocabulary and understanding of problems and required solutions		**Broad Feedback Integration** • authors publishes code change, reviewers volunteer to criticize code • author consolidates broad feedback • achieve satisfactory solution and keep team up to date about changes *Additional TMS structure leveraged:* • shared understanding of problems, shared vocabulary to express issues
HIGH / Differentiated expertise + shared labels + shared meta-knowledge		**Optimized Expert Solution** • targeted selection of most knowledgeable pairing partners • two experts pair program elaborating problem and developing a solution • achieve optimal achievable solution *Additional TMS structure leveraged:* • shared meta-knowledge of who has required expertise		**Expert-Approved Solution** • targeted invitation of one or more renown expert reviewers • author includes targeted feedback • achieve solution that conforms with expert requirements *Additional TMS structure leveraged:* • shared meta-knowledge of who has expertise to perform in-depth review

Fig. 4.3 Functional affordances depend on transactive memory structure

acceptably solutions and peer code review for integrating broad feedback. That is, by gaining a shared language and agreeing on ontological viewpoints regarding a particular task, it becomes possible for pair programming developers to externalize parts of their knowledge and discuss with their programming partner how to approach the task and solve the problem on the basis of both participants' prior knowledge. While these developers may not necessarily be the most knowledgeable team members for the specific task, they can communicate, discuss, and collaborate during pair programming in order to find an acceptable solution that both partners are satisfied with. Shared language and ontology are also a necessary requirement for peer code review to be useful for creating and integrating broad feedback into a piece of code. Peer code review only affords integrating broad feedback if several interested and knowledgeable team members can easily and meaningfully contribute their expertise to an author's piece of code in a peer code review system. Through necessarily written review comments, such easy and meaningful exchange is only possible if reviewers can quickly understand the problem an author tries to solve, think into the author's solution, and can write down their critique in a way that is accessible and helpful to the author. If the respective team members do not have established ways of communicating about a particular type of tasks and corresponding source code or if reviewers cannot articulate their expertise in a way that is understood by the author then the restricted communication possibilities of peer code review render the technique unattractive for collocated ISD teams. Shared labels, incorporating a shared vocabulary and ontological agreement on a task, are therefore indispensable conditions for peer code review to afford the integration of broad feedback.

Finally, if ISD team members not only have differentiated expertise as well as a shared vocabulary and basic viewpoints on a task, they may also possess the last element of a sophisticated transactive memory system: mutual awareness of one another's knowledge (i.e., shared meta-knowledge). Such teams know for a given task which team member is the most adequate expert in the respective area and can most effectively and efficiently perform the task. To these teams, pair programming and peer code review afford also the creation of optimized expert solutions and of expert-approved solutions respectively: in tasks that touch the knowledge areas of not only one but of two experts, shared meta-knowledge allows these experts to find together and pair program in order to create the best possible solution based on the expertise available in the team. Alternatively, one of the experts may develop a solution and invite the other as a reviewer in peer code review, thereby saving the reviewer resources as compared to pair programming but still leverage his or her specialized expertise. Without the meta-knowledge of each others' expertise, pair programming partners and reviewers cannot be identified for either approach. In sum, the more sophisticated an ISD team's transactive memory becomes the more sensible ways of use afford the collaborative quality assurance techniques. Figure 4.3 outlines in detail how different elements of transactive memory structure cause the advanced functional affordances of pair programming and peer code review. The following section substantiates these findings in the light of the four in-depth case studies.

4.2.2.2 Detailed Case Analysis and Supporting Evidence

As can be derived from the case descriptions (cf. Sect. 4.2.1), the four case study teams had strong differences in their transactive memory system and in their ways of applying collaborative quality assurance techniques. Table 4.5 provides an overview of the teams' transactive memory systems based on exemplary evidence, Table 4.4 an overview of the functional affordances of pair programming and peer code review that the four teams perceived and made use of. In the following, details from the case studies are reported that depict the causal influences of the teams' transactive memory on the affordances of collaborative quality assurance techniques. Supplementary examples of the enactment of advanced affordances can also be found in Tables 4.6 and 4.7.

Team COMPILE consisted of specialized developers who could nevertheless easily discuss tasks and knowledge requirements as they possessed an extensive

Table 4.4 Functional affordances in case studies

	COMPILE	BPM	DELIVER	SELL
Application frequency				
– Pair programming		High	High	Moderate
– Peer code review	High	High	Moderate	
Basic affordance				
– Error correction	X	X	X	X
Pair programming advanced affordances				
– Task understanding		X	X	X
– Problem solving		X	X	
– Expert solution		X	(sub)	
Peer code review advanced affordances				
– Intelligibility	X	X	X	
– Broad feedback	X	X	X	
– Expert approval	X	X	(sub)	

X: affordance used; sub: affordance used within sub-teams; empty: technique/affordance not used

Table 4.5 Exemplary evidence for transactive memory of case teams

	Specialized knowledge	Shared labels	Shared meta-knowledge
COMPILE	*Strong specialization:* • Developers primarily work in different components of compiler • Refer to experts when estimating effort of single tasks	*Extensive shared labels:* • Use many idiosyncratic names for components, libraries and functionalities that are known by all team members	*Established meta-knowledge:* • Use expertise maps and update them, product owner can predict who is going to pick which tasks • New trainee provided with expertise map of the team
BPM	*Scant areas with specialist knowledge:* • Only quality experts and developers differ significantly in background knowledge • Aim at homogenization of these two groups by fostering knowledge exchange	*Extensive shared labels:* • Idiosyncratic expressions shared across developers • Developers quickly agree on appropriate design patterns and labels	*Established meta-knowledge:* • Tightly connected developers know the scant expert areas of colleagues well • Share opinions of what knowledge is required for which tasks

(continued)

Table 4.5 (continued)

	Specialized knowledge	Shared labels	Shared meta-knowledge
DELIVER	*Expert areas in two sub-teams:* • Topics still lie with sub-teams that have been merged • Experts for different analysis technologies, server types and project management tools • Scrum master tries to reduce specialization and task differences across sub-teams	*Only few shared labels across sub-teams:* • Across-sub-team: use words that others do not understand and give very detailed explanations	*Low across sub-teams:* • Sub-team externals do not know which different task areas are related to particular server technologies
		Extensive shared labels within sub-teams: • Sub-team: developers share opinions about code aesthetics and preferences in architectural decisions	*Established meta-knowledge within sub-teams:* • Sub-team members know which colleague implemented code fragment 1.5 years ago
SELL	*Low but increasing specialization:* • Scrum master acknowledges that expertise areas differentiated during last half year • Tasks stick with same persons for several weeks to "prevent reinventing the wheel"	*Low shared labels:* • Developers disagree about the meaning of different method names and the function they suggest • No common understanding of architecture and quality criteria	*Little shared meta-knowledge:* • Little exchange about any required expertise • Only one acknowledged expertise area (runtime performance) associated with one expert

shared vocabulary to describe technological components, tasks, and issues. Both face-to-face communication during daily routine as well as communication during peer code reviews were loaded with technical terms and idiosyncratic expressions that the team members had established to describe different aspects of their product, tasks, and development activities. Even during lunch breaks team members would discuss properties and underlying assumptions of the compiler they were developing in a way that was hard to follow for other developers familiar with the employed technologies. Despite their broad and open discussions, all team members had clear areas of expertise in components of the compiler that they primarily worked on as well as in specific technologies in use. It was illustrated in several occasions and in various ways that these areas were known to all team members. For example, a senior team member could easily depict who would most probably work on each of more than 15 open development tasks during the following 2 weeks, despite the

Table 4.6 Exemplary events of actualizing advanced affordances of pair programming

Share task understanding	
Condensed excerpt of event episode	DELIVER across sub-teams: Developers M and B implement small and simple test of a mail service. M knows service well, but not better than fellow sub-team members. No deep or specialized expertise required to complete the task. Discuss work procedures and the use of their programming environment. B learns from M how testing the service works, whereas B shows M a hidden feature of their programming environment
Actualized transactive memory structure	Discuss intensively both the architecture of the mail service and how to best use the programming environment. Initially use different expressions to describe features and characteristics but quickly adopt M's expressions for the service and B's expressions for the programming environment
Effect on transactive memory structure	B and M exchange knowledge that is commonly held in their respective sub-teams, but is new to the programming partner. Discussing features and functions, each one adopts labels from the more knowledgeable partner in the different areas
Joint solution satisficing	
Condensed excerpt of event episode	BPM: Larger test suite has to be build up for new feature. Developers B and A are interested in the feature and pair to implement tests. Turns out that B has slightly more knowledge about the architecture surrounding the feature, A more experience in complex testing, but the two teamed up without regarding this. A shows B newest test tools, B explains how specific error message is rooted in architectural properties. A and B understand each other easily and intuitively. Build complex extension of test suit together
Actualized transactive memory structure	Use common labels and large body of common knowledge to understand each other easily. Specialized knowledge on tests and architecture is discovered and used during task completion immediately
Effect on transactive memory structure	Find out about their slight specializations on testing and architecture and immediately share this knowledge about test tools and architecture to solve problem. Thereby reduce the specialization and create shared expertise on new, large test suite
Optimized expert solutions	
Condensed excerpt of event episode	DELIVER within sub-team: Developers S and J decide in daily team meeting to pair for developing a required code management feature in repository management. S is specialized in repository management, J in code management. Discuss intensively different possible solutions, each one pointing out potential issues in respective expert area. Focus on design and architecture, explain idiosyncrasies of their areas based on metaphors. Argue later on that none of them would have had a chance to implement the solution alone
Actualized transactive memory structure	Knowing each other's specializations, S and J can team up to solve problem that touches both their areas of expertise but no one has an immediate solution for. Shared labels allow using metaphors and intensive discussions. Both partners' expertise is required to find a solution
Effect on transactive memory structure	Explanations of idiosyncratic functions and potential issues in specialist areas convey knowledge and thereby reduce specialization of the explaining expert. Create new, shared knowledge about code management in the repository management

Table 4.7 Exemplary events of actualizing advanced affordances of peer code review

Code intelligibility	
Condensed excerpt of event episode	COMPILE: Developer V investigates an error message thrown by the automated test server. V traces the error back to a specific class he does not know. V uses the peer code review system to first understand the class causing problems and subsequently find out who last changed it. V easily understands what the class does and finds that its author is not part of the team, but team member M served as a reviewer ensuring especially understandable naming and structure. V discusses the issue with M who agrees with V's problem analysis. V fixes the issue. M reviews and approves the solution
Actualized transactive memory structure	Code is understandable to V so that problem analysis and discussion of possible solutions with M are possible based on existing code. M's prior knowledge about the class' original purpose allows him to grasp the problem. The system helps finding M, although V does not have the matching meta-knowledge
Effect on transactive processes	Existing code and documented reviews allow V to determine required expertise, find the respective expert, and include expert feedback in a new solution even without prior knowledge about the class or M's role in its development

Broad feedback	
Condensed excerpt of event episode	BPM: Developer M changes a component that has many interdependencies with other parts of the process management software. M broadcasts review requests to the entire team in order to have several people double-check his changes and provide ideas as well as concerns. Two team members provide reviews with very different foci and express different concerns: one focuses on architectural integration, the other on understandable and maintainable modularization and tests. M revises and the reviewers approve the revision
Actualized transactive memory structure	M does not know of any expert team members for this component, and actually there are none. But common understanding of the code and shared language allow team members with different knowledge areas to express understandable concerns and provide ideas based on their different perspectives
Effect on transactive processes	On their own, team members identify parts in the code where their expertise can help improve the solution. M can retrieve and include their feedback without knowing whom to ask a-priori

(continued)

Table 4.7 (continued)

Expert approval	
Condensed excerpt of event episode	COMPILE: Author T works for 3 days on the extension of an interface and submits it for review. Invites P and A as reviewers and states this also during the team's morning meeting. P and A both have specialized expertise in this area: together with the author, P is one of two knowledgeable experts in this area. While the code change per se is not seen as complicated, it is embedded in highly complex code. A is now product owner but developed the original interface. P perceives that other team members would not have been able to review the change. Both comment on potential errors, enforce naming conventions, and provide suggestions how to ensure desired behaviors. After revising all commented points, author T commits the code to the team's code base the following morning
Actualized transactive memory structure	Shared labels allow COMPILE to communicate about the task and the required expertise. A, T, and P have specialized expertise in the compiler's modules that handle this interface. P and A can highlight minor potential issues as they know functions and assumptions of surrounding components. Sharing the meta-knowledge that this was an expertise area of A, P, and T, the team agrees implicitly that P and A are the best reviewers. T invites them directly
Effect on transactive processes	Peer code review allows T to easily retrieve expertise from experts in surrounding components at the same time. In-depth feedback is documented in the reviews, allowing its retrieval in case of future changes. Future authors, even without prior meta-knowledge, can immediately see that these three experts have been working on the interface before

fact that all developers were free to select the tasks they liked. In another occasion, several developers were discussing the estimated amount of work to complete several tasks, but their estimations diverged strongly. They quickly relied on the different team members' estimations that were most experienced in each particular area:

"C, you are our expert for SWIG [i.e., a specific technology]. Your estimation counts." (Team Lead M, COMPILE)

"M, you know how the debugger input [i.e., a specific component] works, I don't." (Developer C, COMPILE)

While not applying pair programming at all, its sophisticated transactive memory system enabled team COMPILE to make use of all advanced affordances of peer code review. As such, reviewers frequently requested different, more meaningful, names for methods, variables, and classes during peer code review. These were easily adapted by authors as many idiosyncratic expressions and abbreviations were quite common in the team and could be used to describe the semantic contents of different constructs. At the same time, reviewers often ensured that authors reduced repetitions of semantically identical source code and that the principles behind source code modularization were followed by all team members; for example by applying the same design patterns for similar tasks even if they were part of different components. Review comments that indicated different needs for revision were generally very brief but understood nevertheless by authoring team members, independently of differences in their areas of specialization. In fact, ensuring code intelligibility for all members was explicitly argued to be an immediate and desired result of the extensive application of peer code review in the team.

"Code review has also revealed errors, relevant ones in fact. It definitely makes for solid code quality. And in particular it ensures that comprehensibility is taken care of. It thereby facilitates discussions on a topic." (Team Lead M, COMPILE)

Moreover, COMPILE occasionally applied code review to create and integrated broad feedback from multiple, diverse reviewers. This was especially the case if the author of a piece of code was insecure whether his chosen solution for a problem was the best possible one. The author would in such cases mark the review requests for all team members with a special sign that indicated that the proposed solution was preliminary and might become subject to major revisions. Based on various opinions, concisely expressed in review comments, the author would then decide if to revise the existing solution or even to redevelop a new one from scratch. Different specialization backgrounds of developers thereby ensured that they looked at the proposed solution from variegated perspectives while their extensive shared vocabulary allowed them to quickly and concisely provide understandable feedback to the author.

Finally and most frequently, developers of COMPILE directly invited at least one team member they perceived as the most appropriate reviewer for a developed piece of code depending on involved technologies and components of their product.

Often, these expert reviewers would provide in-depth feedback to the author and sometimes this could lead to major revisions as authors were informed of properties of other components they had not known about before. For example, in one occasion developer K had developed a piece of code that aimed at processing particular text commands. In order to break these commands down for further processing, K used an existing parser for text to tokens that had been developed by team member V. Consequently, K invited V to review the code, and V indeed provided expert feedback that led to a larger reconceptualization of the solution approach:

> "[The way you use this class] was not intended. If there [are] more than 4 expected token types (e.g., [...]) the parser omits the suggestion." (Review Comment of Developer V, COMPILE)

K easily enough understood that this property of the parser had been unknown to him because it was buried deep in the parser's source code but rendered parts of his new code fragile and error-prone. V had helpfully made a brief suggestion how to work around the issue. Consequently, K revised the piece of code and had the solution approved again by V before submitting it to the common code base on the same day. While K's knowledge of the parser was limited in this case, the team's transactive memory allowed K to involve V as a subject matter expert in the peer code review. V's expert knowledge not only prevented K from submitting error-prone source code to the team's repository, it also allowed to provide a suggestion for quick but thorough revision of the proposed piece of code.

Similar to COMPILE, team BPM had established an extensive set of shared labels that the team members used to describe technologies, tasks, issues, and specific knowledge areas. Likewise, BPM's members knew very well who of them held specialized expertise in different areas and how to determine tasks that required this expertise. However, in contrast to team COMPILE, BPM did not appreciate or foster such specialization due to its history and negative experiences with specialized expertise. In fact, the team actively tried to distribute specialized knowledge and there was only a decreasing, small amount of well-known areas left in which experts had much more expertise than the rest of the team. That is, team BPM's transactive memory was qualitatively well-developed with closely interconnected developers who could easily communicate about tasks and knowledge requirements and knew about each others' areas of expertise. From a quantitative perspective, however, the specialization areas were not many and further decreasing in number.

Nevertheless, the sophisticated transactive memory system of BPM allowed the team to perceive and make use of all affordances of both peer code review as well as pair programming. Most frequently, BPM applied pair programming to share task understanding and to jointly develop acceptable solutions for problems. Peer code review was most frequently conducted with the goals to ensure code intelligibility and integrating broad feedback. As team members tried to reduce isolated areas of expertise, both pair programming and peer code review in BPM were typically characterized by longer and more extensive exchanges of opinions and friendly arguments between the participants as compared to COMPILE. Team members of BPM could easily express their viewpoints and externalized some of their knowledge making use of the team's extensive shared vocabulary. The creation of expert solutions in pair programming and expert-approved solutions in peer code review was much lower in BPM than in COMPILE as there was only a limited amount of isolated expertise areas that BPM's experts could draw from. Noticeably, team BPM frequently moved from code review for expert approval to pair programming of the respective experts if expert reviewers saw the need for bigger changes. In one occasion, a reviewer who had been invited because of his expertise in and experience with a specific area of the legacy code stated:

> "As easy as you have changed it[,] it isn't. Imagine an user, which has 1000 UME roles/groups. Adding such an amount of principalIds to the SQL statement will lead to a SQLException. You need to generate bundles of executable statements, lets say blocks of 40 principalIds. [I] know, that the old implementation wasn't handling this either, but if we replace this block, we should introduce a working solution. Please contact me to discuss about the best solution." (Review Comment Developer E, BPM)

BPM's transactive memory system thereby allowed the team members to easily query the experts of the remaining areas of specialized knowledge also through peer code review. Nevertheless, BPM switched to pair programming whenever addressing problems that required specialized expertise in order to not only leverage the experts' knowledge to create an optimized solution but also to break open areas of specialized expertise as far as possible.

Consisting of two recently-merged sub-teams, team DELIVER's transactive memory system was fractured at the beginning of the case studies. Developers possessed profound and differentiated expertise about the technologies and infrastructure components they had been using and enhancing in their old teams. Within their sub-teams, developers could still rely on the vocabulary and meta-knowledge they had developed over years before the merger of the teams. As such, architectural properties of the development infrastructure were commonly known, shared labels were used to describe them as well as the technologies applied, and specialized expertise was easily accessible as experts were known to all members of their old teams. However, across these sub-team boundaries team members were still early on in the process of developing a shared vocabulary, and meta-knowledge was not yet in place to reference any experts from the other sub-team.

Applying both collaborative quality assurance techniques in the overall team, DELIVER primarily made use of the advanced affordances of sharing task understanding through pair programming and, to a lesser extent, of ensuring code intelligibility through peer code review. Typically, task understanding would be shared across sub-team boundaries during intensive discussions in pair programming while peer code review for code intelligibility involved both personally invited reviewers from the same as well as members of the other sub-team. Within each of the two sub-teams, developers also made use of their shared vocabulary and extensive meta-knowledge by occasionally conducting pair programming of two experts in order to create an optimized solution and by authors relying on known experts' approval when developing code in their areas of expertise. However, on an overall team level the fractured transactive memory led to problems with advanced affordances of both techniques. The lack of shared labels and meta-knowledge about team members' expertise prevented members of different sub-teams from easily gaining the same preconception of a development task or explicating the required expertise in a way that was understandable for the other sub-team. By consequence, even if experts existed in the different sub-teams, they simply did not find together for pair programming optimized solutions and authors could not invite experts for approval in peer code review. That is, the techniques only afforded these ways of use to the sub-teams, not to the merged team. Sometimes, developers were even misled by their sub-teams' transactive memory to apply the techniques in ways they afforded to the sub-teams but not to the overall team. This was repeatedly illustrated by code changes in peer code review of authors waiting for broad subject matter feedback but receiving only little or none. In these cases, developers from the other sub-team did not gain easy access to the problem at hand or could not explicate their knowledge in a way that was helpful for the author.

Similarly, pair programmers in DELIVER repeatedly failed to jointly develop acceptable solutions if the task at hand fell into the area of the other sub-team that none of the pair programmers belonged to. In one such occasion, developers H and K of DELIVER joined together to develop a smaller portion of new code: they wanted to relax an existing consistency check in one of the code repositories DELIVER provided to other teams. While they were both experienced developers, neither H nor K had ever developed any code for this kind of repository before as it had traditionally resided with the other sub-team. Even though H and K could rely on exemplary source code that had been developed by the other sub-team and only had to be adapted, they could not transform this code into a working solution for the new problem because they lacked basic understanding of the repository's architecture and existing interfaces. They could moreover not understand the documentation of the exemplary code, and various times they went to members of the other sub-team to briefly ask for explanations. Despite the help of these other team members, H and K could not solve their problem together and quit pair programming without a successfully running piece of code. This was because H and K had intended to apply pair programming to jointly develop a satisfactory solution as they used to do within their sub-team but were facing the other sub-team's task based on different technology and a different documentation of source code. They therefore lacked the basic understanding of this technology and could not make sense of given code samples and their documentation. The sophisticated transactive memory on a sub-team level thereby misled the developers to conduct pair programming in a way that was not reasonable in this situation due to lacking transactive memory of the overall team. Other team members had therefore already concluded that for the largest part, sharing task understanding was the major affordance of pair programming when working across sub-teams.

"[On the level of the entire team,] the primary motivation is nearly always distributing knowledge, only very seldom the combination of competences." (Senior Developer J, DELIVER)

Lastly, team SELL's transactive memory was rudimentary and interpersonal relationships of the team were strained. While team members had developed specialized areas of knowledge in the recent past, others could not easily make use of this as there was only little exchange in the team. In more detail, the team members did not have a common understanding of their task areas or the necessary shared vocabulary to easily describe them. Relationship tensions within the team led to boundaries so that single developers communicated only little and did not learn about each other's specializations during daily routine.

SELL did not apply peer code review but conducted pair programming in order to share such task understanding and to come to agreed-on solutions for tasks. Joint solution satisficing was not generally seen as a possible successful application of pair programming. While often the same few developers pair programmed with each other, the most fruitful discussions evolved when developers pair programmed who were not typically doing so. It took these pairs noticeable effort to discuss tasks as the partners often did not understand each other's approaches, referred to different expressions, and had generally very different ideas of how their product should develop in the future. The restricted body of shared labels and the limited meta-knowledge present in the team thereby provided initial obstacles for pair programmers. Nevertheless, these exchanges could be seen as highly positive for the team; even though the lengthy discussions may often not have constituted the fastest way to a solution, single developers learned about their mutual viewpoints and background knowledge and could establish a shared agreement on the code they developed together. For future reference, they could rely on these small increments in shared labels and meta-knowledge about the pair programming partner.

4.2.2.3 Summary

With respect to the influence of team cognition on the task level application of collaborative quality assurance techniques (Research Question 1), this study finds that qualitative improvements in a team's transactive memory structure cause advanced functional affordances of collaborative quality assurance techniques. Results from four cases and the preceding exploratory phase show that if teams lack central elements of a sophisticated transactive memory structure then this also impacts their ability to use collaborative quality assurance techniques. In more detail, a lack in transactive memory constrains teams in the functional affordances of pair programming and peer code review they can perceive and make use of. Existing specialization in different expertise areas, shared labels, and shared meta-knowledge in the team create advanced functional affordances for ISD teams on a task level. Transactive memory must therefore be seen as an enabling and constraining cause of functional affordances of collaborative quality assurance techniques as outlined in Fig. 4.3.

4.2.3   Emergent Effects on Teams' Transactive Memory Systems

Whereas a team's existing transactive memory impacts the task-level goals which the team can reasonably achieve, the continued application of pair programming and peer code review is found to yield also emergent effects on the team's transactive memory system. By studying both, the actual changes in the case teams' transactive memory during single sessions of collaborative quality assurance as well as the changes in their transactive memory systems in the course of the case studies, this study finds that two generative mechanisms underlie the emergent effects of collaborative quality assurance to a team level: homogenization and transparency. This section first presents a brief overview of the findings regarding the two generative mechanisms of team-level effects. Subsequently, more detailed analyses and supporting evidence depict these effects based on the four in-depth case studies.

4.2.3.1   Overview: Homogenization and Transparency

This study finds that two generative mechanisms, *homogenization and transparency*, cause changes in ISD teams' transactive memory systems if they apply collaborative quality assurance techniques. These generative mechanisms underlie both pair programming and peer code review but materialize to different degrees in the two techniques. As such, intensive and ongoing use of pair programming primarily leads to a more homogeneous distribution of expertise within an ISD team whereas the use of peer code review primarily leads to a more transparent utilization of the existing distributed expertise. Through homogenization, pair programming therefore primarily affects the knowledge structure in a team, whereas peer code review affects the transactive processes for information encoding, storage, and retrieval through transparency.

In more detail, intensive and continuous use of pair programming on a team level consists of many instances in which single developers pair program, thereby discussing intensively how to solve problems, externalizing and communicating parts of their expertise to their partners, and coming to mutually accepted solutions. Doing so, team members not only develop a larger shared vocabulary and acceptance of each other's viewpoints; they also transfer parts of their knowledge to their pair programming partners and even jointly extend their expertise with the knowledge they create together. Over time, single developers pair program not with a single but with various team members. They jointly work on different development tasks which leads to the exchange of different parts of their expertise as well as to an extended understanding for one another's skills and experiences. By consequence, existing knowledge as well as meta-knowledge spread in the team, leading to more homogeneity in the expertise and task understanding of the team members. The generative mechanism of *homogenization* therefore describes the transfer and joint creation of expertise, labels for knowledge requirements and tasks, as well as meta-knowledge caused by intensive, task-based interaction of developers. Homogenization thereby affects a team's transactive memory structure by extending the shared labels and shared meta-knowledge in the team on the one hand. On the other hand, it induces redundancy in the expertise of team members and reduces the accuracy with which expertise areas can be attributed to specific team members.

Continued and extensive application of peer code review primarily fosters transparency in ISD teams. The generative mechanism of *transparency* describes the alteration of transactive memory processes to become less dependent on transactive memory structure through the provision of alternative sources for expertise location information. That is, transparency makes a team's transactive memory structure transparent for team members who execute transactive processes for encoding, storing, and retrieving information and allows these processes to be executed relatively independent of extant transactive memory structure. In more detail, transparency generated by direct access to team members' current and previous tasks, their contributions to the work of others, and immediate understandability of their work results enable their colleagues to access these team members' specialized knowledge without much prior conception of their expertise. Transparency unfolds through frequent, team-wide application of peer code review in several ways. First, peer code review systems document which developers actively contribute to different areas of a team's product. In search for an expert in a specific code area, developers can retrieve the information who has last or frequently served in this area as an author or as a reviewer and can contact the respective expert. Even without prior meta-knowledge about this expert's areas of specialization, other developers can thereby find and retrieve his or her expertise without larger efforts. Similarly, broadcasting review requests can be used to elicit hidden expertise from one or multiple team members. While an author may not know whom best to contact for a review, expert reviewers may themselves determine the usefulness of their expertise for a given code change and voluntarily answer to broadcasted review requests. Finally, code that is more accessible and understandable to all team members makes it easier to communicate about the code and the task that incorporates it. Understandable code reduces the required amount of established, shared labels and discussions that must be conducted on a meta-level. With an understandable piece of code at hand, authors and reviewers can immediately discuss task-based solutions and improvements without the need to first describe conceptual and more abstract solutions in much detail. Thereby, it facilitates the retrieval and inclusion of expertise for the task at hand without transferring large amounts of background knowledge first. In sum, peer code review supports transactive processes that rely less on the team's already established transactive memory structure and more on the developers' individual knowledge. Through transparency, peer code review provides lean mechanisms to determine which expertise may be helpful for a given task, find this expertise within the team, and include expertise-based feedback in the solution. Peer code review thereby constitutes an alternative to transactive memory structure as a basis for conducting transactive processes.

Various case events served as a basis for the identification of the two generative mechanisms. As such, the following section presents evidence for the existence and causal workings of homogenization and transparency based on single sessions of collaborative quality assurance, incremental changes in teams' transactive memory, team members' perceptions and descriptions, and changes of the teams' transactive memory systems over the duration of the case studies.[1]

4.2.3.2 Detailed Analysis and Supporting Evidence

Changes in teams' transactive memory structures conceptually consist of incremental units of implicitly or explicitly labeled, task-related, specialized knowledge and associated meta-knowledge (Brandon and Hollingshead 2004). That is, a team's transactive memory structure expands incrementally whenever a new unit of exclusively-held, task-related knowledge and associated, shared meta-knowledge is added to the team's knowledge stock by explicitly or implicitly labeling a team member as an expert for a specific task based on a common understanding that his or her expertise matches the task requirements. This can either happen through creating an entirely new unit of specialized expertise and shared meta-knowledge, or by developing and labeling shared meta-knowledge about existing specialized expertise (in other words, by a team-wide "discovery" of expertise that already existed within the team before). Correspondingly, transactive memory structures incrementally deteriorate whenever associations of tasks, specialized expertise, and expertise holders are destroyed. The latter may happen when either specialized expertise is lost (e.g., by member attrition) or when associated meta-knowledge is damaged (e.g., by team members gaining expertise in others' specialization areas and thereby blurring those others' role as the sole experts for these areas). To find the effects of collaborative quality assurance techniques on teams' transactive memory systems, this study therefore first analyzed incremental changes in the four case teams' transactive memory structures based on the expertise they contributed to and knowledge they exchanged during the single, observed event episodes where teams made use of advanced functional affordances of the techniques.

With regard to pair programming, all event episodes showed strong commonalities in terms of incremental changes in transactive memory. Interestingly, these commonalities were not dependent on the specific advanced functional affordances of the technique that were actualized in the event episode. During intensive discussions, pair programming partners generally came to adapt their task-related vocabulary to their programming partners'. Where one partner was clearly more experienced in a task area, the less experienced developer typically adopted the

---

[1]In addition, also the interviews of the exploratory phase were re-analyzed based on the conceptualization of the generative mechanisms gained from the case studies. Supporting evidence was found in various interviews. For the sake of conciseness, however, the following section focuses exclusively on evidence from the four cases.

partner's established labels to describe tasks, problems, and solutions. In many cases, the intensive discussions during pair programming episodes additionally helped the programming partner's to discover aspects about each other's expertise they had not been aware of before the pair programming session. Within the pair, these developers could thereby associate one partner's expertise to a specific type of task based on the meta-knowledge created during pair programming. At the same time, however, parts of the discovered expertise were immediately externalized and shared with the programming partner: when one partner's specialized expertise was a necessary part of task completion, the expert typically not only solved the task but also provided detailed explanations and background information on taken decisions, properties of existing and related code, and why to prefer a particular solution. The expert thereby transferred parts of the specialized expertise to the less experienced partner during pair programming. While this led to a better task understanding on the latter's side and to mutual agreement with respect to the chosen solution, it also blurred the clear association of the more experienced partner with expertise in the specific area: now, also the less experienced partner had worked into the specifics of the topic. Both task knowledge as well as labels to describe tasks and required expertise thereby became more homogeneous and overlapping when developers conducted pair programming. Table 4.6 substantiates these findings with condensed excerpts of exemplary event episodes when teams actualized different advanced functional affordances of pair programming.

Over time, single developers did not only pair program with a single partner but, working on multiple tasks sequentially, also with others. By consequence, shared labels, expertise, and meta-knowledge were transported by the single developers to their other team members. Thereby, changes in the distribution of knowledge and associated meta-knowledge also emerged to a team level and clearly affected the teams' transactive memory structure by homogenizing expertise across the different developers.

This stepwise emergence was exemplified by team BPM when they had to implement a small functional change to their process management software for a key customer. This change entailed a complex architectural modification at the back end: after sketching out the detailed requirements of the task, it was broken down into several work packages consisting of a quick fix that could rapidly be provided to the customer but was not architecturally sound, the creation of a test suit for the final implementation to test if it still integrated issue-free with other components, and the actual conceptualization and implementation of the final solution. The three work packages were addressed by different developers but developer A was involved in all three of them. In the morning, developers A and B conceptualized and implemented a test suite in pair programming. Especially developer B could contribute much expertise to this task as he had been working for years on several of the components that would most probably have to be changed. B was recognized as the most knowledgeable team member in this area. During pair programming, B told A about the specifics of several interdependencies between different components that had previously not been known to A, and neither to any other team member actually. At the same time, developer M implemented the quick fix and requested A to conduct a peer code review of it because the author knew that A was working on the test suite task with B in the morning. After this peer code review, A pair programmed with J in the afternoon to actually create the final solution that would be rolled out in the future. During this pair programming session, developer A communicated most of the knowledge about component interdependencies he had gathered from B in the morning to developer J, so that they could account for the interdependencies in the implementation of the solution.

The intensive, task-based discussions that are inherent to pair programming and the rotation of pair programming partners thereby had clear consequences for team BPM: substantial parts of expertise on architectural interdependencies between different components of the business process management software had been spread from one expert to several other developers. These developers thereby not only adopted B's labels for specific interdependencies but also homogenized expertise in the sense that developer B was now not the uncontested expert for those interdependencies anymore.

On a higher level, this effect of homogenization could also be observed with respect to the four teams' transactive memory over the duration of the case studies. As such, team BPM had not had many expert areas with exclusively-held specialized expertise even at the beginning of the case studies. But at the end, they argued that there were only "one or two" broad areas with isolated expertise of a single team member left; and they were going to reduce these even further. Team DELIVER, previously consisting of two quite separate sub-teams and gradually relying more and more on pair programming, had substantially extended the commonly shared body of knowledge for all team members by the end of the case studies. Especially with regard to central technologies and software solutions, they had established a common understanding and shared labels that allowed them to communicate about task-related issues across the formerly strong boundaries of the sub-teams' task areas. Finally, team SELL moderately applied pair programming and personal relations in the team remained tense over the duration of the case studies. Noticeably, SELL's team members exchanged less knowledge during pair programming sessions as pair programmers were mostly concerned with finding the right words to communicate their ideas to their counter parts and coming to mutually agreed approaches in addressing the problems at hand. Despite of the interpersonal relationships remaining tense, team members perceived by the end of the case studies that they were more readily able to access expertise held by other team members and that there was a small nucleus of technological knowledge that was shared across large parts of the team. In fact, this may indicate that, while homogenization took place in all case teams that applied pair programming, especially team SELL gained improvements to its transactive memory system: even personally distant team members started to access one another's expertise. While team DELIVER's extensive pair programming sessions had resolved most boundaries between the sub-groups, it had also partially homogenized the formerly specialized expertise within the sub-teams. In several areas that had previously constituted expert areas of one well-known team member, expertise had now been shared and there was partial redundancy in knowledge areas. Tasks that had fallen clearly into the expertise area of a single team member were now associated with the working areas of several team members and could be addressed by all of these developers. Finally, also team BPM actively applied pair programming with frequently changing pair programming partners in order to share knowledge. The creation of redundant expertise in their team was a welcome result for both teams BPM and DELIVER.

> "We generally intend to rotate and mix [pair programming partners] as we try to distribute knowledge, especially for those topics that unilaterally come from one of the [former] teams." (Team Lead DELIVER)

Arguably, these homogenization effects on a team level constitute an integral part of the application of pair programming in general. As pair programming partners jointly work on a task and intensively discuss its solution, they adapt their language to each other, express and exchange parts of their knowledge, and may revise the meta-knowledge of required expertise and expertise holders for this type of task. Applying pair programming in a team with rotating partners and for different tasks, these dyad level effects successively emerge to the team level. In more detail, the effect on the team level transactive memory system is twofold. It leads to (1) a more homogeneous and team-wide shared understanding of tasks as developers start to use the same labels and descriptions for tasks, associated issues, and expertise requirements; and (2) a more homogeneous body of distributed expertise, consisting of less task areas that are associated with the specialized expertise of a single developer and more task areas in which multiple developers hold partially redundant expertise. In the following, this study refers to the described mechanism as *homogenization*. The team level effect of homogenization materializes as a change to a team's transactive memory structure, that is a change in the team's body of shared labels, specialized expertise, and shared meta-knowledge. While a team's transactive memory system may benefit from a convergence of shared labels and meta-knowledge, the creation of expertise redundancy within a team entails increased inaccuracy of task-expertise-person associations and may therefore even constitute a deterioration of the transactive memory system.

With regard to the team level effects of the continuous application of peer code review, this study finds changes to teams' transactive memory structure to be much less pivotal. Instead, peer code review appears to establish mechanisms for bypassing transactive memory structure when conducting transactive memory processes. In more detail, relying on peer code review enables teams to store and retrieve adequate expertise for a task even though there is not necessarily a specialized expert known to be associated with this kind of task. That is, as they incorporate peer code review in their daily development activities, teams get to a lesser extent forced to rely on shared labels and meta-knowledge in order to encode, store, and retrieve information.

The analysis of task level event episodes showed that, independent of the functional affordances that a team made use of, peer code review often led to the inclusion of specialized expertise that would not have been accessible by leveraging the transactive memory structure (Table 4.7 provides exemplary excerpts of event episodes for all advanced affordances of peer code review, the relevant parts of transactive memory structure, and the effect of peer code review on the actually realized transactive processes). This bypassing of a team's shared body of labels and meta-knowledge was found to be rooted in procedural and technical aspects of peer code review. Peer code review facilitated quick and task-based feedback from multiple team members to the author of a code change, given that reviewers could gain immediate access to the workings of the code. Therefore, authors strove to structure, describe, and package their code a-priori in a way that allowed reviewers to give feedback on semantics of the code rather than on stylistic aspects. In addition, reviewers demanded changes in aspects that were not easy to understand and thereby ensured that revised versions were more readily accessible from their points of view. Consequently, team members of the case teams BPM and COMPILE had developed implicitly shared coding styles and their code became more similar and understandable to all team members. This is different from the development of shared labels as these coding norms did not serve to describe tasks or special knowledge requirements but rather determined what source code was expected to look like in order to be "readable" in the future. While shared labels constitute the transactive instrument to determine whether a fellow team member's expertise fits a task, readable code by contrast allowed potential reviewers to determine more easily if their own expertise was helpful for the task.

During the case studies, the three teams applying peer code review showed strong differences with respect to the author-reviewer relationships and their shared coding styles. In team COMPILE, each team member frequently participated in peer code reviews with each of the others. That is, all developers were frequently interconnected via peer code review. Team DELIVER dramatically increased the amount of pair programming they conducted, and dramatically decreased the amount of peer code review until there was nearly no peer code review conducted in DELIVER anymore. In team BPM, on the other hand, there were several team members who participated in peer code reviews only with one or two particular colleagues over the duration of the case studies. Compared to COMPILE, these team members of BPM perceived it as much harder to directly understand source code of most of their colleagues. In pair programming sessions, BPM's members typically did not have any difficulties as their colleagues explained decisions and code based on the extensive shared labels. Consequently, the tight and frequent interconnection of COMPILE appeared to foster the creation of a commonly accepted and readable coding style even more than many pair programming sessions of rotating partners over time.

In peer code review, team BPM relied on the broadcasting of review requests and had potential reviewers determine on their own whether their expertise could help improve a piece of code. Authors' preconceptions of their team members' expertise did therefore not influence who responded to their requests, and they received feedback even from team members they previously did not associate with expertise in a specific area (cf. Table 4.7 for an example). Similarly, both teams COMPILE and BPM used in various occasions historical data from their peer code review systems to discover which team members had previously worked as authors and reviewers in particular areas of existing code, assuming these could be the most expert reviewers available (cf. Table 4.7). In both cases, the routinized application of peer code review therefore circumvented the need for already established meta-knowledge about other team members' specialized knowledge for the retrieval of expertise regarding tasks at hand.

While such "discovered" expertise arguably also constituted a change in the teams' meta-knowledge, this effect was only minor compared to the transfer of knowledge in pair programming. Authors who received brief, written feedback on their proposed solution from an unexpected reviewer only rarely reported that this feedback changed their picture of the reviewer's expertise. By contrast, the intensive discussions and stepwise communication of background information typical for pair programming resulted in much stronger impressions already at a dyadic level which could then emerge to a team level. In fact, also developers emphasized that peer code review provided them with a very good overview of the current state of ongoing work on their software product and with the possibility to retrieve the names of team members that contributed to specific parts in the past based on the documented reviews but only if desired. That is, team members most often did not bother remembering in detail who had worked on each task exactly as they could always rely on their peer code review systems to quickly find experienced developers for all parts of the existing code.

"We used to be four, now we are eight. This drives complexity.[...] Still, with the help of peer code review we are able to keep an overview of what is going on in this team of eight. That's quite a big deal! I'd say, as far as possible, I do have a rough understanding what is going on in the code." (Team Lead COMPILE)

This effect was especially pronounced in team COMPILE. While the team already had a sophisticated transactive memory structure in place, they conducted most of the code-related transactive processes via their peer code review system. Being aware that not all expertise of the team members was captured in existing code of their product, they occasionally conducted meetings to create and update "exper-tise maps". During these meetings, each developer outlined especially technological and domain-specific knowledge areas s/he had recently worked into but had not yet incorporated them into any source code. Implicitly, COMPILE acknowledged thereby that expertise which had already been incorporated into source code could easily be retrieved via peer code review while newly gained expertise that had not yet influenced peer code reviews was better dealt with through an explicit update of the transactive memory structure.

While the case teams that applied pair programming reduced the knowledge specialization within their teams through pair programming, team COMPILE, that relied exclusively on peer code review, stuck with its sophisticated transactive memory structure and did not intend to reduce the specialization of team members. Quite the contrary, team members of COMPILE even gained new specializations and made them available through peer code review whenever possible. As such, developer K of team COMPILE had been working on improving the runtime performance of their compiler by using a new library. After implementing a prototypical solution and going through several rounds of revisions with one reviewing colleague, K decided that the desired performance improvement could not be realized with this library. K archived the code reviews with a short note that performance improvements would not work with this library, so that colleagues would be able to easily find the changes and to contact K in the future if they require more in-depth expertise. The peer code review system thereby served as a storage for meta-knowledge of K's expertise in the new library. When searching the team's code repository for this library in the future, other developers could find K's prototypical solution, see that K held expertise in this library, and decide whether K's expertise could help improve the outcome of their own task. Although the team's transactive memory structure did not contain meta-knowledge associating K with this library as only a single other team member had seen any of it, transactive processes conducted through the peer code review system would consequently still retrieve K's expertise in the library.

Overall, peer code review thus fosters the execution of transactive memory processes for information encoding, storage, and retrieval that are less dependent on the actual transactive memory structure of shared labels, specialized knowledge, and shared meta-knowledge in a team. Peer code review effectively bypasses the transactive memory structure of a team: it connects team members in search and in possession of expertise on the basis of their previous and current work areas as well as their self-assessed relevance of expertise for a given solution. In contrast to the homogenizing influence of pair programming, peer code review thereby alters the transactive processes of a team's transactive memory system but leaves its transactive memory structure unchanged. This study refers to this mechanism as *transparency* because the transactive memory structure becomes partly indecisive and transparent for the execution of transactive processes.

4.2.3.3 Summary of Emergent Effects

With respect to the emergent effect of collaborative quality assurance techniques on team cognition (Research Question 2a), this study finds that two distinct generative mechanisms underlie the influences of continued application of pair programming and peer code review on ISD teams' transactive memory systems: homogenization and transparency. Homogenization constitutes the primary effect of pair programming on a team's transactive memory structure. As pair programming entails intensive face-to-face discussions about tasks, issues, and solution approaches of changing partners over time, developers adapt their language and task understanding to each other but also transfer large parts of their specialized expertise to other team members. This leads to a more homogeneous task understanding, more even distribution of knowledge, and the existence of redundant expertise. Transparency constitutes the primary effect of peer code review on a team's transactive memory system as a whole. As peer code review entails the direct search, retrieval, and persistent recording of relevant expertise within a peer code review system, it allows for conducting these transactive processes relatively independent of a team's existing body of shared labels and shared meta-knowledge (i.e., its transactive memory structure). Making use of advanced affordances, peer code review systems fill over time with the historical reviews provided by team members in their different areas of expertise. Authors can use this data to quickly search recent reviews in a specific area of source code in order to find appropriate colleagues that may review their code and provide specialized expertise. Authors thereby circumvent the need for shared labels and meta-knowledge for finding an expert in their team but can directly address him/her based on information drawn from the peer code review system. By consequence, routinized and continued application of peer code review with all team members bypasses a team's transactive memory structure and allows for sophisticated information storage and retrieval even without appropriate shared labels and meta-knowledge in place.

While pair programming also leads to slight changes in transactive processes and peer code review to slight changes in transactive memory structure, these effects are found negligible compared to the major effect of each technique. Consequently, this study finds that the generative mechanisms of transparency and homogenization are both present in the application of each collaborative quality assurance technique, but homogenization in pair programming and transparency in peer code review are exceedingly more effective than their respective counterpart.

4.2.4 Summary and Critical Assessment

Insights from the four in-depth case studies are twofold. First, a team's transactive memory exerts causal influence on the task level affordances of collaborative quality assurance techniques applied in the team (Research Question 1). As such, the existence of specialized knowledge in a task allows teams to share task understanding via pair programming and to create intelligible source code via peer code review. On top of specialized knowledge, shared labels for describing task properties, knowledge requirements, and problems enable developers to use pair programming for joint solution satisficing and peer code review for broadly integrating opinions and information from and for multiple team members. With additional shared meta-knowledge regarding a task, developers can successfully apply pair programming for creating optimized expert solutions and peer code review for creating expert-approved solutions. The task-relevant transactive memory of an ISD team thereby decides whether or not advanced affordances of the techniques can be enacted successfully.

Second, findings from the case studies suggest that ongoing use of pair programming successively homogenizes labels, knowledge, and meta-knowledge whereas peer code review partially decouples transactive processes from transactive memory structure in an ISD team (Research Question 2a). As peer code review systems fill with data from previously conducted peer code reviews, developers can use these systems to directly retrieve comments of old reviews on the one hand and find expert reviewers based on their previous contributions on the other hand. Doing so, developers can locate and retrieve specialized expertise for a specific piece of code even though they may not have the shared meta-knowledge and labels that would allow them to find expert reviewers via the team's transactive memory system. By consequence, they substitute transactive memory structure with data from their peer code review systems. Pair programming, by contrast, changes ISD team's transactive memory structure by homogenizing shared labels and meta-knowledge on the one hand, and creating redundant expertise on the other hand.

The circular connection of these two findings regarding Research Questions 1 and 2a deserves some elaboration: while a team's transactive memory structure causes the task level affordances of collaborative quality assurance techniques, the techniques' continued application causes changes in the transactive memory system in turn. In more detail, only the continued actualization of advanced affordances yields the emergent effects on a team's transactive memory: only advanced affordances of pair programming encompass the significant knowledge transfer that leads to homogenization, whereas only the advanced affordances of peer code review create a body of historical reviews in which members with specialized expertise can be identified as task experts. The actualization of advanced affordances is therefore a prerequisite for the emergence of effects on the transactive memory system. There is, however, no evidence that particular advanced affordances of a single technique have different emergent effects. Consequently, it does not seem to play a role for the emergent effects which particular one of the advanced functional affordances of a technique is enacted most. In more detail, the application of pair programming successively creates knowledge redundancies as not only labels and meta-knowledge but also actual task knowledge become more homogeneous. This suggests that extensive application of pair programming may actually lead to a deterioration of specialized expertise and accordingly of advanced affordances of pair programming: as developers gain increasingly overlapping knowledge from one another they may not be able to refer to specialized expertise anymore for specific tasks. For the application of collaborative quality assurance techniques, this may mean that teams could eventually be left with basic task level affordances only. By contrast, transparency caused by the actualization of advanced affordances of peer code review leads to a decoupling of transactive processes from transactive memory structure. Teams that frequently apply peer code review over time consequently become able to use their peer code review systems in place of a transactive memory structure for identifying experts. Regarding the application of collaborative quality assurance techniques, this may suggest that these teams can make use of advanced affordances of peer code review even for tasks that are not covered by their transactive memory. In this respect, the findings of the case studies suggest that extensive and continued application of peer code review may reinforce its positive effects on information storage and retrieval, whereas extensive and continued application of pair programming may actually cannibalize the positive effects of its application. The following sections present the results of a questionnaire-based survey that consequently examined the quality impacts of both techniques against this backdrop.

Limitations of Case Studies

The critical realist case studies were conducted with four ongoing, collocated ISD teams who had all received trainings in collaborative quality assurance techniques. By consequence, findings generated from these four cases may not necessarily transfer to all ISD teams in general. For example, in teams working across geographical, temporal, and cultural distances, team-wide pair programming may be impossible or restricted to collocated sub-groups whereas peer code review was actually developed for such distributed settings. At the same time, extant literature holds that team cognition in globally distributed ISD teams is severely impacted by spacial and temporal distances (e.g., Espinosa et al. 2007; Oshri et al. 2008). Future research should therefore more closely examine the application of collaborative quality assurance techniques and its effects in teams that comprise geographically distributed members. Similarly, prior research suggests that team cognition in temporary project teams and newly established work groups differs from team cognition in ongoing, long-lasting teams (e.g., Austin 2003; Choi et al. 2010; Majchrzak et al. 2007). Future research should consequently investigate if collaborative quality assurance techniques actually hold the same functional affordances for short-lived teams and whether they lead to the same socio-cognitive effects of homogenization and transparency in that context.

All case studies were moreover conducted with ISD teams who extensively relied on pair programming, peer code review, or both techniques in their daily practice. No teams were studied that rejected both techniques or applied them only marginally. Although the consistency of results across the different cases and the exploratory phase can be seen as initial evidence for transferability, the specific context of ISD teams who clearly adopted at least one of the techniques could arguably limit the generalizability of findings. To address this shortcoming, a questionnaire-based survey study was conducted next that incorporated answers from a larger number of ISD teams in very different contexts who applied the techniques to freely varying degrees.

4.3 Survey Study

The presentation of qualitative analyses of this study has so far focused on Research Questions 1 and 2a. Regarding Research Question 1, findings showed that a team's transactive memory system creates advanced functional affordances of collaborative quality assurance techniques on the level of single tasks. Regarding Research Question 2a, results indicated that the ongoing enactment of advanced affordances results in emergent effects on a team's transactive memory system in turn. In particular, analyses identified two generative mechanisms, homogenization and transparency, that cause impacts on a team's transactive memory system. Following a sequential mixed-methods research design, this study proceeds by presenting the results of a questionnaire-based survey study of ISD team members, team leads, and product managers that served two purposes: (1) corroborate the existence of homogenization and transparency as mechanisms that cause emergent changes in a team's transactive memory system when collaborative quality assurance techniques are applied (Research Question 2a); and (2) show that these mechanisms help better understand the quality impact of collaborative quality assurance techniques (Research Question 2b). This section first presents concepts fundamental to the survey study of transactive memory systems from a critical realist perspective and provides an overview of the research model underlying the survey. Subsequently, this section develops a coherent set of hypotheses from extant theory and from the proposed generative mechanisms of homogenization and transparency. Next, operationalizations and measurement properties are discussed and assessed in the light of the conducted survey. The hypotheses are evaluated following established guidelines by Gefen et al. (2011) and Ringle et al. (2012) and lastly discussed regarding their validity and impact.

4.3.1 Conceptual Foundations and Overview of Research Model

Based on the two generative mechanisms identified in the case work so far, this study proceeds by analyzing the presence of these mechanisms as well as the quality impacts of collaborative quality assurance techniques in a broad variety of ISD teams. However, this study's underlying ontological and epistemological stance, critical realism, poses constraints to such an endeavor. In fact, the assumptions of nondeterminism and of the fallibility of human knowledge forbid a direct confirmation or disconfirmation of generative mechanisms in quantitative studies without being trapped in epistemic fallacy (Mingers 2004; Zachariadis et al. 2013). Especially the properties of complex social constructs, such as a team's transactive memory system, can only hardly be assessed accurately based on individuals' opinions as these are dependent on the personal history of an individual, distinct from other individuals' personal perspectives and experiences, and inherently fallible (Mingers 2001, 2004). Nevertheless, social structures such as a team's transactive memory do influence individuals' perceptions of these structures as well as their resulting actions, albeit not always in a deterministic and statistically reliable manner (Archer 1998; Mingers 2001). Quantitative studies alone may therefore not serve for causal explanation of a phenomenon or disconfirmation of generative mechanisms. However, they can serve to identify *demi-regularities* (Zachariadis et al. 2013) that support existing causal explanations and can help refine these explanations by uncovering unexpected relationships (Venkatesh et al. 2013).

In line with these thoughts, this survey study focuses not on the team level construct of a team's transactive memory system but rather on the individual level perceptions of the effectiveness of a team's transactive memory system. Moreover, the qualitative analyses did not indicate that the single advanced affordances of each technique differ in the emergent effects they cause (cf. Sect. 4.2.4). Findings indicated that repeated enactment of any advanced affordance of pair programming leads to homogenization whereas all advanced affordances of peer code review result in transparency. This survey study is primarily interested in the emergent effects on team cognition and quality. Consequently, it does not differentiate between single functional affordances but examines only the overall extent to which team members conduct collaborative quality assurance with each technique. This appears reasonable based on the assumption that team members who generally apply pair programming or peer code review more often should, by tendency, also make more frequent use of advanced affordances of the respective techniques.

While the previous, qualitative steps of this study have carved out the detailed team level workings of homogenization and transparency caused by collaborative quality assurance techniques, this survey shows that team members' perceptions as well as changes to the resulting software largely behave as would be expected under the light of the two generative mechanisms of homogenization and transparency. In doing so, this study also takes important results from prior work as well as extant theory on transactive memory systems and ISD teams into account. As such, transactive memory systems were first observed in intimate couples (Wegner et al. 1985), and extant theory holds that effective transactive memory systems develop particularly in groups with close personal relationships (Hollingshead 2000). Moreover, literature emphasizes that modularity drives the quality of software products (Maruping et al. 2009a) and is a central mechanism for knowledge coordination in work groups and organizations (Brusoni and Prencipe 2001; Gagsch 1980; Kilmann 1984) that may possibly rival knowledge coordination through transactive memory systems. Therefore, this survey builds on the body of existing research and includes effects of and on the relationship quality of ISD team members and the modularity of the software they develop.

Figure 4.4 depicts the research model that is developed in the following section, Table 4.8 outlines the corresponding construct definitions. The model follows extant theory in proposing that interpersonal relationship quality drives the perceived effectiveness of a team's transactive memory system (H1) which, in turn, improves software quality (H2). Based on the theoretical mechanisms resulting from the qualitative analyses of this study, the model argues that homogenization through pair programming reduces the perceived effectiveness of a team's transactive memory system as knowledge redundancies make the transactive memory system inaccurate (H3). This effect is argued to be especially strong if team members have close interpersonal relationships that would allow them to easily query one another for specialized expertise (H4). Software modularity is proposed to drive software quality (H5) and to reduce the quality effect of transactive memory system effectiveness (H6). Moreover, homogenization through pair programming is argued to foster agreement in architectural decisions and rules that emerge as the product grows, thereby reducing misunderstandings about how to modularize and inhibiting the erosion of modularity due to bad design decisions of individual developers (H7). Results from the case studies suggest that transparency through peer code review partially decouples a team's transactive processes for encoding, storing,

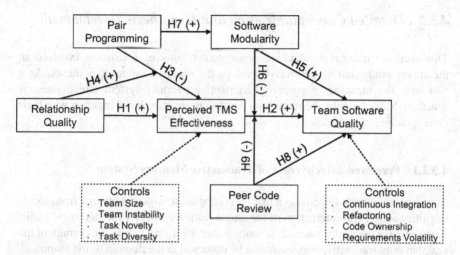

Fig. 4.4 Developed research model

Table 4.8 Construct definitions

Construct	Definition	Based on
Perceived transactive memory system effectiveness	Developers' assessment of the extent to which their team possesses and effectively coordinates differentiated and credible expertise	Majchrzak et al. (2013b), Lewis (2003)
Team relationship quality	The extent to which team members have positive, friendly feelings toward one another	Guinan et al. (1998), Liang et al. (2010)
Team software quality	The extent to which an ISD team produces software that is responsive to customer demands, operationally effective, and maintainable over time	Liang et al. (2010)
Peer code review	The extent to which developers conduct peer code review with one another in their team	Self-developed
Pair programming	The extent to which developers conduct pair programming with one another in their team	Maruping et al. (2009a)
Software modularity	The degree to which the components of a software produced by an ISD team can be separated and recombined effectively	Schilling (2000), Lau et al. (2007, 2009)

and retrieving information from its established transactive memory structure. In other words, peer code review *substitutes* the established transactive memory in creating software. Following this reasoning, peer code review is argued to drive software quality (H8) while reducing the positive quality influence of transactive memory effectiveness at the same time (H9). In the following, these hypotheses are developed in detail.

4.3.2   Detailed Conceptualization and Hypothesis Development

This section outlines the detailed conceptualizations of constructs involved in the survey study and successively develops the research model hypotheses. As a first step, the meaning of perceived transactive memory system effectiveness is specified. Subsequently, the remaining constructs are introduced together with their corresponding hypotheses.

4.3.2.1   Perceived Effectiveness of Transactive Memory System

Transactive memory systems as a team level cognitive structure emerge from socio-cognitive action and interaction of the single team members. From a critical realist perspective, a team's transactive memory is thereby a structure in the domain of the real, but only transactive processes can be observed in the domain of the empirical. While transactive processes have been directly observed and interpreted in the critical realist case studies for single instances of pair programming and peer code review, this is hardly possible when studying large numbers of different teams in a field setting. To study the effects of pair programming and peer code review on the extent and effectiveness of a team's transactive memory in this context, it is therefore necessary to elicit subjective opinions of single individuals. Individuals, however, necessarily have a stratified perspective on the social structure of a transactive memory system. As a consequence, even though assuming best efforts, individuals may only report their subjective opinions on team level structures and resulting processes.

This study conceptualizes *perceived transactive memory effectiveness* as an individual team member's perspective on the team's transactive memory structure and the effectiveness of transactive processes based on this structure. This is different from the intent to measure the real structure of a team's transactive memory system as it acknowledges the interpretive function that a team member executes when reasoning about and reporting on the actual structure. Nevertheless, the latent structure of the transactive memory can be reasonably assumed to affect individuals' perceptions of it (Archer 1998). While not deterministically and biased by individual experiences and interpretations, improvements in transactive memory by tendency increase an individual's perceptions of transactive memory effectiveness. At the same time, changes in a group's transactive memory structure emerge from the changes to single group members' knowledge stock, labels, and meta-knowledge (Kozlowski and Klein 2000). By consequence, it appears most meaningful to focus on the perceived effectiveness of transactive memory systems on an individual level for two reasons: (1) these perceptions can more realistically be assessed in a broad survey study than the real underlying transactive memory structure and (2) individuals' perceptions are more immediately affected by changes to knowledge, labels, and meta-knowledge; they constitute the basis for emergent effects on the real transactive memory structure and can therefore provide more immediate insights.

4.3.2.2 Team Relationship Quality

Transactive memory systems have first been observed in intimate couples (Wegner et al. 1985) and have only later on been examined in work groups that do not necessarily show such intimate personal relationships (Hollingshead et al. 2011; Lewis and Herndon 2011; Peltokorpi 2008; Ren and Argote 2011; Wegner 1987). Some scholars traditionally argued that transactive memory systems are particular to groups with personally close relationships and high intimacy (Hollingshead 2000). In fact, positive affections between team members appear to foster transactive memory systems development as they increase interpersonal trust, thereby making team members more willing to rely on one another's expertise and to contribute their own knowledge (Akgün et al. 2005). Although less intimate relationships have also been associated with cognitive diversity that may constitute a desirable extension of a group's body of differentiated expertise (Rau 2005), negative affections between team members are typically seen as negative for a groups' transactive memory. They can prevent teams from retrieving information, even from retrieving information that is commonly known to be available in the team (Liang et al. 2010; Rau 2005).

Close personal relationships, by contrast, bring about explicit and implicit communication and exchange of information between the related persons. In closely related work groups, individuals moreover tend to align their expectations as well as evaluations of single team members' contributions to team-task accomplishment (Hollingshead 2001). What is more, positive affection leads individuals to reflect more on others' strengths and weaknesses and fosters altruistic behavior; thereby, positive affection may facilitate the mutual recognition of expertise, the forwarding of information to appropriate team members, and the provision of individuals' expertise when others look for it (Huang 2009). By consequence, teams with close affective relationships can be expected to develop more effective transactive memory systems and single team members' perceptions can be assumed to reflect this. That allows to put forward the hypothesis:

> H1: The better team members perceive the quality of interpersonal relationships in the team, the more effective do the team members perceive the team's transactive memory system.

4.3.2.3 Software Quality

Teams that work on the same product over longer periods face challenges and goals that are partially different from the ones of teams working in temporary projects (Austin 2003; Choi et al. 2010). As such, the fixed time line of ISD projects typically leads to an evaluation of software development teams not only based on the results of their work but also based on their adherence to the project's time line and its predefined resources, that is their process efficiency (Faraj and Sproull 2000; Guinan et al. 1998; Nidumolu 1995). By contrast, software development teams that develop, maintain, and extend a software product, potentially over several years, are much less bound to the short-framed time restrictions of a typical ISD project. For these teams, it is more desirable to create a product that can be maintained efficiently, effectively satisfies customer demands, and can easily be extended in the future. That is, software quality becomes more important for these teams as compared to ISD project teams. Consequently, and also due to the fact that this work centers around collaborative quality assurance techniques, software quality is treated as the central dependent and economically relevant variable of this survey study.

Software quality refers not only to the absence of programming errors but also to the adequacy of the software for internal and external software stakeholders (Sommerville 2012, p. 712). Thereby, internal software quality refers to properties of a software product's source code that facilitate its maintenance over time and flexibility for change (Mc Connell 2004, p. 483). This includes that source code be written, formatted, and documented in a way that allows for grasping its purpose and implementation specifics, thereby facilitating the identification of hidden flaws, changes, and extensions in the future. In addition, high-quality software meets customer demands in that it is responsive to user needs and is efficient in its operation (Liang et al. 2010). Numerous studies have shown that, in order to create a software product with these characteristics, software development teams rely on the effective combination of differentiated expertise through their transactive memory systems (Faraj and Sproull 2000; Lin et al. 2011; Oshri et al. 2008). Assuming that single team members' perceptions of transactive memory system effectiveness are strongly influenced by the team's real transactive memory, these perceptions can arguably be used to predict the actual quality of their resulting software. Consequently, this study hypothesizes as follows.

> H2: The more effective team members perceive the transactive memory system of a team, the better is the software quality provided by the team.

4.3.2.4 Homogenization Through Pair Programming

Results of the four in-depth case studies suggest that the application of pair programming affects a team's transactive memory structure through homogenization. As single team members engage in pair programming, they intensively discuss the task at hand and possible solutions based on their prior knowledge and expertise. Doing so, developers are forced to come to shared expressions and labels for the problems and solutions they discuss. While each of them brings forward arguments and contributes information to achieve a mutually accepted solution, pair programming partners learn about each other's expertise but also explicitly exchange knowledge, partially from their areas of specialized expertise. As team members pair program with multiple partners over time, these labels, knowledge, and meta-knowledge spread from one dyad to the next and emerge to the team level, thereby inducing changes to the team's transactive memory structure. In sum, pair programming homogenizes all three elements of a team's transactive memory structure: team members develop shared labels and meta-knowledge about one another's expertise, but also homogenize their stock of knowledge and create redundant expertise. While homogenization as a generative mechanisms may not be directly observable, its observable effects on the effectiveness of teams' transactive memory systems should provide corroborating evidence for the existence of this mechanism.

Redundant knowledge can yield positive effects on a team's performance under certain conditions (Gupta and Hollingshead 2010; Hollingshead et al. 2011; Wegner 1987). As such, teams with sophisticated transactive memory systems with clearly differentiated expertise rely primarily on the respective experts when working on tasks in different areas. By consequence, these teams' task performance is tied closely to the single experts' performance; and disturbances of the transactive memory system, for example by membership attrition, can yield extreme impacts on team performance (Lewis et al. 2007). Teams that rely on more redundant knowledge, on the other hand, can compensate better for the loss of single members as other team members may substitute for their role in the transactive memory system (Gupta and Hollingshead 2010; Hollingshead et al. 2011). Similarly, redundant expertise can enable that team members mutually verify the correctness of one another's work results and provide backup for knowledge retrieval processes (Ellis et al. 2003; Wegner 1987). However, these activities based on redundant expertise are only effective and efficient if a team's task structure allows for clearly distinguishing between right and wrong solutions and if the team does not need to manage large amounts of information so that specialization does not appear crucial (Gupta and Hollingshead 2010). As neither of these assumptions can be made for tasks of ISD teams, these direct positive effects of large redundancies in team knowledge may not hold for the type of teams addressed in this study. Consequently, the homogenization and creation of redundant expertise inherent in pair programming may rather have negative consequences for ISD teams.

Early literature on transactive memory systems talked about the value of redundant knowledge in a team's transactive memory structure. As such, Wegner (1987) even defined a special type of transactive memory systems that relied to a large part on redundant, as opposed to differentiated, expertise: "An *integrated transactive memory* occurs when the same items of information are held in different individual memory stores and the individuals are aware of the overlap because they share label and location information as well" (Wegner 1987, p. 204). Only few later studies, however, have found mentionable positive effects of large amounts of redundant expertise in transactive memory systems. More commonly it is held that high levels of redundancy worsen a group's performance on knowledge tasks (Hollingshead 2000; Ohtsubo 2005; Wong 2008) while expertise differentiation lowers cognitive load on individuals and increases task performance of ISD teams (Chen et al. 2013; Espinosa et al. 2007; Faraj and Sproull 2000; Hsu et al. 2012; Lin et al. 2011; Maruping et al. 2009b) as well as of general work groups (Austin 2003; Hollingshead 1998a; Jarvenpaa and Majchrzak 2008; Kanawattanachai and Yoo 2007; Liang et al. 1995; Majchrzak et al. 2007; Moreland and Myaskovsky 2000). This is because redundant expertise reduces the accuracy of a group's transactive memory system: as expertise areas of single team members blur, it becomes harder and more communication-intensive to find the right team member when looking for or remembering information in specific areas (Peltokorpi 2008). Redundant expertise thereby increases the cognitive load on each team member who cannot focus on a specific expertise area anymore, and it is typically associated with reduced performance in the team members' focal areas of expertise (Hollingshead 2000). These findings are in line with recent studies that find expertise redundancy to reduce agile ISD teams' efficiency (Fægri et al. 2010).

Beyond the negative effects of redundant expertise, however, teams need to develop shared labels and shared meta-knowledge in order to be able to effec tively retrieve expertise from their single, specialized members (Wegner et al. 1985). Shared abstract concepts referring to a team's task domain, that are for example established during joint team trainings, facilitate the creation of shared labels and meta-knowledge (Hollingshead 1998b; Liang et al. 1995; Moreland and Myaskovsky 2000). In fact, only a shared base of transferable, abstract conceptions ultimately allows teams to effectively use their transactive memory system not only for standard tasks but also for innovative, non-routine tasks in related domains (Akgün et al. 2005; Lewis et al. 2005; Ren et al. 2006). If team members fail to establish enough common ground for shared labels and meta-knowledge, knowledge specialization can isolate team members (Jones and Kelly 2013) and reduce the effectiveness of information retrieval in a teams (Gupta and Hollingshead 2010). Ilgen et al. (2005) summarized parts of the extant research in this stream stating that "Structures that created specialized loners failed to learn because of the noncommensurate nature of their experiences, and teams structured in terms of overly broad generalists failed to learn because of information overload" (Ilgen et al. 2005, p. 532). Consequently, effective teams typically develop a differentiated knowledge structure based on shared labels that incorporate commonly accepted "higher-order information" about the team's tasks, topics, and interrelations thereby balancing integrated and differentiated elements of their transactive memory structure (Hollingshead et al. 2011).

Especially for teams that have not yet worked together or that cannot access their distributed expertise due to other reasons, establishing shared labels and meta-knowledge is of utmost importance (Rulke and Rau 2000). Although communication constitutes a necessary element of this process (Hollingshead 1998b; Kanawattanachai and Yoo 2007), communication and member familiarity alone do not suffice for establishing shared labels and meta-knowledge (Jackson and Moreland 2009; Moreland and Myaskovsky 2000). Instead, it requires exchange on task-related topics and interactions that allow for implicitly or explicitly inferring team members' expertise areas and informal roles (Huckman et al. 2009; Ren et al. 2006; Rulke and Rau 2000). While negative affections in teams can inhibit such interactions (Huang 2009; Rau 2005), exchange on single tasks can nevertheless be enforced by specific collaboration techniques. As such, cross-training single team members in one another's job can enforce the development of shared labels and meta-knowledge in spite of prior relations and may therefore be especially suited to foster transactive memory structure development (Ellis et al. 2008). By consequence, the homogenization of labels, knowledge, and meta-knowledge within teams that conduct pair programming can be expected to have a dual effect. On the one hand, redundant knowledge created and shared through pair programming may negatively influence a team's transactive memory system, lead to less accuracy of task-expertise-person associations, and reduce transactive memory system effectiveness. On the other hand, homogenization through pair programming may be beneficial for teams' transactive memory systems if they do not incorporate large exchanges of task level knowledge. Prior studies and also results from this study's in-depth case work suggest that pair programming team members who have tense interpersonal relationships struggle more in coming to shared points of view of tasks and possible solutions than affectively close pair programming dyads. As developers with tense interpersonal relationships invest more time in coming to general agreement on problems and possible solutions, they exchange less task level knowledge than close partners. Ceteris paribus, pair programmers with tense relationships may therefore create more shared labels and meta-knowledge and less redundant expertise than personally close dyads. In sum, negative interpersonal relationship quality may therefore reduce the amount of redundant expertise created in pair programming teams while close relationships may foster such redundancy. Assuming this is reflected in developers' perceptions, this study consequently hypothesizes:

H3: The more extensively team members conduct pair programming, the less effective do the team members perceive the team's transactive memory system.

H4: Close interpersonal relationships positively moderate the negative effect of pair programming on perceived transactive memory system effectiveness.

4.3.2.5 Software Modularity

Modularity is "a continuum describing the degree to which a system's components can be separated and recombined, and it refers both to the tightness of coupling between components and the degree to which the 'rules' of the system architecture enable (or prohibit) the mixing and matching of components" (Schilling 2000, p. 312). Modularity of software thereby facilitates the recombination of existing components and allows for changes to the inner workings of single components without affecting others. Defects in existing components can therefore be repaired more easily (Subramanyam et al. 2012) and lead to less severe consequences than in less modular software (Maruping et al. 2009a). In addition, modularity enables more fine-grained changes and thereby allows for capitalizing on contributions even from developers who may not have a detailed understanding of an entire software product but only of single components (Baldwin and Clark 2006). While this helps reduce development effort and increases development efficiency (Gomes and Joglekar 2008; Subramanyam et al. 2012), modularity can also positively affect products from a customer's point of view. As such, higher modularity allows for easier exchange of single components and thereby for later and better decisions about the exact specifications of required modules (Lau et al. 2007). By consequence, product modularity enables the creation of more innovative products and increases the flexibility to react on customer service demands, ultimately leading to improved quality from a customer's perspective (Lau et al. 2007, 2009). Software modularity therefore arguably improves internal as well as external software quality.

The modularity of a software is largely determined by the system architecture which defines the elements of the software's codebase, their interactions, and rules for their composition (Baldwin and Clark 2006; Shaw and Garlan 1996). The majority of the decisions about this architecture are traditionally made up-front before the details and inner workings of a software are designed and implemented. By consequence, "the architecture of a codebase is not a matter of natural law but, is to a large degree, under the control of the initial designers of the system" (Baldwin and Clark 2006, p. 1117). However, the architecture, and thereby also the modularity of a software, is not totally static, but it evolves as developers add, change, and remove components of the codebase (Waterman 2014). In fact, architectures can evolve over time to become more or less modular, albeit with strong path dependencies created by the initial architecture (Schilling 2000). Single software developers and ISD teams can therefore become explicitly or implicitly responsible for the "emergent architecture" of their product.[2] Changes toward more modularization may be based on rational grounds such as the need to serve customers with distinct requirements or the necessity to rely on developers who are proficient only in small parts of a software (Baldwin and Clark 2006; Schilling 2000). However, such evolution may also result from the socially created and fallible nature of human knowledge. For example, single developers may misunderstand their product's implicit rules of modularization when adding, changing, or removing components thereby gradually watering down the architectural principles underlying the product's structure and reducing its modularity. On the other hand, entire ISD teams may be well aware of these underlying principles, be it implicit or explicit ones, and may over time even increase their product's modularity by reworking existing code that violates architectural rules when they encounter it (Waterman 2014). Through pair programming and the inherent homogenization of labels, knowledge, and meta-knowledge in ISD teams, developers may achieve a team-wide shared perspective on architectural rules and principles of modularization, on how new functionality fits into the existing modular structure, and on how old code could better be structured in a more modular way. By consequence, these developers may violate less architectural rules and press on modularization in a desirable way based on shared labels and redundant knowledge. Additional efforts for pair programming within the boundaries of single components may thereby be outweighed by reduced integration efforts across different components (Dawande et al. 2008). As more developers become knowledgeable in different components, these components may be developed more quickly in parallel based on redundant knowledge, thereby

---

[2]In fact, early agile software development literature has proposed to reduce up-front architectural activities to a minimal necessary amount and to have subsequent architectural decisions be made by ISD teams when the concrete need arises. This has led to a reluctance in adopting agile ISD methods in industries that traditionally rely on robust architectures such as embedded systems development (Ronkainen and Abrahamsson 2003). For a detailed discussion of findings on emergent and up-front architectures in software development teams see Waterman (2014).

allowing the team to rely more confidently on highly modularized structures. This reasoning parallels findings that emphasize pair programming dyads produce better software designs than their least experienced individual member (Canfora et al. 2007; Lui et al. 2008; Mangalaraj et al. 2014). Although such incremental changes may only have weak impacts compared to the initial architecture of the system (Schilling 2000), homogenization may still have a positive effect on the modularity of software developed in a team.

A central function of architectural modularization is coordination (Gagsch 1980; Kilmann 1984; Simon 1969). Coordination of work and coordination of knowledge lead to a reduction of cognitive load on individuals: "architectural knowledge is needed to let each designer know what he or she needs to know, and nothing more, about other components' specifications (i.e. the interfaces)" (Brusoni and Prencipe 2001, p. 181). Modularity, not only of their software product but also of the associated development tasks, thereby allows ISD teams to reduce effort and time required to develop an entire software through concurrent work on relatively independent components on the one and specialization gains on the other hand (Gomes and Joglekar 2008). With a highly modular software architecture, single developers may consequently specialize in different components and work only on tasks that concern these components. In this respect, software modularity constitutes a knowledge coordination mechanism functionally similar to an ISD team's transactive memory system; it allows for coordinated assignation of tasks to team members that possess matching expertise to complete them effectively and efficiently. In fact, this may lead to the conclusion that the modularity of a team's software and its transactive memory system constitute competing mechanisms to increase team performance, either by specialization in particular knowledge areas or by specialization in physical modules of the team's product. By consequence, software modularity may weaken the positive effect of a team's transactive memory with respect to the team's work results. This study therefore puts forward the following three hypotheses.

H5: The more modular the software produced by a team, the better is the software quality.
H6: Software modularity negatively moderates the positive effect of perceived transactive memory system effectiveness on software quality.
H7: The more extensively team members conduct pair programming, the more modular is the software produced by the team.

4.3.2.6 Transparency Through Peer Code Review

Results of the four in-depth case studies suggest that the application of peer code review affects a team's transactive memory system through transparency, that is by partially decoupling transactive processes from the team's transactive memory structure. The use of peer code review systems as a technological artifact plays a central role in this effect. Extant research on transactive memory systems has addressed the impact of technology on the development and workings of transactive memory systems from distinct perspectives. First and foremost, technology has been studied as a facilitator for transactive memory system development in work groups as well as in larger organizational units (Nevo and Ophir 2012; Ren and Argote 2011). Technologies such as knowledge management systems and expert directories can provide individuals with explicit meta-information about who knows what; they thereby support team members in learning about the expertise of their co-workers and encoding this information in their transactive memory system (Choi et al. 2010; Nevo and Wand 2005; Peltokorpi 2004; Yuan et al. 2007). Technology can also facilitate computer-mediated communication to retrieve information from remote team members (Oshri et al. 2008; Su 2012). Recent technologies like social media additionally provide social cues that facilitate the psychological decision processes of individuals when they decide whom to supply with information and from whom to request information (Nevo et al. 2012). This entire stream of research implicitly holds that information systems and communication technologies complement the transactive processes conducted face-to-face between individuals and help create, update, and sustain effective transactive memory structures (Oshri et al. 2008; Ryan and O'Connor 2013). This conception of complementarity appears to hold for the groups studied in this stream of research: typically teams working in settings challenging for transactive memory system development such as of global distribution (Kotlarsky and Oshri 2005; Lewis 2004; Oshri et al. 2008; Su 2012), a strong lack of tacit knowledge (Nevo and Wand 2005), or temporary projects (Lewis 2004; Yuan et al. 2007). By contrast, this study is concerned with ongoing, collocated ISD teams that have plenty of opportunity to conduct the activities central to transactive memory system development: exchanging codified as well as tacit knowledge, learning about one another, and learning about their tasks during face-to-face conversations (Lewis 2004; Peltokorpi 2008). In comparison, effects of peer code review systems in these teams may be of minor importance for initial transactive memory development.

Contrasting thoughts of complementarity, other scholars have reasoned about the possible substitution of transactive memory systems through technology (Lewis and Herndon 2011). As such, some studies found that transactive memory systems can be more effective when teams have little explicit information available (Griffith and Sawyer 2010) and that teams sometimes rely on information systems to keep track of specialized expertise rather than building up a transactive memory structure (Gray 2000). Griffith and Sawyer (2010) argue that this effect may be based on coordination costs: explicit knowledge may be more efficiently retrieved from an accessible information system than from team members because the required transactive processes incur coordination costs (Griffith and Sawyer 2010). However, research on "transactive" knowledge management systems such as expert directories that primarily explicate who holds knowledge in an area have not consistently shown direct positive outcomes (Child and Shumate 2007; Nevo and Ophir 2012). This may be because knowledge only becomes useful for a team when it is not only located but also retrieved and applied to a team task (Choi et al. 2010). While many information systems may foster single, specific transactive processes under certain conditions, few cover the entire range of encoding, storage, and retrieval processes that are incorporated in a transactive memory system. Consequently, Lewis and Herndon

(2011) suggest "that technology substitutes such as repository-based systems and systems that predominately locate expertise are deficient (and will not reliably predict performance or other outcomes observed in the TMS literature) because these systems do not effectively emulate or facilitate transactive processes. [...] Incorporating the functions of transactive processes in information technology involves modeling the transactive aspects of learning, storage, and retrieval (i.e., cognitive activities that result from interactions between people, or between a person and a system)" (Lewis and Herndon 2011, p. 1262).

Results from the in-depth case studies suggest that peer code review as technique, based on underlying peer code review systems, allows for exactly such an emulation of transactive memory: authors in teams that rely on peer code review may gain new knowledge while working on a task and implementing the respective source code as well as during discussions with reviewers. Expertise of other team members may be located either by searching old reviews and revisions in the system, by identifying relevant parts of existing code in the system together with the team members who last worked on it, or by simple broadcast of review requests. Once knowledge is retrieved from reviewers, an author directly applies it to create a revised version of the code change at hand. Finally, a revised and accepted piece of code which is understandable to a number of team members is stored in a traceable way together with data about its author, its reviewers, and the review comments. Future authors can therefore more easily understand this piece of source code, find team members experienced in this code, and rely even on review comments that were made during former reviews. By consequence, intensive, continued, and team-wide peer code review partially decouples these transactive processes from the underlying body of meta-knowledge held by developers and makes an ISD team's transactive memory structure partially transparent for its members. Peer code review thereby partially substitutes transactive memory structure in its function of coordinating expertise in the creation of good software. Following Lewis and Herndon (2011), this partial substitution should lead to a dual effect: on the one hand, higher levels of peer code review should be associated with more positive outcomes, that is better software quality; on the other hand, the utility of a team's established transactive memory should decrease with increasing levels of peer code review and peer code review should be particularly effective in teams with a less sophisticated transactive memory. Consequently, this study puts forward the following hypotheses.

H8: The more extensively team members conduct peer code review, the better is the software quality provided by the team.
H9: The extent of peer code review conducted negatively moderates the positive effect of perceived transactive memory system effectiveness on software quality.

4.3.2.7 Control Variables

Prior research on transactive memory systems and quality assurance in ISD teams has proposed several explanations for team work results and transactive memory systems development. To ensure that effects addressed at the core of this study are relevant over and above these extant explanations, this survey controls for a set of variables. First, Maruping et al. (2009a) study agile development not on a technique level but on a methodology level. They find that using agile methods has positive effects on teams' software quality while frequent changes in requirements impact these quality measures negatively. The latter is also in line with research on transactive memory systems which finds task volatility to negatively impact team performance (Akgün et al. 2006; Ren et al. 2006). To ensure explanatory quality above the findings of prior research, this study controls for the quality effects of requirements volatility and of agile ISD techniques that have been found significant, namely of continuous integration, refactoring, and code ownership (cf. Maruping et al. 2009a).

A number of team and task characteristics has repeatedly shown explanatory value for transactive memory system development (for reviews see Hollingshead et al. 2011; Lewis and Herndon 2011; Nevo and Ophir 2012; Peltokorpi 2008; Ren and Argote 2011). This study therefore controls for a number of established team and task variables that may vary meaningfully in ongoing, professional ISD teams that are located in the same office space. As such, larger groups have constantly been shown to face more difficulties in establishing as well as sustaining a working transactive memory system (Nevo and Wand 2005; Ren et al. 2006). Although a team as an institution may carry on, single team members may leave it, thereby rendering the remaining team's transactive memory ineffective (Lewis et al. 2007). This study therefore controls for the effects of team size and team instability on perceived transactive memory system effectiveness.

With regard to ISD teams' development tasks, two previously examined factors may be of particular interest: the novelty and the diversity of tasks that a team has to deal with. Teams that have to complete a large amount of different tasks face difficulties in establishing and maintaining expertise responsibilities because of the sheer number and variety of activities that are conducted by different team members over time (Lewis and Herndon 2011). Finally, teams that constantly need to work on novel tasks cannot easily develop routines and establish adequate expertise because novel tasks often require novel knowledge and existing expertise is not necessarily useful (Akgün et al. 2005; Ren et al. 2006). Consequently, this study also controls for task novelty and task diversity.

4.3.3 Operationalization and Measurement Model

A survey instrument was developed to test the research model with individual software developers working in ISD teams in the target company. The instrument consisted of three types of questionnaires per ISD team, each one completed by either team members (i.e., individual developers), the team lead, or the team's product manager (cf. Sect. 3.6). Wherever possible, validated survey measures from extant research were utilized or adapted. New measurement items were developed for internal and external software quality as well as for team members' participation in team-wide pair programming and peer code review. Items were generated based on the exploratory interviews and the critical realist case studies. Measures were adapted and refined to ensure content validity, convergent validity, discriminant validity, and stable psychometric properties following the process outlined in Sect. 3.6. Table D.1 of the appendix outlines the final list of measurement items as well as the organizational role that provided the respective ratings.

Overall software quality was measured in two distinct but equally necessary dimensions: internal and external software quality (cf. Sect. 2.1.3). These dimensions of quality are in line with prior ISD research and practice (cf. Salleh et al. 2011; Mc Connell 2004). External quality was measured from the perspective of a product manager as the satisfaction of customer needs and the delivery of required functionality. Internal quality was measured in terms of maintainability and readability of developed source code as well as in terms of the adherence to company-internal task completion criteria. Although there are numerous other criteria of software quality proposed in research and practice (e.g., Mc Connell 2004; Salleh et al. 2011; Schmitz et al. 1982) the chosen measures appeared adequate as they arguably reflect the internal and external facets of software quality well. The internal and external quality dimensions were aggregated to a reflective second-order construct. A reflective specification of the latent second order construct is appropriate from both a theoretical as well as a statistical point of view (Bollen 2002; Cenfetelli and Bassellier 2009; Lewis and Herndon 2011): (1) it is by these very variables that one can *infer* that a team produces high quality software; (2) the theoretical reason that internal and external quality appear together lies in the fact that a team produces high overall quality (i.e., internal and external quality *covary* as a function of the overall quality of software produced by a team); (3) while these constructs are not necessarily independent when observed in isolation, they are independent after controlling for a team's overall software quality (i.e., apart from the reason that a team produces high quality software, there is no theoretical reason for the internal and external quality variables to vary with each other). As product managers potentially coordinate many teams that develop their software, they arguably have a broader view on this product and its single components than do teams who work in single parts of the software. Moreover, product managers may be more capable to compare the quality of software delivered by different teams from an external perspective than team members or team leads because of the product-wide perspective they take due to their role. Product managers therefore provided ratings for their teams' software quality, the software products' modularity, as well as for the volatility of requirements. Measurement items for requirements volatility and software modularity were adapted from Maruping et al. (2009a) and Lau et al. (2007, 2009) respectively.

The extent of pair programming and peer code review conducted by a developer with his or her team was naturally assessed by each single team member. Pair programming was measured as the amount of code developed in a pair and the number of colleagues regularly engaged in pair programming. To measure peer code review, random identifiers were assigned to the single team members. Then each developer rated for three pre-assigned colleagues the extent to which they frequently reviewed each other's code. The three relations that each developer was assigned to were calculated a priori and were composed so as to cover the maximum possible amount of dyadic relationships per team. In addition, team leads provided information on the use of code review systems so that the amount of peer code review conducted in a team could clearly be distinguished from simply looking at one another's code and from conducting centralized meeting-based code reviews as defined by Fagan (1986): developers' scores for peer code review greater than 0 (strongly disagree) were only considered if the team leads reported that the team used a peer code review system and conducted peer code review primarily based on this system (i.e., if less than 20 % of all "code reviews" in the team were conducted offline outside the peer code review system). Other answers were treated as 0 (strongly disagree).

In line with recent studies, perceived transactive memory system effectiveness was measured based on the scale developed by Lewis (2003) and conceptualized as a formative second order construct based on reflective measures for specialization, credibility, and coordination of knowledge in the team (Majchrzak et al. 2013b). This scale measures both the perceived differentiation of transactive memory structure and the perceived effectiveness of transactive processes based on this structure at the same time (Lewis 2003; Lewis and Herndon 2011). It is the most widely applied measurement of transactive memory effectiveness in questionnaire surveys (Nevo and Ophir 2012; Ren and Argote 2011). Relationship quality within the team was measured with four items as defined by Guinan et al. (1998). Both affective relationship quality and perceived transactive memory system effectiveness were assessed by each developer individually. Measures for refactoring, continuous integration, shared code ownership, and requirements volatility were adapted from Maruping et al. (2009a) and Nidumolu (1995). Like other development activities, refactoring was rated by single team members. Continuous integration and shared code ownership, resembling norms and characteristics of the development process, were rated by team leads. Team size, membership attrition, and ratings for novelty of tasks were also provided by team leads. Task novelty was measured based on the scale of Nidumolu (1995). Team instability was calculated as the number of team members that left the team during the preceding 12 months divided by the total number of team members at the time of data collection. Several indicators were dropped after data collection because of low loadings on their focal construct or high cross-loadings with other constructs (cf. Table D.1 of the appendix). This procedure is well established in IS literature and is in line with current research on transactive memory systems and general team cognition (Gray and Meister 2004; Jarvenpaa and Majchrzak 2008). Table D.1 of the appendix depicts the resulting items together with the informant role that rated them.

4.3.4 Results

As described in Sect. 3.6, the developed research model was tested based on data collected within the same case company that also participated in the qualitative phases of this study. Individual team members, team leads, and product managers completed the developed questionnaires. Validation and evaluation of measurement and structural model followed established guidelines by Ringle et al. (2012), Gefen et al. (2011), and Hair et al. (2009).

4.3.4.1 Measurement Model Validation

A confirmatory factor analysis was conducted for all first order constructs based on the retained items in order to establish convergent and discriminant validity (Hair et al. 2009). All indicators loaded significantly ($p < 0.001$) on the respective constructs with loadings well greater than 0.5 and mostly minor cross-loadings below 0.5 (cf. Table D.4). All indicator cross-loadings were more than 0.2 lower than actual loadings which is commonly seen as sufficient to indicate convergent validity (Hair et al. 2009). Nevertheless, indicator cross-loadings were partially greater than 0.5 for internal (intq) and external quality (extq) as well as for relationship quality and knowledge coordination. This can be a symptom of multicollinearity and warrants closer examination through a full collinearity test (Kock and Lynn 2012). Consequently, a full collinearity test was conducted for these first order variables with a variation of the hypothesized model that contained the first order dimensions of transactive memory and overall software quality in place of the second order constructs. Block variance inflation factors for all structural paths and full collinearity variance inflation factors for all first order variables were examined accordingly (Kock and Lynn 2012). All block variance inflation factors were smaller than 1.6, all full collinearity variance inflation factors were smaller than 2.2. All the relevant factors were thereby well below the conservative threshold of 2.5 which indicates the absence of multicollinearity in these constructs. Table 4.9 also lists the full collinearity variance inflation factors that have been argued to suffice as indicators (Kock and Lynn 2012).

For all first order constructs, composite reliability was well greater than 0.8 and the average variances extracted above 0.5. Cronbach's α (Cr. α) was greater than the common threshold of 0.7 for all reflectively specified constructs except for credibility. In face of the validity of all other reliability coefficients, this minor deviation from guidelines (Cr. $\alpha_{cred} = 0.677$, cp. Table 4.9) appears tolerable. In sum, reliability and convergent validity could be established. Also discriminant validity could be verified as the square roots of the average variances extracted were comfortably greater than any inter-construct correlations (cf. Table 4.10).

Regarding the measurement model validation for the second order constructs of perceived transactive memory system effectiveness and software quality, a two-step approach was taken. Composite scores were calculated for the reflectively

Table 4.9 Reliability and validity of measures

	pp	pcr	rel	mod	ci	ownshp	ref	spec	cred
Composite reliability	0.924	0.967	0.948	0.912	0.979	0.865	0.906	0.861	0.823
Cronbach's alpha	0.875	0.949	0.927	0.871	0.956	0.765	0.844	0.757	0.677
Average variances extracted	0.803	0.907	0.821	0.721	0.958	0.682	0.762	0.674	0.609
Full collinearity VIFs	1.222	1.484	1.829	1.268	1.088	1.366	1.097	1.149[b]	1.475[b]

	coord	intq	extq	tms	qual	vol	div	nov
Composite reliability	0.888	0.882	0.934	0.76[a]	0.91	0.896	0.872	0.884
Cronbach's alpha	0.81	0.798	0.905	0.527[a]	0.802	0.824	0.801	0.802
Average variances extracted	0.725	0.715	0.779	0.521	0.835	0.742	0.634	0.719
Full collinearity VIFs	1.924[b]	2.269[b]	2.276[b]	1.721	1.484	1.244	1.295	1.248

Notes: n = 452

[a]Not meaningful for formative construct

[b]Assessed in first order model without latent second order constructs

Table 4.10 Inter-construct correlations and square root of AVE

	Median	Mode	pp	pcr	rel	mod	ci	ownshp	ref	cred	intq	vol	div	novel	spec	coord	extq
pp	-0.129	-1.263	**0.896**														
pcr	-0.649	-0.649	0.329	**0.952**													
rel	0.215	0.918	0.047	0.121	**0.906**												
mod	0	0	0.118	0.042	-0.003	**0.849**											
ci	0.325	0.325	0.026	0.129	-0.064	-0.095	**0.979**										
ownshp	0.432	0.721	0.047	0.328	0.219	0.017	0.099	**0.826**									
ref	-0.066	-0.644	0.203	0.086	0.01	0.024	0.032	0.104	**0.873**								
cred	0.061	0.061	0.072	0.049	0.494	-0.012	-0.032	0.116	0.044	**0.78**							
intq	0.036	0	0.164	0.238	0.257	0.31	0.026	0.062	0.047	0.073	**0.846**						
vol	0	0	0.084	-0.026	0.071	-0.131	-0.154	0.038	-0.022	0.04	-0.016	**0.861**					
div	0.17	0	-0.148	-0.351	-0.088	-0.173	0.006	-0.314	-0.04	-0.047	-0.143	0.087	**0.796**				
novel	-0.128	-0.872	0.023	-0.007	-0.022	0.097	-0.12	-0.226	-0.143	-0.005	-0.054	0.185	0.006	**0.848**			
spec	0.343	0.343	-0.119	-0.144	0.127	-0.075	0.007	-0.101	0.01	0.255	-0.09	0.071	0.099	-0.032	**0.821**		
coord	0.318	0.653	0.163	0.17	0.618	0.062	0.005	0.11	0.076	0.438	0.338	0.057	-0.162	-0.085	0.118	**0.851**	
extq	0.107	0	0.05	0.098	0.251	0.301	-0.025	0.076	0.098	0.143	0.67	-0.174	0.067	-0.026	-0.039	0.302	**0.883**

Note: Square roots of average variances extracted (AVEs) shown on diagonal. Median and mode for standardized values

measured first-order variables based solely on the outer model, and these factor scores were used for further estimations of the structural model (cf. Chin 1998; Ringle et al. 2012). This approach is valid because the structural model cannot influence the measurement model if applying PLS regression as an outer model algorithm (Kock 2013). For the reflective second order construct of software quality, composite reliability and Cronbach's α were higher than the thresholds of 0.8 and 0.7 respectively (composite reliability $_{qual} = 0.91$, Cr $\alpha_{qual} = 0.8$), factor scores for internal and external quality loaded significantly (p < 0.001), average variance extracted (AVE) was greater than 0.5 (AVE $_{qual} = 0.84$) and its square root was well greater than any inter-construct correlations (Table 4.10). In sum, construct validity and reliability could be assumed for the reflectively specified second order construct of software quality.

For the formative second order construct of perceived transactive memory effectiveness, weights of the first order constructs specialization (spec), coordination (coord), and credibility (cred) were highly significant (p < 0.001). As indicated in Table D.3, they had standard errors smaller than 0.07, effect sizes greater than 0.2, and showed variance inflation factors (VIFs) below 2.5 (Full Collinearity VIF$_{TMS}$ = 1.66, cf. Table D.3). This indicated non-redundancy of dimensions of the formative construct (Cenfetelli and Bassellier 2009) and ultimately construct validity as well as the absence of multicollinearity (Kock and Lynn 2012; Kock 2013; Petter et al. 2007).

Lastly, the absence of common method bias (Podsakoff et al. 2003) was assessed via a full collinearity test through the assessment of full collinearity variance inflation factors as proposed by Kock and Lynn (2012). For all constructs, full collinearity variance inflation factors were well below both thresholds, the commonly accepted one of 3.3 and the more conservative one of 2.5 (cf. Table 4.9). This indicates the absence of common method bias in a variance-based approach to structural equation modeling such as PLS (Kock and Lynn 2012).

4.3.4.2   Structural Model Evaluation

Figure 4.5 shows the resulting standardized path coefficients (b = β), significance levels, and explained variance for the hypothesized effects. Table 4.11 outlines indicators that give hints towards model fit in PLS although there is no overall goodness of fit measure comparable to covariance-based structural equation modeling (Gefen et al. 2011; Kock 2013). Occurring together and significantly, high average path coefficients (APC = 0.166, p < 0.001) and average adjusted and unadjusted R^2 values (ARS = 0.227, AARS = 0.220, p < 0.001) indicate that the addition of each latent variable to the model adds predictive as well as explanatory quality to the model rather than inducing spurious effects on R^2 values (Kock 2013). The same holds true for Tenenhaus' goodness of fit measure (Tenenhaus GoF = 0.424) which is well above the threshold of 0.36 suggested by Wetzels et al. (2009). In addition, average block variance inflation factor (AVIF) and average full collinearity variance inflation factor (AFVIF) values well below 3.3 (cf. Table 4.11) indicate the absence

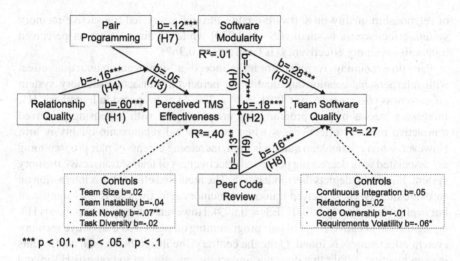

*** p < .01, ** p < .05, * p < .1

Fig. 4.5 Research model evaluation with PLS

Table 4.11 Model fit indicators for variance-based structural equation modeling

Index	Value
Average path coefficient (APC)	0.128 (p < 0.001)
Average R-squared (ARS)	0.230 (p < 0.001)
Average adjusted R-squared (AARS)	0.221 (p < 0.001)
Average block VIF (AVIF)	1.059 (acceptable if <= 5, ideally <= 3.3)
Average full collinearity VIF (AFVIF)	1.303 (acceptable if <= 5, ideally <= 3.3)
Tenenhaus GoF (GoF)	0.414 (small >= 0.1, medium >= 0.25, large >= 0.36)

of both vertical and lateral collinearity (Kock and Lynn 2012). In sum, all indicators suggest good model fit.

In line with prior literature, hypotheses H1 and H2 are both supported. Interpersonal relationship quality (rel) has a strongly significant effect on perceived transactive memory effectiveness ($p < 0.01, \beta = 0.60$) which is in turn significantly related to software quality ($p < 0.01, \beta = 0.18$). Both the direct effect of relationship quality on perceived transactive memory effectiveness and relationship quality's indirect (mediated) effect on software quality are significant ($p < 0.01, \Delta R^2_{TMS} = 0.364, \Delta R^2_{Qual} = 0.029$). This provides evidence for the hypothesized mediation effect of interpersonal relationship quality on software quality through perceived transactive memory system effectiveness (Kock and Gaskins 2014). Effect sizes represent the proportion of variance of a dependent variable explained by a predictor variable. Cohen (1988) classifies effect sizes ($ES = f^2$) as negligible ($ES < 0.02$), small ($0.02 <= ES < 0.15$), moderate ($0.15 <= ES < 0.35$) and large ($ES >= 0.35$). Accordingly, the indirect effect of relationship quality on software quality through perceived transactive memory system effectiveness is small (ES = 0.029) while its direct effect on perceived transactive memory effectiveness is large (ES = 0.367).

Pair programming is found to have indeed a significant interaction effect with interpersonal relationship quality on perceived transactive memory system effectiveness ($\beta = -0.16, \mathrm{p} < 0.01, \Delta R^2 = 0.025$) as proposed in hypothesis H4. Increasing extents of pair programming are associated with increasing perceived transactive memory effectiveness when interpersonal relationship quality is low. However, when relationship quality is high, increasing extents of pair programming are associated with decreasing perceived effectiveness of teams' transactive memory system. Figure 4.6 depicts this moderation. The mediated effect of this interaction on software quality via perceived transactive memory effectiveness is also significant but negligible in size (p < 0.01, ES = 0.003). However, contrary to hypothesis H3, no significant negative effect of pair programming on perceived transactive memory system effectiveness is found. Quite the contrary, the insignificant path coefficients is even positive. While this does not impact the rejection of hypothesis H3 in any way, it lends further support to H4: while H4 had originally been hypothesized as a positive moderation of a negative main effect, results found a significant negative moderation of an (insignificant) positive relationship. That is, the statistical effect of an interaction term with negative impact on perceived transactive memory effectiveness is found as expected per H4. Consequently, hypothesis H3 is rejected while hypothesis H4 is supported.

In line with hypotheses H8 and H9, peer code review is found to show two significant effects: on the one hand there is a positive effect (p < 0.01, $\beta = 0.16$)

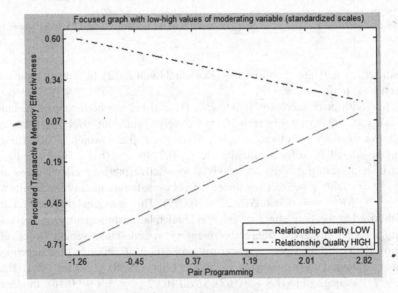

Fig. 4.6 Interaction of relationship quality and pair programming

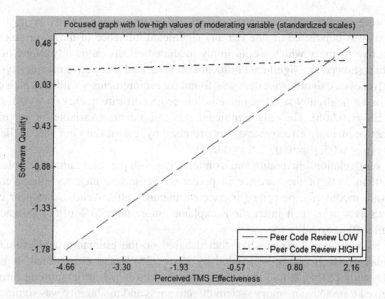

Fig. 4.7 Interaction of peer code review and perceived TMS effectiveness

on software quality, and on the other hand peer code review shows a negative interaction effect with perceived transactive memory effectiveness on software quality ($p < 0.05, \Delta R^2 = 0.02$). Both effects are small in size ($ES_{PCR} = 0.029, ES_{PCRxTMS} = 0.020$). Figure 4.7 depicts this expected interaction effect. Closer examination shows that in a setting with a high level of peer code review there is only marginal improvement of software quality based on increased perceived effectiveness of transactive memory. By contrast, increasing perceived transactive memory effectiveness has a large effect on software quality in the near absence of peer code review.

In line with hypothesis H5, higher modularity of the software a team develops is associated with higher overall quality of the team's software ($p < 0.01, \beta = 0.28$). There is also an expected negative interaction effect ($p < 0.01, \Delta R^2 = 0.088$) of perceived transactive memory effectiveness and modularity on software quality (H6). That is, quality improvement effects of better transactive memory systems appear to diminish with increasing modularity of the software product. Both hypotheses H5 and H6 are therefore supported.

Hypothesis H7 argued that increased levels of pair programming should lead to higher modularity of the software under development. Indeed, results show that there is significant positive effect of pair programming on modularity ($p < 0.01, \beta = 0.12$). However, this effect is too small to be of commendable explanatory relevance ($ES = 0.014$).

Finally, none of the control variables for continuous integration, refactoring, and shared code ownership showed any significant influence on software quality. This was a strong mismatch with prior agile ISD literature that strongly suggested

they were important for software quality (Maruping et al. 2009a). A post hoc
analysis was conducted to rule out any significant influence of these variables on
transactive memory which would imply mediated effects on quality. None of the
variables showed any significant influence on perceived transactive memory system
effectiveness. A significant effect was found for requirements volatility which only
exercised a negligibly sized negative influence on software quality ($p < 0.1, \beta = 0.06, ES = 0.006$). The only significant effect of a control variable for perceived
transactive memory effectiveness was exercised by task novelty but was negligible
in size ($p < 0.05, \beta = 0.07, ES = 0.004$).

In sum, relationship quality and its interaction with pair programming explained
more than 39 % of the variance in perceived transactive memory effectiveness.
Software modularity, perceived transactive memory effectiveness, and peer code
reviews as well as their interactions explained more than 26 % of the variance in
overall software quality.

A mediation analysis was conducted based on the estimation and evaluation
of indirect effects as recommended by Kock (2013) and exemplified in Kock
and Gaskins (2014). While the total indirect effect of pair programming through
perceived transactive memory system effectiveness and modularity was significant,
it was negligible in size ($ES < 0.02$). The same holds true for the indirect
effect of the interaction term (i.e., mediated moderation) of pair programming and
interpersonal relationship quality on software quality through perceived transactive
memory system effectiveness ($ES = 0.003$). Table 4.12 depicts all direct and
indirect total effects including their significance levels and effect sizes.

Table 4.12 Mediation analysis: total direct and indirect effects

	tms		mod		qual	
	β	ES	β	ES	β	ES
pp	0.046 (ns)	0.003	0.118***	0.014	0.043***	0.005
rel*pp	−0.15****	0.024			−0.028***	0.003
rel	0.599****	0.364			0.106****	0.029
tms					0.177***	0.037
pcr					0.157****	0.029
pcr*tms					−0.128**	0.02
mod					0.282***	0.094
mod*tms					−0.268****	0.088
tsize	0.016 (ns)	0.0			0.003 (ns)	0.0
instab	−0.045 (ns)	0.002			−0.008 (ns)	0.0
novel	−0.066**	0.004			−0.012 (ns)	0.001
div	−0.023 (ns)	0.002			−0.004 (ns)	0.0
ci					0.002 (ns)	0.0
ownshp					−0.012 (ns)	0.001
ref					0.018(ns)	0.001
vol					−0.062*	0.006

Entries show total effects with significance levels and resulting effect sizes
*$p < 0.1$, **$p < 0.05$, ***$p < 0.01$, ****$p < 0.001$, (ns) not significant

4.3.4.3 Robustness Check and Post-Hoc Analyses

This study was conducted analyzing individual level data of software developers working in teams. Relevant indices for simultaneous interrater agreement and interrater reliability (ICC(1) and ICC(2)) indicated that the ratings of perceived transactive memory system effectiveness and its first order constructs could not reliably be aggregated to a team level (Bliese 2000). While this is not surprising from a critical realist point of view, it encompassed the necessity to conduct robustness checks on an individual level for the individuals' responses who were actually clustered in teams. When evaluating such data, non-independence of observations has to be taken into account, as for example ratings of the same transactive memory system provided by different team members are not independent from one another. Technically, this means that a regression analysis may result in an overestimation of significance for single structural paths because the error terms of individual ratings are correlated. Such non-independence can be accounted for by conducting robust regression analyses that allow error terms to co-vary freely within certain clusters (Huber 1967; Rogers 1993). However, structural equation modeling software does currently not provide the possibility to conduct robust analyses accounting for clustered data. Such a robust path analysis was consequently conducted for clusters consisting of the single ISD teams employing the software Stata 13.[3]

In order to ensure that individual-level error in answering questions was accounted for, variable scores of the latent variables were estimated for each developer with PLS regression in WarpPLS. That is, the measurement model was estimated with the above mentioned PLS regression algorithm. The structural model was then estimated stepwise in Stata based on these latent variable scores via ordinary least squares regression analyses with robust standard errors clustered by single teams. The results of these regressions can be found in the appendix of this study in Table D.5.

Estimating the research model with clustered error terms for individual developers working in the same teams had the following effects. First, as expected, path coefficients and explained variance (R^2) stayed stable for clustered and unclustered regression analyses and matched the results provided by WarpPLS's estimation of the structural model. Second, no control variables retained any significant influence, neither on perceived transactive memory system effectiveness nor on software quality. Third, whereas nearly all significance levels relating to hypotheses were stable and equal for clustered and unclustered analyses, two significance levels of structural paths in the model changed: (1) the direct effect of peer code review became significant on a 5 % level only instead of a 1 % level in the unclustered

---

[3]http://www.stata.com/.

analysis; and (2) the effect of pair programming on software modularity became insignificant. That is, when accounting for team level differences that are not explicitly part of the model, the effect of pair programming on modularity became insignificant while the quality effect of peer code review stayed significant, albeit on a lower level. As has already been suggested by the negligible effect size in the unclustered analysis, this means that the modularity of a team's software cannot statistically be traced back to the team-wide use of pair programming. However, this result also suggests that modularity may indeed depend on team level aspects which are not part of the tested model.

Additionally, several alternative plausible models were estimated as a robustness check. Models were created to rule out the possibilities of pair programming having a direct influence on software quality and of peer code review having an effect on perceived transactive memory system effectiveness. The respective links (pair programming on software quality and peer code review on perceived transactive memory effectiveness) were tested as part of the full research model as well as with partial models that did not contain any other effects of pair programming and peer code review. As expected, none of these estimations yielded any significant results. It was further controlled for the independence of software modularity from peer code review and the independence of relationship quality from pair programming. Estimations showed that peer code review did not affect software modularity and pair programming did not affect relationship quality. Lastly, alternative models were tested that allowed the control variables for perceived transactive memory effectiveness (team size and instability, task novelty and diversity) and for software quality (continuous integration, refactoring, shared code ownership, requirements volatility) to influence the respective other endogenous variable. No significant effects were retrieved by these estimations. In sum, the results provide confidence that results of the presented research model estimation are quite robust with the exception of the effect hypothesized between pair programming and modularity (H7) which had already yielded only negligibly sized effects in the primary analysis.

4.3.5   Summary and Critical Assessment

The objectives of this survey were to empirically examine the existence of homogenization and transparency as generative mechanisms in collaborative quality assurance techniques and to extend the understanding of quality impacts of pair programming and peer code review by doing so. It was sought to understand the techniques' quality impacts by modeling and testing their influence on the effectiveness of team's transactive memory systems as perceived by software developers and on the resulting software quality. These influences were theoretically based on the mechanisms of transparency and homogenization and formulated in a set of hypotheses. The resulting model explained 40 % of team members' perceived transactive memory system effectiveness and 27 % of team's software quality.[4]

As predicted based on the theoretical mechanism of transparency, peer code review had at the same time a significant positive influence on software quality and a significant negative moderator effect on the relation of perceived transactive memory system effectiveness to software quality. That is, the extensive application of peer code review is associated with improved team outcomes but reduced outcome effects of transactive memory system effectiveness. According to predictions based on the mechanism of homogenization, pair programming interacted significantly with interpersonal relationship quality: pair programming fostered perceived transactive memory system effectiveness when interpersonal relationships were tense while pair programming decreased perceived transactive memory system effectiveness when interpersonal relationships were close.[5] Contrary to predictions, pair programming did not have any significant and reasonably sized influence on perceived transactive memory system effectiveness or on software modularity over and above the interaction effect with relationship quality. In fact, mediation analysis showed that even this moderator effect of pair programming and relationship quality through perceived transactive memory system effectiveness had only a negligible effect on software quality. Lastly, software modularity was found to affect software quality positively and to negatively moderate the relation of perceived transactive memory system effectiveness on software quality. Figure 4.8 depicts the support for hypothesized effects based on estimations via PLS and subsequent robustness checks.

4.3.5.1 Transparency Through Peer Code Review

These results broadly support the theoretical argument that peer code review decouples transactive processes from transactive memory structure through transparency. The developers' perception of the effectiveness of their teams' transactive memory systems serves as a predictor of the teams' software quality. Increasing levels of peer code review in a team, however, compensate this effect partially: higher levels

---

[4]R^2 values of this magnitude for team outcomes are common in top tier IS journals and are also reached in previous studies on the performance effects of team cognition. As such, Maruping et al. (2009b) explain 30 % of software project technical quality, Faraj and Sproull (2000) explain 30 % and 32 % of team effectiveness and efficiency respectively, Choi et al. (2010) explain 24 % of teams' performance, and Liang et al. (2010) explain 27 % software quality.

[5]The significant observed moderator effect of interpersonal relationship quality (H4) was negative contrary to the positive hypothesis. This sign change resulted from an insignificant sign change in the main effect of pair programming on transactive memory system effectiveness (H3). As the main effect was insignificant but carried a different sign than its hypothesis, the significant moderator effect of H4 also carried a different sign while semantically still resembling exactly the hypothesized effect. For this reason, the moderator effect of interpersonal relationship quality can be seen as supported despite the altered sign.

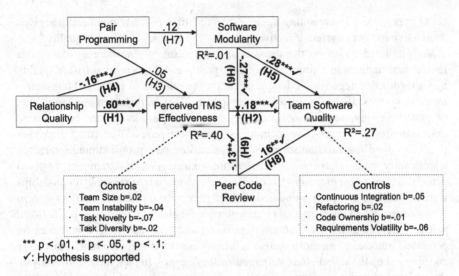

Fig. 4.8 Evaluation of hypothesized effects after robustness checks

of perceived transactive memory system effectiveness in teams that conduct little peer code review are associated with higher levels of software quality than in teams that conduct more peer code review. It was argued that this effect stems from the fact that frequently applied team-wide peer code review allows teams to encode, store, and retrieve information relatively independent of their transactive memory structure. In fact, by exercising two effects at the same time (i.e., a direct positive effect on quality and a negative moderation of perceived transactive memory system effectiveness on quality), peer code review complies with the description of a substitute for transactive memory systems given by Lewis and Herndon (2011): peer code review reduces the impact of transactive memory on an aspect of team performance and at the same time predicts this performance aspect itself. It is however not only the technological artifact of a peer code review system that is found to impact quality as would be suggested by the idea of "technological substitutes" proposed by Lewis and Herndon (2011). It is much rather the frequent and team-wide application of the peer code review technique that impacts quality and reduces the effect of perceived transactive memory system effectiveness on quality. That is, the effects were stronger for developers who reviewed code from more team members and who had more team members review their own code than they were for developers who had review relationships only with isolated, single colleagues. This has theoretical impact: the search for technological substitutes may be misled when the different ways of application of these artifacts are not accounted for. Results from the case studies suggest that only the frequent and team-wide application of peer code review, based on peer code review systems, allows teams to conduct transactive processes reliably through these systems. Where developers could not rely on reasonably quick answers to review requests, teams gradually abandoned their review systems. Where developers could not be sure to reach all team members through their review request, they had little chance to retrieve expertise without knowing the respective expert. That is, peer code review *systems* may allow ISD teams to conduct transactive processes without relying on established meta-knowledge but only peer code review as a technique, with frequent and team-wide exchanges in reviews and revisions, appears to actually lead to the expected outcome improvement and reduced outcome effects of transactive memory structures. Future research should therefore not solely focus on technology when investigating potential substitutions of transactive memory structure but should focus equally well on the applications of the respective technology. In fact, especially the theory of functional affordances appears very promising for concurrently studying exactly such interaction of socio-cognitive structure, socio-technical interaction, and physical aspects related to technology.

4.3.5.2 Homogenization Through Pair Programming

Regarding the homogenizing effects of pair programming, the survey results demand for more differentiated interpretation. First and foremost, the interaction of pair programming and interpersonal relationship quality exactly matches the results expected based on the mechanism of homogenization. Under low relationship quality, pair programming exercised positive effects on perceived transactive memory system effectiveness, whereas this effect reversed for high relationship quality. Importantly, this does not mean that pair programming improves interpersonal relationships as has been argued in prior literature (Salleh et al. 2011). Such direct effects were proven insignificant in the robustness checks. Instead, distributed and differentiated expertise of the single team members is perceived to become useful when more pair programming is conducted even though affective relationships between the developers may remain tense. That is, a useful homogenization of labels and meta-knowledge indeed appears to outweigh the creation of redundant expertise when pair programming helps team members overcome the blocking influence of negative affections and make one another's expertise accessible without necessarily improving affections. This perspective on relationship-related effects of pair programming thereby reconciles conflicting findings in pair programming research that demand positive interpersonal relationships as a prerequisite for pair programming on the one hand and see relationship quality as a result of pair programming on the other hand (Salleh et al. 2011).

At the same time, there were no significant effects of pair programming over and above its interaction with relationship quality. Whereas this was in contrast to the predictions regarding software modularity and perceived transactive memory system effectiveness, the non-existence may in fact be understood based on the premises of homogenization. As such, this study argued that homogenization inherent to pair programming should have a negative effect on perceived transactive memory system effectiveness because of the creation of redundant expertise. However, pair programming was also argued to homogenize labels and meta-knowledge which could be beneficial to transactive memory system development and use. Clearly, these effects are in conflict regarding the perceived effectiveness of a team's transactive memory system. The interaction with relationship quality lends strong support to this argument as it accounts for situations in which team members cannot retrieve one another's knowledge because of interpersonal barriers that block the creation of shared labels and meta-knowledge. It appears therefore reasonable that homogenization's conflicting changes in teams' transactive memory structure would not result in any effects on perceived transactive memory system effectiveness beyond the resolution of blocking influences of relationship quality: beyond this resolution, negative and positive effects may simply outweigh each other, leaving the total effect insignificant.

Moreover, higher levels of pair programming were predicted to slightly increase software modularity. While initial analyses found a minor significant effect, this effect did not prove robust and was marginal in size. Also prior literature has argued that the vastly dominant influence on software modularity is exercised by a software product's initial designers rather than by developers who work on the product later on (Baldwin and Clark 2006). There is consequently reason to belief that developers, independent of the techniques they apply, may not be able to overcome the path dependencies created by initial designers. The absence of any effect of pair programming as the most widely-applied agile development technique (Dybå et al. 2007) may thereby even call the idea of "emergent architecture" as proposed by agile ISD literature (Waterman 2014) into question. Future research may want to investigate whether any other agile ISD techniques are in fact related to architectural properties like software modularity or if software architecture still remains in the hands of architects whose up-front decisions suppress any mentionable emergent architectural changes.

Interestingly, pair programming was not found to have a mentionable effect on software quality. Whereas direct and indirect quality effects of pair programming were insignificant after robustness checks, its interaction with relationship quality on quality was significantly mediated by perceived transactive memory system effectiveness. However, this effect was only marginal in size so that this survey is in line with prior studies that did not find quality gains resulting from pair programming (Balijepally et al. 2009; Salleh et al. 2011). Nevertheless, homogenization through pair programming and its interaction with relationship quality clearly seem to affect perceived transactive memory system effectiveness. That is, pair programming may be much more relevant for the constitution of a team's transactive memory than for the software quality produced in this team. Prior literature suggested that transactive memory systems can be especially useful not only for effectiveness gains but also for efficiency improvement (Faraj and Sproull 2000). Future research should therefore investigate if pair programming as the most widely-adopted agile ISD technique has more significant effects on measures such as ISD teams' speed and reliability due to its impact on transactive memory structure.

4.3.5.3 Software Modularity

Software modularity is found to have a similar compensatory effect as does peer code review: software modularity is positively associated with software quality while negatively moderating the influence of perceived transactive memory system effectiveness on quality. This has consequences for transactive memory systems theory. The findings may indicate that modular software allows developers to specialize in different modules to a degree that knowledge coordination through a transactive memory system becomes partly dispensable because tasks can be doubtlessly assigned to the responsible module developers and expertise in different modules does not need to be shared across the team. That is, modularization may constitute a rival mechanism to transactive memory systems when it comes to reducing cognitive load on individuals by specializing in different areas. While software modularity allows for easier specialization in physical modules of a team's product, transactive memory allows for specialization in different areas of expertise that may or may not be tied to physical modules. This is especially interesting in the light of transactive memory literature that has created partially conflicting results and recommendations. On the one hand, literature on transactive memory systems highlights that for developing and leveraging a transactive memory, teams should have highly interdependent tasks (Brandon and Hollingshead 2004), which would imply that specialization in modules without overlap should be detrimental to performance. On the other hand, transactive memory literature emphasizes that specializing in distinct knowledge areas is beneficial for jointly produced outcomes of groups (Hollingshead 2000), which would apply to software developers who specialize in different modules that need to fit together. Future research should therefore investigate how teams should balance their investments in creating highly modular software on the one hand and closely collaborating to develop, update, and refine their transactive memory system on the other hand.

4.3.5.4 Limitations of Survey Study

This survey has a few key strengths and limitations that need to be highlighted. First, this survey was conducted based on field data from software developers and ISD teams which leads to high external validity. However, all data was collected from German locations of a single software company in which also the qualitative parts of this work were conducted. While this allowed for controlling for contextual factors that might have impacted a multi-firm study, future investigations should replicate the findings to ensure their robustness across firms and cultures. Second, the presented survey examined the effects of homogenization and transparency on teams' transactive memory systems theoretically and empirically on an individual level. While high-class IS research often fruitfully examines transactive memory systems from an individual level perspective (e.g., Jarvenpaa and Majchrzak 2008; Kotlarsky et al. 2015; Majchrzak et al. 2013b), transactive memory systems are essentially a team level phenomenon. In line with critical realism's skepticism of objective and unbiased assessments of social structures, this research regarded it as more truthful and valid to examine each individual's perception of the effectiveness of his or her team's transactive memory system one by one rather than creating arguably dubious aggregations of their perceptions to represent the real team level transactive memory system. Nevertheless, this study evaluated the possibilities of statistical aggregation to a team level for robustness checks. Concurrent interrater agreement and interrater reliability (i.e., ICC) were however problematic for perceived transactive memory system effectiveness as a potential team level variable. The resulting robustness checks by means of clustered standard errors that were conducted instead are well established in literature and provide confidence in the robustness of individual level results. This study moreover collected data from multiple respondents in different organizational roles at one point in time. While product managers provided responses for aspects relating to the software product and quality, team leads provided background information about tasks and the use of peer code review systems whereas developers reported on relationships and their application of collaborative quality assurance techniques. It constitutes a limitation of the presented survey that these data were collected at a single point in time only. Albeit common practice in IS research, the statistical examination of the hypothesized emergent effects based on a single snapshot is more restricted than in longitudinal research designs of multiple data collections. Future research should aim to follow such longitudinal designs. Nevertheless, the use of the specific respondent roles increases the validity of responses and reduces concerns regarding common method bias. Lastly, this survey focused on software quality as the dependent variable influenced by transactive memory system effectiveness and collaborative quality assurance techniques. Literature on transactive memory systems has suggested that not only team effectiveness but also team efficiency can be increased by means of knowledge coordination. Future research may therefore want to examine further outcome variables that may help extend our understanding of the socio-cognitive effects of collaborative quality assurance techniques.

Chapter 5
Discussion of Findings

So far, results from three distinct but interconnected research phases of this study have been presented. This chapter briefly reiterates the purpose of this study and integrates the distinct phases' findings into one coherent picture with regard to the relations between team cognition and the application of collaborative quality assurance techniques in ISD teams. Subsequently, contributions to theory and managerial implications of this study are discussed in the light of prior and possibilities for future research. This chapter concludes by pointing out the limitations of this study.

5.1 Integration and Interpretation of Findings

This study was motivated by the question how team cognition influences the use and the effects of software development techniques in ISD teams. An investigation of the collaborative quality assurance techniques of pair programming and peer code review in collocated ISD teams appeared particularly worthwhile for several reasons: (1) these techniques capitalize on the joint cognitive accomplishments of several developers, but the role of team cognition in this process is unclear, (2) they both constitute major investments for ISD teams that engage in them, and (3) they represent widely adopted, contemporary ISD techniques that have been proposed as mutual substitutes in collocated settings. It was reasoned that team cognition may constitute a major influence when developers decide whether and how to apply collaborative quality assurance techniques to single tasks and that an ongoing application of collaborative quality assurance techniques may lead to emergent effects on team cognition. More specifically, this study therefore investigated how team cognition affects the task level appropriation of pair programming and peer code review on the one hand, and how continued application of these techniques affects team cognition and performance in ISD teams on the other hand. Theory on transactive memory systems and the concept of functional affordances were

© Springer International Publishing Switzerland 2016   173
K. Spohrer, *Collaborative Quality Assurance in Information Systems Development*,
Progress in IS, DOI 10.1007/978-3-319-25163-9_5

harnessed to conceptualize and investigate these phenomena. An epistemologically clear distinction of transactive memory structure and transactive memory processes was provided based on a critical realist account of transactive memory systems and applied to expertise in ISD teams. The concepts of functional affordances, material properties, and symbolic expressions were extended to cover not only technology but also technology-based ISD techniques such as the ones in the focus of this study. Light was subsequently shed on team cognition and collaborative quality assurance techniques in a mixed-methods study consisting of three sequential research phases which all examined collocated ISD teams and their use of pair programming and peer code review.

The first purpose of this study was to understand the influence of team cognition on the appropriation of collaborative quality assurance techniques (Research Question 1). Results show that the application of collaborative quality assurance techniques is not a homogeneous phenomenon. On a task level, ISD team members decide whether to apply a collaborative quality assurance technique based on the specific goals they can, in their own perceptions, reasonably achieve with a technique. These reasonably achievable goals are found to vary between different teams and between the two collaborative quality assurance techniques of pair programming and peer code review. Whereas the techniques are both found to afford basic error correction for ISD teams' source code, each one also provides distinct advanced affordances. On a task level, ISD teams apply pair programming not only to correct errors but also to share task understanding, to jointly create acceptable solutions for problem, or to create optimized expert solutions. Contrastingly, peer code review is applied to ensure code intelligibility, to broadly solicit and integrate feedback, and to create expert-approved solutions. These distinct possibilities for goal-directed applications of collaborative quality assurance techniques are found to originate from two root causes: immutable, material properties of the techniques and the respective teams' transactive memory systems. Material properties physically enable and constrain all actions that can be taken within the scope of an ISD technique, whereas each task level application of the techniques leverages different elements of a team's transactive memory structure: where ISD teams lack shared meta-knowledge, shared labels, or specialized expertise, both collaborative quality assurance techniques gradually lose their potential for achieving more advanced goals than the correction of programming errors. Distinctive advanced affordances of pair programming and peer code review result also from the techniques' different material properties. These characteristic physical, temporal, and basic behavioral properties define the immutable elements of a technique that do not allow for variation and do not require further interpretation. They thereby differentiate one technique from the other and cause potential applications of these techniques that go beyond simple error correction. Symbolic expressions, that is values and hints toward specific desirable ways of application, result from team members' interpretation of the these immutable elements as well as trainings in the techniques. Where developers perceive and adopt these values, they can more readily find advanced affordances provided by a technique. Material properties consequently determine a space of general actions that can possibly be executed as part of a technique while transactive memory structure determines which information can possibly be exchanged during such activities; these facts are detected and interpreted based on limited, value-laden perspectives of developers. By consequence, ISD teams with a more sophisticated transactive memory structure objectively have and subjectively perceive more possibilities to solicit and exchange information during different activities of collaborative quality assurance. They can therefore use the techniques to work towards more and distinct reasonably achievable goals.

In sum, this study finds that ISD teams' transactive memory structure and material properties of different collaborative quality assurance techniques create a space of objectively possible task level applications in the context of an ISD team. These objectively possible applications are perceived and interpreted by single developers from their personal, subjective perspectives on the techniques and on the teams' transactive memory. In consequence, developers perceive collaborative quality assurance techniques to be more or less useful for reaching different task level goals from their individual perspectives. Nevertheless, relatively stable patterns of appropriation emerge as symbolic expressions embedded in the techniques steer individuals' perceptions toward specific directions that hint at what may be seen as "faithful" appropriation of the techniques.

The second purpose of this study was to understand emergent effects of the application of collaborative quality assurance techniques in ISD teams on team cognition as well as on performance (Research Questions 2 a & b). Findings show that two generative mechanisms underlie all observed advanced affordances of pair programming and peer code review: homogenization and transparency. These generative mechanisms are found to affect ISD teams' transactive memory systems when collaborative quality assurance techniques are applied frequently by an entire team. Through homogenization, pair programming creates overlap in team members' meta-knowledge and labels but also induces expertise redundancy. In line with this conception, pair programming is found to have ambivalent effects on a team's transactive memory: while shared labels and meta-knowledge can foster the coordination of differentiated knowledge, expertise redundancy reduces differentiation and thereby effectiveness of a team's transactive memory system. This leads to the insight that significant effects of pair programming are dependent on the specific context of an ISD team. Pair programming is found most effective where a lack of shared labels and meta-knowledge in ISD teams inhibits effective knowledge coordination. Results suggest that one such inhibitor is negative affection between team members. Teams with distant interpersonal relationships can therefore improve their transactive memory through the homogenizing effects of pair programming whereas teams with close interpersonal relationships hurt their transactive memory system with frequent pair programming that induces redundancy and inaccuracy in their transactive memory. Overall, these ambivalent effects may constitute the reason why pair programming is found to lead to marginal quality improvements only.

By contrast, the generative mechanism of transparency inherent in peer code review is found to decouple ISD teams' transactive processes from their transactive memory structure. Frequent and team-wide peer code review improves software quality delivered by an ISD team while decreasing the quality-relevant effects of its transactive memory system. Applying peer code review as a technique that incorporates the use of a peer code review system, developers are found to store information in and retrieve information from these systems. In particular, peer code review encompasses mechanisms for finding and engaging team members that hold valuable expertise to review and improve a piece of code. By consequence, teams that apply peer code review become partially independent from their transactive memory structure for coordinating differentiated expertise of their single members. That is, the teams' transactive memory structure becomes partially transparent and less relevant for these transactive processes. In line with this reasoning, perceived transactive memory system effectiveness is found to relate less strongly to software quality when developers conduct peer code review often and with many team members. That is, the software quality of a team depends less on the effectiveness of its transactive memory system if the team conducts more peer code review. By consequence, this study finds peer code review acts a partial substitute for sophisticated transactive memory structure.

5.2 Contributions to Theory and Directions for Future Research

Referring to information systems development, Mangalaraj et al. (2014) argue that "theoretically anchored empirical research on this topic is, at best, sparse, especially in premier IS journals" (Mangalaraj et al. 2014, p. 269). Explaining the appropriation and impacts of collaborative quality assurance techniques based on theory of transactive memory systems and the concept of functional affordances, this study first and foremost contributes to the small but growing body of theoretically anchored empirical research on information systems development, especially on practices and processes in ISD that rely on the joint accomplishments of individual ISD team members. It thereby stands in the tradition of prior work such as Maruping et al. (2009b), Balijepally et al. (2009), Vidgen and Wang (2009), He et al. (2007), and Mangalaraj et al. (2014). Hopefully, this study contributes to extending the theoretically sound basis for empirical investigations in ISD and helps establish a stronger theoretical framework of information systems development. It makes a number of more specific contributions to literature on information systems development, transactive memory systems, and functional affordances which are highlighted and discussed in the following in the light of prior literature and extant theory.

Moving Team Cognition into the Explanatory Center of Research on Collaborative Quality Assurance Techniques and Their Effects in ISD Teams

This study contributes to ISD literature by directly answering a recent call for team cognition-based research that helps understand collaborative quality assurance techniques in ISD (Davern et al. 2012). A substantive body of literature exists that examines collaborative quality assurance techniques, particularly pair programming. However, with extremely few exceptions, these studies do not focus on the team level but exclusively look at dyads of often inexperienced developers. This study acknowledges, theoretically as well as empirically, that collaborative quality assurance techniques are generally used in enduring ISD teams of professional software developers and that the size of such teams is typically larger than two. Results not only indicate that team cognition influences how developers in ISD teams can actually apply collaborative quality assurance techniques, but also that team cognition is pivotal to the techniques' effects on software quality in ISD teams. By consequence, this study calls several aspects of extant theory into question. First, like previous research, this study indeed finds that pair programming increases knowledge transfer between individuals; however it strongly contradicts the assertion that knowledge transfer constitutes a positive performance effect per se which is widely assumed in ISD literature (e.g., Cockburn and Williams 2002; Hulkko and Abrahamsson 2005; Vidgen and Wang 2009; Salleh et al. 2011; Rigby et al. 2012; Bacchelli and Bird 2013). In fact, *pair programming* is found to exert ambivalent pressures on an ISD team's transactive memory system by fostering it with more homogeneous shared labels and meta-knowledge on the one hand while deteriorating it through more homogeneous task knowledge and expertise redundancy on the other hand. In accordance with this finding, results do not suggest that there is any positive effect of frequent and team-wide pair programming on the overall quality of software produced in a team. While this absence of quality effects conflicts with large parts of prior studies on dyadic level effects of pair programming (cf. Hannay et al. 2009; Salleh et al. 2011), it is more in line with recent studies which underline that pairs of programmers typically do not exceed the quality achievements of their best individual developers (Balijepally et al. 2009; Mangalaraj et al. 2014). It further complies with results by Fægri et al. (2010), who highlight that knowledge redundancy in ISD teams, induced by frequent role changes and work on other experts' tasks, may incur coordination costs that are not outweighed by performance improvements. Results of this study therefore broaden our understanding of pair programming by taking a team cognition perspective to extend theory to an ISD team level and suggest that the empirically observed absence of quality impacts of pair programming is rooted in ambiguous effects of homogenization on a team's transactive memory.

Findings moreover suggest there is at least one situation in which the positive effects of homogenization through pair programming outweigh the negative ones: when interpersonal relationships in an ISD team are strained, pair programming can help improve knowledge coordination despite of negative affections between team members. When interpersonal relationships are very close, however, pair programming can significantly deteriorate the team's transactive memory. This may appear surprising in the light of a number of dyadic level studies that find a "feelgood factor" (Müller and Padberg 2004, p. 151) between pair programming developers is relevant for their joint performance (Müller and Padberg 2004; Madeyski 2006; Salleh et al. 2011). Close personal relationships are thereby argued to improve the performance of single pairs, whereas this study finds that close personal relationships can turn pair programming into a deteriorating factor for the entire team's transactive memory. Interpreting this finding together with the rest of this study, it strongly suggests that dyadic level results on the effectiveness of pair programming may not easily transfer to the team level. While pair programming may be applied on a dyadic or task level to achieve a number of goals, only one of them being the achievement of optimal quality, its emergent effects on a team level do not appear to go hand in hand with these dyadic level goals. Personally close teams that decide to rely heavily on pair programming in order to achieve excellent software quality may in fact gradually deteriorate their transactive memory structure and thereby ultimately worsen their performance. Estranged teams that pair program for the sheer need for quality assurance, on the other hand, may actually gain significant benefits from the inherent homogenization of labels and meta-knowledge, consequently improving their ability to effectively coordinate knowledge even across interpersonal boundaries and paving the way for increased team performance. Taking a team cognition perspective, this study therefore calls extant knowledge on the effectiveness of pair programming into question. Findings on dyadic effects of pair programming may not necessarily translate to a team level, and dyadic level effects can apparently even be reversed when examining dyads as a part of a larger team. Future research should therefore cautiously examine extant research on single pairs and investigate its transferability to entire ISD teams.

This study contributes particularly to the emergent stream of research on *peer code review* applied in for-profit organizations by moving ISD teams and their cognition into the focus of theory and analysis. First, finding a clear positive effect of frequent and team-wide peer code review on internal and external software quality delivered by ISD teams, this study supports and extends the findings from open source (Rigby 2011; Beller et al. 2014; McIntosh et al. 2014) and prior organizational studies (Bacchelli and Bird 2013; Rigby and Bird 2013). Second, this study further finds that quality improvement through peer code review partly stems from the transparency it creates in an ISD team's transactive memory. Broadcasting review invitations or examining persistent data from previous reviews and revisions, authors can quickly elicit relevant expertise in their team, retrieve review comments from their expert colleagues, and directly address their critique in a revised solution. Findings show that peer code review can thereby partially compensate for deficiencies in a team's transactive memory structure. On the one hand, this distinguishes peer code review in organizational, collocated ISD teams from large open source communities where finding a reviewer with appropriate expertise often constitutes an overly complicated venture (Wang and Carroll 2011; Thongtanunam et al. 2015). On the other hand, it supports previous assertions that knowledge exchange constitutes a pivotal element of organizational peer code review and that peer code review may increase the mutual awareness of developers (Rigby and Bird 2013; Bacchelli and Bird 2013). However, it also calls to attention that prior research has looked at knowledge exchange largely as an attribute relevant to single peer code review sessions and to individual developers instead of acknowledging the wider implications for ISD teams' knowledge structure and software quality: differences in teams' transactive memory structures lead to specific constraints in conducting peer code review and allow for gaining different benefits from the application of peer code review. Future research on the outcomes of peer code review should take this specific context much more into account and should critically examine results from the open source context in the light of this study before deciding whether they are directly transferable to ISD teams in for-profit organizations. Lastly, prior research acknowledges, assesses, and presents developers' different motivations to conduct peer code review as static properties of the peer code review technique (Bacchelli and Bird 2013). Results of this study indicate that the motivations to use peer code review are neither static nor context-free. In fact, the usefulness attributed to peer code review for a specific task is found to depend on a teams' transactive memory but also on the presence of alternative ways to achieve the same goals. For example, where collocated ISD team members can choose between pair programming and peer code review for sharing elementary task understanding between two developers, they are found to rely more probably on pair programming than on peer code review, although prior research proposes sharing of understanding as a general motivation for applying peer code review (Bacchelli and Bird 2013; Rigby and Bird 2013). Future research should therefore differentiate more clearly between the different contexts that developers work in and should especially extend the body of team level investigations.

Explaining Task Level Appropriation of Collaborative Quality Assurance Techniques with Functional Affordances and Team Cognition

With the establishment of agile software development, ISD teams all over industry gained large amounts of autonomy to choose the development techniques they want to apply in order to achieve their goals (Janz and Prasarnphanich 2003, 2009). Making use of this autonomy, many ISD teams have subsequently refrained from adopting entire new methodologies but chose to apply single techniques in a selective manner according to their assessments what suited them best (Dybå and Dingsøyr 2008; Maruping et al. 2009b). Such adoption is however not a purely dichotomous decision whether or not to apply an ISD technique. Instead, ISD teams appropriate techniques to their needs in different ways (Fitzgerald et al. 2006) and go beyond the application of a "textbook 'vanilla' version" (Wang et al. 2012, p. 23) of these techniques. Numerous extant studies are concerned with proposing different patterns of adaptation of agile ISD methods in organizations (cf. Dingsøyr et al. 2012), but little is known why ISD teams actually appropriate techniques in different ways. Some scholars argue that the context in which ISD techniques are applied may conflict with the techniques' original purpose, leading to appropriation or abandonment of the technique (Senapathi and Srinivasan 2012; Cao et al. 2013). While such a perspective may allow for understanding each case of a single team that appropriates ISD techniques, it does not allow for understanding why there appear to be more general patterns in which teams tend to appropriate ISD techniques in a few distinctive but often similar ways (Wang et al. 2012).

This study contributes to research on the appropriation of ISD techniques by explaining why collocated ISD teams are enabled and constrained in successfully applying two particular techniques for different tasks based on two factors: their transactive memory on the one hand and material as well as relational properties of the techniques on the other hand. The techniques' material properties create the same, real constraints for every team regarding the behaviors that are possible within the scope of the technique. But they also carry values and implicit hints toward reasonable behavior (i.e., symbolic expressions) which can be interpreted by single developers. While these interpretations do not deterministically lead to the same result for different individuals in different teams, their rootedness in material properties steers individuals in similar contexts *by tendency* toward similar interpretations of a technique. At the same time, increasing sophistication of a team's transactive memory structure enables the team to encode, store, and retrieve more information during the interactions within the scope of each technique. Together, these factors create a set of possible applications of collaborative quality assurance techniques that make the techniques more or less useful for different teams in achieving different goals. While there is no deterministic process that makes teams appropriate collaborative quality assurance techniques for all reasonable tasks, the interaction of properties of the techniques and teams' transactive memory provides the objective grounds for the subjective decisions whether and how to apply the techniques to a task. By tendency, interpretation-based appropriations align with the real, objective possibilities. This explains why different ISD teams appropriate the same technique differently for their tasks on the one hand while at the same time similar patterns of appropriation appear in many teams on the other hand.

This study thereby extends prior research on the appropriation of ISD techniques by providing causal explanations for the application of pair programming and peer code review in ISD teams based on transactive memory and functional affordances. It incorporates previous studies' reasoning that context may create the shaping structures for the appropriation of an ISD technique (Senapathi and Srinivasan 2012; Cao et al. 2013) and provides a clear conceptualization of this phenomenon based on literature on functional affordances and on transactive memory. Whereas prior work identifies heterogeneous appropriations of ISD techniques without causal explanations (Wang et al. 2012) or provides only limited, case-specific understanding (Senapathi and Srinivasan 2012; Cao et al. 2013), this study introduces team cognition and functional affordances as mechanisms that generally enable and constrain the actual application of collaborative quality assurance techniques in all ISD teams. Future research should take this conceptualization and examine its transferability to the appropriation of other collaborative ISD techniques and ISD techniques in general. Especially the concepts of material properties, symbolic expressions, and functional affordances proposed in this study may directly transfer to ISD techniques in general and may help establish a general explanation of the appropriation of ISD techniques based on teams' variable contexts. Moreover, future research should investigate whether the influence of team cognition on the appropriation of ISD techniques is similarly strong for all techniques. Particularly the appropriation of techniques such as refactoring that rely less on the joint cognitive accomplishments of individuals and more on individual performances may depend less on team cognition than on the isolated cognitive resources of individuals.

Explaining Why Pair Programming and Peer Code Review Differ Beyond Being Functional Substitutes with Regard to Error Correction

Since the appearance of pair programming as a collaborative quality assurance technique in ISD teams, research and practice have been interested in the question whether benefits of pair programming outweighed its substantial costs, a question still discussed today (Cockburn and Williams 2002; Gallis et al. 2003; Dybå et al. 2007; Balijepally et al. 2009; Sun 2011; Mangalaraj et al. 2014). While much research focuses on the evaluation of work results of pairs of programmers as compared to solo programmers (Balijepally et al. 2009), some scholars approach the question looking for alternative ISD techniques that could possibly substitute pair programming while incurring lower costs (Mangalaraj et al. 2014). Peer reviews were early on proposed as a potential alternative to pair programming (Paulk 2001). Mentionable experimental studies evaluate pair programming in comparison to more or less formal inspections by peer developers (Müller 2004, 2005; Tomayko 2002; Phongpaibul and Boehm 2006; Winkler and Biffl 2006). Findings from this stream of literature suggest that ISD teams do not find more defects during formal, meeting-based source code inspections with several team members as defined by Fagan (1986) than single pairs of developers do (Tomayko 2002; Winkler and Biffl 2006; Phongpaibul and Boehm 2006). Moreover, such inspection meetings often incur even higher costs than continuous pair programming (Phongpaibul and Boehm 2006). Quick and informal offline reviews of a single, nearby team member, by contrast, resemble pair programming in terms of defect detection and time effort (Müller 2004, 2005). While none of these empirical studies addresses informal, technology-supported peer code review as defined in this study, other scholars compare pair programming and peer code review conceptually based on anecdotal evidence (Rigby et al. 2012): their analysis suggests that pair programming typically causes higher costs and requires more investment from involved developers than peer code review but also leads to better outcome quality and supports team-building.

This study informs research on alternative techniques to pair programming by setting adoption and effects of pair programming in contrast to peer code review in professional, collocated ISD teams. Findings suggest that there is an overlap in the basic functional affordances of pair programming and peer code review. If applied solely for error correction, ISD teams indeed use these practices often interchangeably. However, each technique also has a set of idiosyncratic advanced functional affordances which it affords to ISD teams depending on their transactive memory. These distinctive affordances are found to result from the techniques' material properties and a team's transactive memory. ISD teams that want to leverage advanced affordances of pair programming or peer code review cannot substitute one for the other reasonably. Moreover, the effects of frequent and team-wide use of the techniques are found to differ enormously. While pair programming is found to homogenize expertise, labels, and meta-knowledge in a team, peer code review is found to partially substitute transactive memory structure and to directly improve code quality. Literature on alternatives to pair programming consequently learns that peer code review may serve as a substitute for pair programming on a task level when the only goal is error correction, but emergent effects of both techniques differ strongly.

Application and Extension of the Concept of Functional Affordances to Study ISD Techniques Instead of Technologies

Prior work on functional affordances in IS research nearly exclusively focuses on the ontological, cognitive, and behavioral consequences that result from distinct design features of different information systems in various contexts (Bernhard et al. 2013; Strong et al. 2014; Pozzi et al. 2014; Robey and Anderson 2013). Extant literature fruitfully theorizes why the same technology may provide different functional affordances to individuals, groups, or organizations and how individual level affordances emerge to produce effects on collective levels (Leonardi and Barley 2010; Goh et al. 2011; Volkoff and Strong 2013; Strong et al. 2014). However, some scholars criticize this stream of research for partly oversimplifying organizational reality. They argue that the presently exclusive focus on the affordances of only technology falls equally short in capturing the full phenomenon of organizational practices and their inherent socio-technical interactions as does a focus on social behavior which reduces technology to an invariant, external influence on organizational routines (Robey and Anderson 2013). Findings of several scholars enormously enrich research on functional affordances by showing how functional affordances of technology interact with organizational routines and how they influence their mutual evolution (Volkoff et al. 2007; Volkoff and Strong 2013; Leonardi 2011, 2012; Goh et al. 2011). However, none of these scholars venture that routines and practices themselves may actually have different affordances and that technology may be just an important but partial aspect of such affordances (Robey and Anderson 2013). Interestingly, Davern et al. (2012) do not delve deep into theory on functional affordances, but they suggest that especially ISD techniques may have functional affordances which facilitate team cognition and deserve to be researched.

To the best of the author's knowledge, this study is the first to pick up these ideas and answer calls for research that conceptualizes functional affordances not as a concept relational between technology and its users but as a concept relational between technology-based organizational practices and the actors who conduct these practices (Robey and Anderson 2013). Thereby, this study broadens the scope of functional affordances from the study of technology appropriation and evolution to the study of team level ISD techniques that encompass the use of technology. The value of this perspective becomes clear when looking at the example of pair programming: it helps us understand that it is not the sole existence of two developers and of a work station computer which affords them immediate concrete outcomes such as error correction, sharing task understanding, or joint solution satisficing. Whereas their existence is a necessary condition, it does not directly enable or suggest them to aim for specific outcomes. However, when sitting together at this work station, using it to write source code and to talk about this code, then these outcomes become immediately achievable and concrete. The explanatory value of functional affordances of a technique that encompass the use of technology consequently goes far beyond the explanatory value of functional affordances of technology only.

Moreover, extant IS research on functional affordances particularly highlights that organizational routines and practices change and evolve, partially in concert with information technology that supports or hinders them (e.g., Volkoff et al. 2007; Volkoff and Strong 2013; Leonardi 2011, 2012; Goh et al. 2011). However, little is known about the parts of practices that stay the same. This study addressed this problem for the collaborative quality assurance techniques of pair programming and peer code review. It argues that collaborative quality assurance techniques have an immutable core that actually defines the technique as a structure in the domain of the real and does not change. To extend the concept of functional affordances to ISD techniques and to incorporate this reasoning of an immutable core, this study adapted the concepts of material properties and symbolic expressions to cover the material and the relational aspects of ISD techniques. The core of a technique is accordingly seen as an immutable, material nucleus including physical, temporal, and basic behavioral constraints. Only beyond this core, individual actors can decide consciously or unconsciously how to behave and how to make use of a technique, but symbolic expressions embedded in the core by tendency cause these actors to decide for similar behaviors. This study therefore contributes to prior literature on functional affordances by adapting and extending the concepts of material properties and symbolic expressions to match collaborative quality assurance techniques. It stands to reason that this conceptualization also extends to other ISD techniques and organizational practices. Future research should transfer the adapted conceptualizations of material properties and symbolic expressions to other techniques and critically examine their usefulness and validity.

Lastly, this study also contributes to literature on functional affordances by taking a team cognition perspective recently called for in ISD literature (Davern et al. 2012). There is much research on emergent functional affordances of technology on an organizational level (e.g., Volkoff et al. 2007; Goh et al. 2011; Volkoff and Strong 2013; Strong et al. 2014), whereas only few scholars focus on the group level in their research (Leonardi 2012; Majchrzak et al. 2013a; Malhotra and Majchrzak 2012). While there is general agreement that functional affordances and individuals' cognition are closely interrelated (Robey and Anderson 2013), cognitive structures and processes in collective entities are paradoxically addressed only scarcely. In line with more conceptual theorizing, the little extant empirical work on groups emphasizes the need for convergence in single individuals' perceptions and the use of technology affordances as a prerequisite for group level impacts (Strong et al. 2014); given this, however, technology can alter the knowledge exchange processes in groups (Leonardi 2012). This present study goes beyond prior research in two aspects: (1) this study shows that emergent effects of frequent and team-wide use of functional affordances not only impact the processes of knowledge exchange but also the team level structure of distributed knowledge (i.e., a team's knowledge, labels, and meta-knowledge); (2) showing and explaining that different qualities of transactive memory structure generate different affordances of pair programming and peer code review, this study clarifies how team level cognition affects task level functional affordances in the first place. In sum, this study adds to our understanding of what actually has functional affordances (not only technology does but also techniques do), why they exist (because of interacting mechanisms rooted in techniques' material properties and in team level cognitive structure), and which emergent effects they can produce (changes in transactive memory structure as well as transactive memory processes).

Technical Substitutes of Transactive Memory Structure

In a seminal review of research on transactive memory systems, renown scholars highlight the shortcomings of contemporary IT which prevent it from substituting transactive memory systems. In more detail, Lewis and Herndon (2011) emphasize that current IT fails to substitute group level transactive memory systems because of its inability to emulate transactive memory processes. This study now finds that peer code review exerts exactly such a substitutive effect on ISD teams' transactive memory through the mechanism of transparency. Making frequent and team-wide use of advanced affordances of peer code review, ISD teams build up a base of prior reviews in their peer code review system and develop a shared style of coding. As a result, each piece of source code becomes easily understandable to all team members and accessible via the peer code review system. By consequence, developers can look up previous code changes in areas related to their current task, can identify colleagues who contributed as authors or reviewers to these areas, can retrieve these colleagues' expertise via review requests, and can also examine and understand the genesis of current code. Developers are thereby enabled to execute transactive processes for knowledge coordination relying on data of the peer code review system instead of relying on their meta-knowledge about their colleagues' expertise (i.e., their team's transactive memory structure). However, only if a team conducts peer code review frequently and includes all members in collaborative quality assurance, this keeps data in the peer code review system up to date and a useful representation of the current state of distributed expertise in the team. That is, without any enforcement and only due to actions that are inherently part of peer code review, this "externalized transactive memory" grows and immanently keeps up to date. This study thereby finds that the actions and interactions that are part of the peer code review technique build, update, and use the transactive qualities of data in the peer code review system. This suggests that a search for purely technological alternatives to transactive memory systems, as has been proposed by Lewis and Herndon (2011), may be doomed to failure. Instead, the socio-technical behaviors in the scope of collaborative techniques, including prescribed interactions with technology, may constitute the procedural elements that are required to make technology afford knowledge coordination without transactive memory. Future research should examine this proposition in the context of other techniques that appear promising. For example, Kotlarsky et al. (2014) examine a number of practices that result en passant in codified meta-knowledge of who holds expertise in a particular area, and Nevo et al. (2012) show that interpersonal relations are very influential on individuals' decision whether to rely on such codified meta-knowledge. Future research may therefore aim to understand which generalizable material properties of a technique, including the use of technology, afford the codification, effective maintenance, and use of this codified meta-knowledge. These results may then be a starting point for innovative design science research to create more effective and efficient techniques.

Moreover, the results of this study indicate that software product modularity exerts a similar compensatory effect on the effectiveness of teams' transactive memory systems as does transparency (cf. Sect. 4.3.4). This is interesting, as it may suggest that there is another rival mechanism to transactive memory systems for effective knowledge coordination: in more decoupled and less coherent software structures, developers may be able to specialize on tasks related to a physical software module rather than specializing in a specific area of expertise that may or may not relate to a module. Ultimately, modular structures may thereby reduce the overall need for knowledge coordination and exert similar quality effects as transparency. This raises questions for future research as to how to balance interdependency and product modularity in ISD teams from a team cognition perspective (cf. Sect. 4.3.5). One reason why prior research does not find this effect, may lie in the particular context of this study: this is one of few studies on transactive memory systems that examines established teams who are engaged in developing and maintaining products over time rather than temporary project teams (Ren and Argote 2011; Choi et al. 2010). Specialization in particular modules may take time and may therefore only be observable in teams that continuously work on the same product over time. These results therefore call for further research on modularity and transactive memory in ongoing ISD teams.

Lastly, Ellis et al. (2008) reason that role changes and cross training in teams should help them develop a transactive memory system. The results of this study suggest that this assumption needs careful further examinations. On the one hand, pair programming, with its close collaboration and role changes between partners, is indeed found to be beneficial for knowledge coordination through transactive memory when personally distant relationships impede knowledge coordination. On the other hand, pair programming is however found to be detrimental for transactive memory effectiveness if no such inhibitors exists. It appears therefore crucial to apply the recommended cross-trainings and role changes of Ellis et al. (2008) with great care and only as long as they are needed to overcome inhibiting personal distances between team members. Future research should more closely elaborate on these ambiguous effects and find measures that help teams decide whether and how intensively they want to apply techniques such as pair programming.

5.3   Contributions to Practice

The findings of this study have a number of implications for ISD practice. They inform practitioners in ISD firms, both on a managerial and on a team level, about adoption and effects of pair programming and peer code review. They moreover help developers of peer code review tools to better understand the requirements of for-profit organizations as compared to their traditional clients in open source communities.

5.3.1   Implications for ISD Managers

Peer code review has gained broad acceptance in large software developing enterprises such as Google, SAP, Microsoft, Facebook, Erickson, Sony, and AMD (Rigby and Bird 2013; Bacchelli and Bird 2013). Even in companies where formal code inspections as proposed by Fagan (1986) used to be discarded for their overhead and lack of agility, peer code review in its modern form has gained many advocates on management and team levels (Bacchelli and Bird 2013; Rigby et al. 2012). In contrast to formal inspections, quality assurance with peer code review is part of ISD teams' daily routine and aims to collaboratively ensure quality before anyone external to the team is faced with deficient source code. However, there is a dearth of research on the use and effects of peer code review in for-profit organizations. From this study, ISD management learns that *peer code review* is indeed an effective measure to directly improve external as well as internal code quality in ongoing, collocated ISD teams. Importantly, this study shows that effective peer code review requires voluntary feedback from pro-active reviewers. An introduction of peer code review can therefore not be imposed upon ISD teams but must be conducted with their full support. Failing this, peer code review becomes only a detection mechanism for basic defects but does not yield improved solutions or long-term benefits regarding maintainability.

This study also informs ISD managers about the frequently-assumed positive outcomes of *pair programming*. Prior studies largely ignore that pair programming is typically applied not only between a pair of developers but in a team of more than two members (Coman et al. 2014). Whereas prior studies on pair programming are often overly enthusiastic, this study advises for some caution. While ISD teams do use pair programming, at least to some degree, for detecting errors and ensuring solution quality, there are also effects on the teams' cognitive abilities. This study suggests that pair programming may be very beneficial for team building and knowledge coordination in teams with tense interpersonal relationships. For very close teams, by contrast, it may in fact have negative consequences to rely heavily on pair programming: becoming more and more homogeneous, they loose their ability to build on strong experts in specific areas. Moreover, this study cannot identify a clear quality improvement effect resulting from frequent and team-wide pair programming. ISD management may therefore want to encourage teams not to rely exclusively on pair programming. Allowing and fostering pair programming for team building and work satisfaction should be complemented by and aligned with possibilities for developers to create unique, in-depth expertise for specific areas of their products.

Peer code review may moreover provide help for ISD managers who treat *to balance work load* in single components over more than one team. Even if component experts belonging to a specific team may not have the time to implement a desired feature, they may serve as reviewers for proposed implementations. Management could consequently give feature implementation tasks also to less experienced teams that could then acquire expert feedback on their solutions through peer code review. This would move firm-internal division of work more into the direction of contribution management in open source communities (Lee and Cole 2003).

Lastly, ISD management learns that *substituting costly pair programming* with more lightweight peer code review is not feasible. While both techniques provide features for simple error correction, their main benefits lie beyond this, and benefits are different for the two techniques. For team building and increased knowledge coordination in personally distant teams, only pair programming shows mentionable effects. In order to immediately increase code quality delivered by an ISD team, the introduction of peer code review appears more promising, even for teams that may not be able to conduct pair programming, for example because of global distribution.

5.3.2 *Implications for ISD Teams*

Although pair programming and peer code review have been broadly accepted in industry, not all ISD teams have gathered experiences with these techniques, yet.

ISD teams that are at the point of deciding whether to introduce pair programming or peer code review learn that three factors limit what their team can reasonably achieve by applying each of the techniques: while both can serve for simple error correction, all advanced affordances of the techniques depend on the team's transactive memory, its tasks, and its adoption of values underlying the techniques. Teams and Scrum Masters may reflect on their current tasks and the distribution of knowledge in their team to identify how sophisticated their transactive memory is with regard to their different tasks. Based on this assessment, ISD teams can determine whether they can feasibly make use of advanced affordances like the creation of exceptional expert solutions or expert approval in their tasks. Importantly, all advanced affordances rest on the premise that the techniques be applied in line with the values they embed: if pair programmers do not value critical discourse and peer code review teams do not value the variety of opinions and perspectives, they will not achieve more than some defect detection. Such a-priori considerations may consequently support better decision making whether a team can successfully adopt a technique or not.

ISD teams that already apply the techniques learn about the consequences of their use. As such, teams that are personally close and still want to preserve a mentionable level of specialization and knowledge coordination learn that they should not rely exclusively on pair programming for all tasks. ISD teams that already use peer code review learn that they should make sure that all team members are engaged in peer code review over time. Only if the most expert team members volunteer to provide review comments on their topics the review process creates good results. This is also a requirement when teams intend to rely more on the persistent data in their peer code review system to identify experts in different code areas. All outcomes beyond error detection of both techniques rest on the premise that they be conducted frequently and not only by single enthusiasts but by all team members. Teams should therefore try to involve all their members.

5.3.3 Implications for the Development of Peer Code Review Systems

Also developers of peer code review tools can benefit from this study that is one of the first to examine the use and effects of peer code review in for-profit organizations. Prior work emphasizes on the commonalities of peer code review in open source and for-profit organizations (Rigby and Bird 2013; Rigby et al. 2012). This study sheds light on one of the core differences between these two forms of software development: in organizations, peer code review is used by ongoing teams instead of loosely-connected contributors. Developers of peer code review systems firstly gain an important sales argument: the team-wide and frequent use of peer code review does indeed affect internal and external software quality in professional ISD teams. Secondly, however, peer code review must compete against other ways of collaborative quality assurance in collocated for-profit teams.

This study highlights the distinctive features of peer code review as compared to pair programming. Whereas prior work recommends to extend peer code review systems with more synchronous communication capabilities in order to satisfy understanding needs of reviewers in such settings (Bacchelli and Bird 2013), this study strongly opposes such recommendations. Findings suggest that exactly the material properties of peer code review differentiate its affordances from the ones of pair programming. When teams can choose between pair programming and peer code review for satisfying understanding needs, they opt for pair programming. The strengths of peer code review in such settings, by contrast, lie in its possibilities to provide in-depth analyses without the constraints of direct, synchronous interaction between author and reviewer. Working detached from the process of solving a problem, multiple reviewers can more easily bring in their different perspectives to create a richer, more diverse picture than in a session of pair programming. In fact, peer code review may constitute exactly such a cooperative way of contribution that extant literature asks for as a necessary complement to pair programming (Coman et al. 2014). Moreover, this study shows that much of the value of peer code review for ongoing teams lies in the persistent data of prior reviews: by examining prior reviews in a specific code area, developers can quickly find expertise in their team without necessarily holding extensive meta-knowledge. Lastly, peer code review keeps developers in for-profit ISD teams up-to-date about their team members' current tasks as well as about changes in code areas they are interested in. Findings from extant studies suggest that such awareness is a valuable resource for teams (Bacchelli and Bird 2013). Developers of peer code review systems may therefore want to reject the idea of becoming more synchronous and alike to pair programming. Instead, peer code review tools should be extended in their core strengths by providing more functionality to conduct quick examinations of existing review data, effectively storing old review data, retrieving expertise and expertise areas, and leveraging different reviewers' diverse perspectives.

5.4 Limitations of Mixed Methods Study

A number of limitations need to be considered when interpreting the integrated findings of this mixed methods research. First, this study focused on two particular collaborative quality assurance techniques in ISD teams, namely on pair programming and peer code review. By consequence, the generalizability of this study's findings is limited to these techniques. Although peer code review is a central pillar of quality assurance in nearly all open source projects and is becoming increasingly popular in for-profit organizations (Lee and Cole 2003; Rigby and Bird 2013; Bacchelli and Bird 2013) while pair programming is the most widely adopted agile ISD technique (Dybå and Dingsøyr 2008), this research design leaves out many other prominent ISD techniques. Future research should therefore adapt this study's generic conceptualizations of material properties, symbolic expressions, and functional affordances to other particular ISD techniques or even ISD techniques in general. Future work should critically examine the explanatory value of these concepts for investigations beyond pair programming and peer code review. While the mechanisms of homogenization and transparency may be specific to the two techniques under investigation, this study shows that understanding the effects of ISD techniques on team cognition can significantly improve our understanding of ISD team performance. Further investigations into the interplay of team cognition and ISD techniques appear consequently very promising.

Second, this entire study was conducted with experienced developers from a large ISD enterprise with all developers working at the same locations in Germany and single teams working physically close together. One may argue that this empirical basis provides more external validity than the frequently-chosen student samples and short-lived project groups that are common in research on collaborative quality assurance techniques as well as team cognition (Hannay et al. 2009; Austin 2003; Choi et al. 2010). Nevertheless, these factors definitely influenced the findings of this study and therefore constitute boundaries to the generalization of results. Future studies should consequently pick up and critically evaluate the findings made in the presented context. For example, the company's products mostly consist of enterprise software. Compared to other pieces of software, like smartphone applications for example, these products are larger and have arguably higher complexity. The influence of team cognition that allows teams to build, maintain, and extend their knowledge about business processes as well as legacy code may be especially pronounced and relevant in this context. Future research may want to transfer this investigation to the context of smaller firms with less complex products in order to ascertain these suppositions. Moreover, it may be fruitful to vary the cultural context of this study because especially socio-technical ISD techniques such as pair programming and peer code review that build on criticizing one another's work results may be appropriated and actualized very differently in cultural contexts that are traditionally not so blunt in their critique.

Third, based on the theory of transactive memory systems, this study took a view on team cognition that emphasizes on the individual contributions of every single team member to a team's overall cognitive accomplishments. By consequence, this study implicitly ascribed paramount value to specialization and individual expertise that require team level coordination in order to be effective. Other theoretical perspectives on team cognition, such as the concept of shared mental models, emphasize much more on the value of overlapping expertise and shared knowledge that is held by all team members (Mohammed and Dumville 2001). With regard to the team level outcomes of collaborative quality assurance techniques, this study moreover focused primarily on the quality of source code produced by an ISD team. These choices were made based on explicit reasoning and led to respectable theoretical and empirical results. Nevertheless, future research should investigate the phenomena from other theoretical angles and observe effects on other outcome measures. This may lead to further insights into important questions such as how much of an ISD team's knowledge resources should actually be shared when targeting different outcome measures and how collaborative quality assurance techniques can aid in achieving an effective balance between shared and specialized knowledge.

Fourth, the sequential order of research phases in this mixed methods study inherently leaves some questions open for further investigation. A sequential mixed methods design with a quantitative corroboration following a qualitative exploration and four in-depth case studies helped to gain a detailed understanding of the application of collaborative quality assurance techniques, to subsequently theorize the effects of this application, and to finally corroborate the theorized mechanisms. However, each of the individual research phases of exploration, case studies, and survey faced particular threats to validity and generalization (cf. Sects. 4.1.5, 4.2.4, and 4.3.5). The sequential research design helped to compensate in later phases for some limitations of earlier ones. For example, both the initial exploration and the case studies were conducted only with teams who applied at least one of the collaborative quality assurance techniques. In the survey study, there were no such restrictions which thereby lowered the danger of selection bias that may have been induced in the previous qualitative steps. Similarly, data sources and analysis techniques varied considerably throughout the different phases in order to reduce the chance of common method bias. However, due to its final position in the sequence of research phases, no further steps could account for limitations and open questions that remained from the survey study. For example, only a subsequent qualitative inquiry could possibly help better understand why not all hypotheses of the survey study could be corroborated. In fact, some scholars recommend to rely on concurrent mixed methods designs to account for such limitations (Venkatesh et al. 2013). Future research may want to follow their advice and examine particularly the theoretical mechanisms behind the rejected hypotheses of this study.

Fifth, by following a mixed methods design, this study does not fit clearly into one of the established quantitative and qualitative research traditions in IS (Lee and Baskerville 2003; Venkatesh et al. 2013). The research design of this study aimed at gaining rich insights into team cognition and its interrelation with collaborative quality assurance techniques by combining quantitative and qualitative research methods in a mixed methods study. While mixed methods research designs have gained popularity during the last years, the largest body of new studies still consists of either purely qualitative or purely quantitative studies (Mingers 2003; Wynn and Williams 2012). Scholars relate this dominance of the extremes to differences in underlying epistemic assumptions and especially to differences in validity criteria for evaluating research (Tsang 2014; Venkatesh et al. 2013). In line with this reasoning, this study conducted three investigations that each conformed to the established validity criteria of qualitative or quantitative research traditions respectively. Nonetheless, qualitative evidence, which served as a primary source of insight for the effect of team cognition on task level appropriations, may not match the expectations of quantitative researchers; accordingly, quantitative evidence, which served as a primary source of insight for the quality effects of the techniques, may not match the expectations of qualitative researchers. Future research may therefore want to examine appropriation effects within a quantitative and quality effects within a qualitative research paradigm respectively.

Lastly, this study focused only on task and team level aspects of the application of pair programming and peer code review. Prior research on collaborative quality assurance techniques has mostly ignored the fact that these techniques are typically applied in teams in a continuous manner over time. This study identified team level effects of the ongoing application as well as team level factors that influence task level appropriation of the techniques. While this appears an appropriate focus for understanding effects on and within ISD teams, it may also be necessary to look at the organizational level in more detail. For example, peer code review may carry the potential to introduce new forms of division of labor in ISD firms; an effect that needs to be studied on an organizational level rather than on a team level. Conducting explorations, case studies, and a survey primarily targeting ISD teams, this study was not able to report on such organizational level effects in more detail. Further research should therefore be conducted that takes also organization level effects into account.

Chapter 6
Conclusion

This study was motivated by the question how team cognition influences the use and the effects of software development techniques in ISD teams. It was reasoned that team cognition may constitute a major influence when developers decide whether and how to apply ISD techniques to single tasks on the one hand, whereas ongoing and team-wide application of ISD techniques may lead to emergent effects on team cognition on the other hand. Two important and widely-adopted collaborative quality assurance techniques were examined in more detail: pair programming and peer code review. An analysis of extant literature showed that prior work generally ignored that collaborative quality assurance techniques are applied within the boundaries of ISD teams and may therefore be affected by and affect team cognition. What is more, research on team cognition in ISD teams is scarce, and studies connecting ISD techniques to team cognition are hard to find. Consequently, this study investigated how and why team cognition affects the task level appropriation of pair programming and peer code review on the one hand, and why continued application of these techniques affects team cognition and performance in ISD teams on the other hand.

The theory of transactive memory systems and the concept of functional affordances were harnessed and adapted for these investigations. A mixed-methods study, consisting of three sequential research phases, was conducted that examined collocated ISD teams and their use of the collaborative quality assurance techniques. An interview-based, qualitative exploration was followed by in-depth case studies of four ISD teams and a questionnaire-based survey with more than 600 individual respondents. It was found that a team's transactive memory is a determining factor in how the team can apply collaborative quality assurance techniques on a task level. A set of stable, specific possibilities for goal-directed applications of pair programming and peer code review was identified. The common possibility to detect errors in source code is but one of them. Beyond error correction, each technique provides idiosyncratic advanced possibilities of application. These include the sharing of task understanding through pair programming and the creation of

© Springer International Publishing Switzerland 2016

K. Spohrer, *Collaborative Quality Assurance in Information Systems Development*,
Progress in IS, DOI 10.1007/978-3-319-25163-9_6

intelligible code through peer code review. Whether or not a team can make use of these advanced possibilities is largely determined by its transactive memory because it determines how knowledge can be shared between involved developers.

The second purpose of this study was to understand emergent effects of the ongoing, team-wide application of collaborative quality assurance techniques in ISD teams on team cognition and performance. It was found that pair programming homogenizes an ISD team's cognitive resources, including team members' views of one another but also their individual expertise. Pair programming was therefore found beneficial for teams' transactive memory only in situations where tense interpersonal relationships would otherwise block knowledge coordination. In situations of close interpersonal relationships, it was found even detrimental to maintaining an effective transactive memory. Peer code review, by contrast, was found to aid ISD team members in using one another's knowledge cooperatively without the need to know exactly who knows what. Peer code review is accordingly found to improve the internal and external software quality delivered by ISD teams whereas pair programming is not found to directly impact software quality.

In summary, this study is one of the first to examine the interplay of team cognition and teams' use of ISD techniques; an important topic that prior literature had mostly ignored. Findings indicate that team cognition and ISD techniques are indeed closely interconnected within the boundaries of ISD teams: team cognition influences the appropriation of ISD techniques for different tasks, and the ongoing application of ISD techniques yields emergent effects on team cognition. This study has focused on two particularly important ISD techniques for collaborative quality assurance, namely pair programming and peer code review. Future research should build on the given insights in order to better reflect the role of team cognition in research on ISD teams and how they generate value from the knowledge and actions of their single members.

Appendix A
Extant Literature

The following Table A.1 gives a brief overview of extant research on peer code review. Little research has focused on the peer code review in for-profit organizations. Prior studies have focused on different aspects. Primarily, literature sought to identify generalizable patterns of how peer code review is applied within and across open source communities. Few have investigated the degree to which peer code review is adopted in for-profit organizations or even appropriated to suit developers' specific needs. Research on the outcome of applying peer code review has largely ignored for-profit settings. Lastly, there is extremely little use or development of theory in this stream of research and results remain often descriptive rather than explanatory.

© Springer International Publishing Switzerland 2016
K. Spohrer, *Collaborative Quality Assurance in Information Systems Development*,
Progress in IS, DOI 10.1007/978-3-319-25163-9

Table A.1 Prior studies on peer code review

Study	Research approach	Research design	Data & analysis	Focus	Theory	Community/ company	Level of analysis	Key findings
Bacchelli and Bird (2013)	Empirical	Multimethod exploration	Observations, interviews, survey	Adoption, application, outcome	Grounded theory	Microsoft	Individual	Motivation for PCR is primarily defect detection, but also aims for knowledge transfer in teams; PCR increases team awareness of one another's activities and helps create alternative solutions; tools restrict developers in communication bandwidth; understanding the code is crucial for reviewers and takes them the longest time
Beller et al. (2014)	Empirical	Case study	Archival data analysis	Application		Tycho	Review comment	Types of review comments are similar to industry findings: largely about code structure, representation, and documentation; only 25 % are about functionality
Bernhart et al. (2010)	Technology design	Engineering		Application				Propose alternative review tool
Bettenburg et al. (2013)	Empirical	Descriptive case study	Archival data analysis			Android, Linux	Project/ community	Describe review process as part of contribution management process
Bosu and Carver (2014)	Empirical	Network analysis	Archival data analysis, social network analysis	Application, outcome			Community	Reputation matters, core developers receive quicker reviews

Study								
Lee and Cole (2003)	Empirical	Case study	Archival data analysis	Application, outcome	Org. knowledge creation	Linux	Community	PCR is a coordination and knowledge creation mechanism; PCR constitutes a central knowledge creation mechanism in OS communities; fosters evolutionary development of products
McIntosh et al. (2014)	Empirical	Case study	Archival data analysis	Outcome		Qt, VTK, ITK	Software component	PCR participation and PCR coverage predict defect rate after software release
Müller (2004)	Empirical	Experiment	Student sample	Outcome			Individual	PCR is marginally more efficient than pair programming, both are similar in effectiveness
Müller (2005)	Empirical	Experiment	Student sample	Outcome			Individual	PCR and pair programming create similar overhead and task performance
Pangsakulyanont et al. (2014)	Technology design	Engineering		Application		Qt	Review comment	OS reviews contain many off-topic comments; propose tool to distinguish important from unimportant comments
Phongpaibul and Boehm (2006)	Empirical	Experiment	Student sample	Outcome			Review session	PCR is less effective but more efficient in defect detection than pair programming; cultural background (here Thailand) may influence adoption of either technique

(continued)

Table A.1 (continued)

Study	Research approach	Research design	Data & analysis	Focus	Theory	Community/ company	Level of analysis	Key findings
Phongpaibul and Boehm (2007)	Empirical	Experiment	Student sample	Outcome			Review session	Replicate findings of Phongpaibul and Boehm (2006) in India; cultural differences not analyzed due to methodological limitations
Rigby et al. (2008)	Empirical	Case study	Archival data analysis	Application, outcome		Apache	Community	PCR should encompass early, frequent reviews of small, independent, and complete contributions; review requests should be broadcasted, but few self-selected reviewers should answer per change
Rigby et al. (2012)	Conceptual	Conceptual		Adoption, application, outcome				Ensure frequent, incremental reviews from volunteering experienced experts; PCR is a lightweight substitute for pair programming
Rigby and Bird (2013)	Empirical	Case study	Archival data analysis	Appropriation		OS projects of Microsoft, Google, AMD et al.	Project/ community	Projects differ in appropriation of PCR but convergence to a common core is observed; reviewers learn to know new code areas through PCR

Rigby (2011)	Empirical	Multimethod case study	Archival data analysis, inferential statistics, content analysis			Apache, Subversion, Linux, Gnome	Community	PCR in OS is effective and efficient if conducted early and frequently based on small, independent, and complete code changes that receive feedback from few volunteering expert reviewers after broadcasted requests
Stamelos et al. (2002)	Empirical	Quantitative exploration	Archival data analysis	Outcome		100 Linux applications	Project	Code quality established through PCR in OS lacks behind industry standards
Sutherland and Venolia (2009)	Empirical	Exploratory survey	Questionnaire, observations, interviews	Appropriation		Microsoft	Review session	Collocated teams often switch between PCR and face-to-face meetings if necessary; information explicated during PCR is seldom retrieved or used after reviews
Thongtanunam et al. (2014)	Technology design	Engineering		Application				Create visualization tool for data mining PCR repositories

(continued)

Table A.1 (continued)

Study	Research approach	Research design	Data & analysis	Focus	Theory	Community/ company	Level of analysis	Key findings
Thongtanunam et al. (2015)	Empirical	Engineering, tool validation	Archival data analysis	Application		Android Open Source, Open Stack, Qt, Libre Office	Code change	Finding reviewers takes often nearly 14 days; finding potential expert reviewers based on prior activity is promising
Wang and Carroll (2011)	Empirical	Case study	Archival data analysis, content analysis	Application		Mozilla, Python	Project/ community	OS PCR is different from formal inspections in companies; conceptually differentiate them in four phases of bug-fixing and review
Yang (2014)	Empirical	Network analysis	Archival data analysis, social network analysis	Application		Android Open Source, Open Stack, Qt	Community	Developers take different roles with regard to what they do in the PCR process; in some cases submitters also review, in others they do not

OS open source, *PCR* peer code review

Appendix B
Initial Exploration

B.1 Interview Guideline

For the convenience of interviewees, 11 of 13 interviews of the initial exploration were conducted in German, two in English. The following interview guideline for the semi-structured interviews was in German. For interviews in English, the questions were translated on the fly by the interviewer. In several cases, the guideline was not followed strictly in sequence. Instead, questions were asked in the flow of the conversation and emphasis was put on different topics as they came up. Nevertheless, it was made sure that all questions of the guideline had been asked by the end of each interview.

Kontext

1. Bitte beschreiben Sie kurz, wie Sie zur Softwareentwicklung gekommen sind!
2. Was ist Ihre derzeitige Rolle im Unternehmen?
3. Bitte beschreiben Sie kurz Ihr derzeitiges Entwicklungsprojekt:

   - Ziel
   - Zeitraum
   - Projektgröße und Beteiligte

4. Bitte beschreiben Sie kurz Ihr Team:

   - Größe
   - Mitglieder
   - Zeitraum der Zusammenarbeit
   - Verteilung Expertise

© Springer International Publishing Switzerland 2016

K. Spohrer, *Collaborative Quality Assurance in Information Systems Development*,
Progress in IS, DOI 10.1007/978-3-319-25163-9

Code Review und Pair Programming im Team

1. Bitte beschreiben Sie, wie ein Code Review in Ihrem Team abläuft!
2. Lesen Sie auch Reviews, die Sie weder gemacht noch veranlasst haben?
3. Setzen andere Teams Code Review genauso ein, oder gibt es Unterschiede? Wenn ja, welche?
4. In welchen Bereichen arbeiten Sie mehr oder weniger als Reviewer?
5. Gibt es Experten, die bei Änderungen in einem bestimmten Bereich mehr als Reviewer dienen?
6. Für welche Aufgaben bietet sich der Einsatz von Code Review an?
7. Was sind die Vorteile des Einsatzes von Code Review?
8. Was sind die Nachteile des Einsatzes von Code Review?
9. Wenn im Code Review Probleme auftreten, inwiefern werden diese analysiert und an andere kommuniziert?
10. Bitte beschreiben Sie, wie Pair Programming in Ihrem Team abläuft!
11. Arbeiten Sie mit bestimmten Kollegen öfter im Paar als mit anderen? Warum?
12. Gibt es andere Paare, die öfter zusammenarbeiten? Wenn ja, welche und warum?
13. Setzen andere Teams Pair Programming genauso ein, oder gibt es Unterschiede? Wenn ja, welche?
14. Erfahren andere Teammitglieder, was im Pair Programming besprochen wurde?
15. Für welche Aufgaben bietet sich Pair Programming an?
16. Was sind die Vorteile des Einsatzes von Pair Programming?
17. Was sind die Nachteile des Einsatzes von Pair Programming?
18. Wenn im Pair Programming Probleme auftreten, inwiefern werden diese analysiert und an andere kommuniziert?

Konkreter Einsatz

1. Bitte beschreiben Sie die letzte Aufgabe, die Sie im Pair Programming bearbeitet haben.

   - Warum wurde im Paar gearbeitet?
   - Was waren die Herausforderungen?
   - War das Pairing erfolgreich?

2. Bitte beschreiben Sie die letzte Aufgabe, bei der Sie Probleme hatten, sie im Paar erfolgreich zu bearbeiten.

   - Warum wurde im Paar gearbeitet?
   - Was waren die Probleme?
   - War das Pairing am Ende erfolgreich?

3. Bitte beschreiben Sie die letzte Änderung im Programmcode, die Sie ins Code-Review-System eingestellt haben und die das Review im ersten Schritt passiert hat.

   - Was waren die Herausforderungen der Änderung?
   - War das Review hilfreich?
   - Wer waren die Reviewer?

4. Bitte beschreiben Sie die letzte Änderung im Programmcode, die Sie ins Code-Review-System eingestellt haben und mehrere Runden Reviews durchlief.

   - Was waren die Herausforderungen der Änderung?
   - Wie viele Runden an Reviews waren nötig?
   - Waren die Reviews hilfreich?
   - Wer waren die Reviewer?

5. Bitte beschreiben Sie die letzte Änderung im Programmcode, die Sie als Reviewer übernommen haben und mehrere Runden Reviews durchlief.

   - Wer hatte die Änderung eingestellt?
   - Was waren die Herausforderungen der Änderung?
   - Wie viele Runden an Reviews waren nötig?

Inwiefern stimmen Sie den folgenden Aussagen zu und warum?

1. In unserem Team weiß jeder, wer in einem bestimmten Bereich Expertise besitzt.
2. Wenn einzelnen Mitgliedern Wissen für eine Aufgabe fehlt, setzen wir auf Pair Programming/Code Review, um die Aufgabe zu erledigen.
3. Spezifisches Wissen wird bei uns oft im Pair Programming/Code Review geteilt.
4. Wir suchen gezielt Feedback von außerhalb unseres Teams.
5. Wir experimentieren mit alternativen Lösungen hauptsächlich im Pair Programming/Code Review.
6. Als Team prüfen wir, was wir aus dem Erreichten lernen können.
7. Als Team können lernen wir mehr durch Code Review als durch Pair Programming.

B.2   Exemplary Coding

Table B.1 Exemplary coding during initial exploration

Interview text	Open codes	Axial codes	Selective codes
"If someone has double-checked it [in peer code review], this gives you a bit of confidence: someone else also thinks you can solve it this way and you have not really screwed up." (Senior Developer D)	Not committing mistakes, less errors in resulting code	Error correction (cons)	Developers use both techniques in order to correct one another's errors collaboratively
"Without it [pair programming] many more errors would slip through." (Senior Developer E)			
"Compared to older code, you realize it gets increasingly similar. [...] And you say, ok, now that I've said 100 times that I'd throw a NullPointerException [...] colleagues start to do it and then they spread the word, and then a third one does it. That's cool!" (Senior Developer F on peer code review)	Repeated interactions, easily readable code, similar coding style across team members	Code intelligibility (cons), continued application (interaction)	As team members repeatedly conduct peer code review, their coding styles become more similar and code becomes intelligible for other team members than the author
"What I have seen so far, the code has gotten much better [through peer code reviews]; more easily readable and better structured." (Agile Method Trainer B)			
"In the end, I set my focus [in peer code review] on clean code. [...] Others watched for typos, my soft spot, others said formatting is important. [...] And of course, there are the functional things you are interested in." (Senior Developer G)	Code focus, variety of perspectives, improved code design	Outcome integrates perspectives (cons), different views and knowledge on same topic (cond), broad participation and acceptance (int)	Authors create better source code after integrating a broad variety of perspectives on the same piece of code
"Also our code design has improved. When I put something there [for review] of which I think it is good, John Doe might say 'Not bad, but try to write it that way then you can test it easier and the design is better' " (Agile Method Trainer B)			
"It is harder if the [pair programming] partner is quiet. [...] I enjoy working with partners who disagree more with me, so that we can discuss and argue, "We should do this way"—"No, that way!" "(Senior Developer H)	Intensity of dispute and interaction, solving unclear problems	Intensive discussion (int), joint solution satisficing (cons), willingness to discuss (int), solution unclear (cond)	Developers conduct pair programming to jointly develop acceptable solutions with their team members based on intensive and critical discussions of alternatives. Problems arise if interaction is not intensive enough
"Questions of design and solution approach are better discussed in pair programming. [...] I think I usually have good ideas but you always miss small nuances. That's what the partner can bring in." (Agile Method Trainer A)			

SD senior developer, *AMT* agile method trainer, *SM* scrum master, *cond* condition, *int* action/interaction, *cons* consequence

Appendix C
Observations and Interviews of In-Depth Case Studies

C.1 Background Meeting with Team Leads

As a first step for each case study, the team lead provided information about the team, its tasks, and the use of collaborative quality assurance techniques in an interview of 35–60 min. These interviews were semi-structured and, for convenience of the interviewees, partly conducted in German based on the following interview guideline. Not all questions were asked in all four interviews. Questions that are not emphasized in boldface were omitted in case of time pressure.

© Springer International Publishing Switzerland 2016
K. Spohrer, *Collaborative Quality Assurance in Information Systems Development*,
Progress in IS, DOI 10.1007/978-3-319-25163-9

ASE PP, PCR CASE STUDIES – BACKGROUND MEETING WITH SCRUM MASTER

What is the team's name? _____

What is the product you develop?

_____

Further information (PDF, wiki, etc.)

____ _____

Which components does the team work on?

_____

_____

_____

_____

ID-Numbers? _____

_____

_____

How many people work in the team?
(Product Owner, Scrum Master, and Developers) _____ members

Since when has the team's composition been stable,
i.e. > 80% same members? _____ months

Major changes in the team set-up in the past? _____

Which type of software do you develop? _____

How many other teams develop at this product? _____

Do you use Scrum in your team (dailies, sprint reviews, roles)? _____

What is the Sprint length? _____

Team cross-functionality ☐ Everyone can pick every backlog item ☐ We have sub-teams.

How interdependent are the development tasks in your team? _____

Do all developers use the same technology stack in the team? _____

More than 80% of the team are located in ...   ☐ Same room   ☐ Same location

                                                  ☐ Same floor   ☐ Same time zone

                                                  ☐ Same building   ☐ Different time zone

Variance in defect messages?   _____

How long is the delivery process, i.e. till you receive customer messages of newly developed code?   _____

Number of active customers?   _____

In which unit is the team?   ☐ Business Suite   ☐ On Demand

                                                  ☐ TIP   ☐ Globl. Services

Which programming language does the team mainly program in?   _____

What were the activities last 2 sprints?   _____ % New coding _____ % Refactoring

                                                  _____ % Extension _____ % Diff. small changes

                                                  _____ % CSN messages _____ % Services

How long is the typical build cycle?   _____ minutes

Which integrations server is used?   _____

Is testing included in the team or is it done externally?   ☐ Team internally   ☐ Team externally

What is the rough ratio of newly developed (last year) code base vs. the legacy code base the team works with?   _____ : _____ (rough estimate, e.g. 1:5)
                                                     new   legacy

Does the team mainly develop for internal or external customers?   ☐   internal   ☐   external

What is the average ratio of completed vs. committed backlog items at the end of a sprint?   _____ : _____ (average)
                                                completed:committed

Do you have any wikis for internal use?   _____

Task Complexity

1. **Arbeitet Ihr als Team an stets ähnlichen Aufgaben?**
2. **Verlangen Eure Aufgaben von Euch oft das Einarbeiten in neue Bereiche?**
3. **Habt Ihr Routine-Aufgaben? Welchen Anteil stellen diese dar?**

Process Feedback

4. **In welchem Umfang bekommst Du Feedback auf Deine Arbeitsweise?**
5. In wie fern erhältst Du Rückmeldung auf die Art und Weise wie Du arbeitest?
6. Gebt Ihr euch gegenseitig Feedback auf die Arbeitsweise?

Outcome Feedback

7. **Erhältst Du von deinen Kollegen Rückmeldung auf Deine abgearbeiteten Backlog Items?**
8. Wie sieht diese Rückmeldung aus?
9. Wann bekommst Du sie?
10. Erhältst Du auch Feedback von außerhalb Deines Teams?

Team Awareness of Feedback

11. Wer (aus dem Team) bekommt mit, wenn Du Feedback erhältst?
12. **Erfährst Du, wenn andere Teammitglieder Feedback über ihrer Arbeitsweise oder ihre Arbeit erhalten?**

Pair Pprogramming

13. **Wie viel Deiner Zeit programmierst Du im Pair Programming?**
14. Gibt es Paare, die öfter zusammenarbeiten? Wenn ja, welche und warum?
15. Kannst Du bitte kurz beschreiben, wie Pair Programming bei Euch im Team abläuft?
16. Gibt es Voraussetzungen, die zwischen den Partnern erfüllt sein müssen?
17. Bei welchen Aufgaben wird Pair programming hauptsächlich eingesetzt?

Code Review

18. **In welchem Umfang setzt das Team Code Review ein?**
19. **Bitte beschreibe kurz, wie Code Review bei Euch im Team abläuft.**
20. **Liest Du auch Reviews, die Du weder gemacht noch veranlasst hast?**
21. **Gibt es Experten, die bei Änderungen in einem bestimmten Bereich mehr als Reviewer dienen?**
22. Für welche Aufgaben bietet sich der Einsatz von Code Review an?
23. Bereitest Du Dich auf Pair Programming oder Code Reviews auf irgendeine Weise vor?

Transactive Memory

24. **Spezialisierung**
    a. **In welchem Bereich würdest Du Dich in Deinem Team als Spezialist bezeichnen?**
    b. **Haben die anderen auch Spezialgebiete? Beispiele?**
25. **Glaubwürdigkeit**
    a. **Was war das letzte Backlog item, das Du gezogen hast, bei dem du nicht sicher warst, ob Du der richtige im Team warst, um es zu bearbeiten?**
26. **Koordination**
    a. **Ordnet Ihr die Backlogitems immer den richtigen Personen zu?**
    b. Arbeitet Ihr als Team Deiner Meinung nach immer effizient und reibungsfrei?

Team Learning Behaviors

27. **Wie teilt Ihr Wissen und Erfahrungen im Team?**
28. **Wenn neue Mitglieder ins Team gekommen sind, wie habt Ihr diesen geholfen, sich schneller zu integrieren?**
29. Nutzt Ihr für Wissenstransfer Pair Programming/Code Reviews?
30. **Probiert Ihr oft neue Ideen und unterschiedliche Lösungsansätze/Methoden aus?**
    a. Eher im Pair Programming oder über Code Review?
31. Analysiert Ihr Fehler, die im Entwicklungsprozess geschehen sind?
    a. Werden Fehler im Team besprochen oder eher allein behoben?
    b. Wenn im Pair Programming Probleme auftreten, werden diese dem Rest des Teams kommuniziert?
32. Würdest Du sagen, Du lernst mehr im PP oder im CR?

Quality

33. **Würdest Du sagen, Euer Team produziert hochwertigen Code bzgl. interner Qualität (Lesbarkeit, Wartbarkeit)?**
34. **Wie siehst Du Eure Ergebnisse hinsichtlich externer Qualität (Kundenzufriedenheit, Funktionalität)?**
35. Würdest Du Euer Produkt und Eure Arbeit als innovativ bezeichnen?

Schluss

Was würde Dir am meisten fehlen, wenn Du kein Pair Programming und kein Code Review mehr hättest?

C.2 Observation Report Sheets

Observation report sheets contained guidelines for note-taking of researchers during the observation of pair programming or peer code review sessions. Each sheet provided sufficient space to take extensive notes regarding each aspect. For reasons of conciseness, space was removed from the following observation report sheets. Different report sheets were used for pair programming and peer code review sessions. Moreover, the report sheets also contained a set of questions that all participants of collaborative quality assurance sessions were asked immediately after task completion. Subsequent to these questions, conversations typically evolved for several minutes in which developers explained specifics of the observed session of collaborative quality assurance and how it differed from their usual application.

Observation Report Pair Programming

Date/Time/Duration: Observer:
Participants: Backlog Item ID:
Team ID: Rotation (times changed)

- Participants Expertise:
- General Activities (discussion first, navigator/driver, rotation style, etc):

  - Feedback given: - from/to
                             - content
                             - frequency
                             - formal/informal

- Knowledge
  Conversion:
- Socialization
- Externalization
- Combination
- Internalization

Transactive Processes: Transactive Memory Structure:

- Related to PP but not part of it:

Questions After Task Completion

Task

- Interdependency: Was/is the solution of this task possible without coordinating with others? Which coordination was required (War/ist die Löösung der Aufgabe ohne Abstimmung mit anderen möglich? Welche Abstimmung war nötig?)
- Complexity: Have you ever solved a similar task before? Was this a routine task? (Hast Du eine ähnliche Aufgabe schon einmal gelöst? War dies eher eine Standardaufgabe?)
- Team Efficacy: Does the result cover the requirements? How sure are you about that? (Deckt das Ergebnis die Anforderungen ab? Wie sicher bist Du?)

Results

- Is the result of high quality? How sure are you about that? (Hat das Ergebnis eine hohe Qualität? Wie sicher bist Du?)
- Is the resulting code easily maintainable? (Wie einfach ist der Code wartbar?)

Pair Programming and Transactive Memory

- Would you say this pair programming session was successful? Why? (Würdest Du sagen, das Pair Programming war erfolgreich? Warum?)
- Why did you do pair programming for this task? (Warum habt Ihr diese Aufgabe im Pair Programming bestritten?)
- Which benefits did you gain from pair programming for this task? Is this different from other pair programming sessions? (Welchen Nutzen hatte Pair Programming für diese Aufgabe? War dies derselbe Nutzen wie in anderen Situationen des Pair Programming?)
- Why did exactly you two pair program together for this task? (Warum habt genau Ihr beiden für diese Aufgabe im Pair gearbeitet?)
- Do you have any particularly relevant knowledge for this task? (Habt Ihr besonders relevantes Wissen für diese Aufgabe?)

Observation Report Peer Code Review

Date/Time/Duration: Observer:
Participant: Backlog Item ID:
Team ID: Change Size:
Activity:

- Author submits
- Reviewer reviews

- Author revises
- Others read change/reviews

- Participants Expertise:
- General Activities (read all changes/reviews first, make in-line comments, etc):

- Feedback given:
  - from/to
  - content
  - frequency
  - formal/informal

- Knowledge
  Conversion:
  - Socialization
  - Externalization
  - Combination
  - Internalization

- Offline
  communication:
  - participants
  - contents

Questions After Task Completion

Task

- Interdependency: Was/is the solution of this task possible without coordinating with others? Which coordination was required (War/ist die Lösung der Aufgabe ohne Abstimmung mit anderen möglich? Welche Abstimmung war nötig?)
- Complexity: Have you ever solved a similar task before? Was this a routine task? (Hast Du eine ähnliche Aufgabe schon einmal gelöst? War dies eher eine Standardaufgabe?)
- Team Efficacy: Does the result cover the requirements? How sure are you about that? (Deckt das Ergebnis die Anforderungen ab? Wie sicher bist Du?)

Results

- Is the result of high quality? How sure are you about that? (Hat das Ergebnis eine hohe Qualität? Wie sicher bist Du?)
- Is the resulting code easily maintainable? (Wie einfach ist der Code wartbar?)

Peer Code Review and Transactive Memory

- Would you say this peer code review was successful? Why? (Würdest Du sagen, das Peer Code Review war erfolgreich? Warum?)
- Why did you do peer code review for this task? (Warum wurde für diese Aufgabe ein Peer Code Review durchgeführt?)
- Which benefits did you gain from a peer code review for this task? Is this different from other peer code reviews? (Welchen Nutzen hatte Peer Code Review für diese Aufgabe? War dies derselbe Nutzen wie in anderen Situationen des Peer Code Review?)
- Author: Why did you invite one/multiple particular reviewers? Who is to read the code change? (Warum hast Du einen/mehrere bestimmte Personen als Reviewer eingeladen, wer liest den Code Change?)
- Reviewer: Why did you receive this review request? Why did you accept? (Warum hast Du das Review erhalten, warum angenommen?)
- Reviewer: Why did you come to your decision about the code (accept or revise)? (Warum hast Du diese Entscheidung getroffen?)
- Do you have any particularly relevant knowledge for this task? (Hast Du besonders relevantes Wissen für diese Aufgabe?)

Appendix D
Questionnaire-Based Survey

D.1 Survey Items and Measurement Model

This section first lists the questionnaire items used in the survey study in Table D.1. Subsequently, it outlines supplemental data for the examination of measurement model validity. Indicator loadings are represented both in unrotated and rotated ways together with indicator weights in Tables D.2, D.3, and D.4. Lastly, Table D.5 provides the results of post-hoc regression analyses with clustered error terms that served to establish the robustness of results.

© Springer International Publishing Switzerland 2016
K. Spohrer, *Collaborative Quality Assurance in Information Systems Development*,
Progress in IS, DOI 10.1007/978-3-319-25163-9

Table D.1 Items in questionnaire

Variable	ID	Indicator	Role	Scale	Adapted from
Pair programming	PP1	How much of your code do you develop with a programming partner?	D	10 point percent	Developed
	PP2	How much of your coding time do you work with a programming partner?			
	PP3	With how many of your team members do you pair program regularly?			
Peer code review	PCR1	(You and colleague A:) We frequently review each other's code	D	7 point Likert	Developed
	PCR2	(You and colleague B:) We frequently review each other's code			
	PCR3	(You and colleague C:) We frequently review each other's code			
Offline reviews	PCROff	If the team also does offline code reviews, how many reviews are not documented in the system at all?	TL	% of reviews	Developed
PCR system use	PCRSys	Does the team use a peer code review system? If so, which one?	TL	Git Gerrit, review board, other	Developed
Team relationship quality	Rel1	The people on this team get on my nerves. (rev)	D	7 point Likert	Guinan et al. (1998)
	Rel2	There is a lot of unpleasantness among people on our team. (rev)			
	Rel3	Dealing with the members of this team often leaves me feeling irritated and frustrated. (rev)			
	Rel4	Often, I am disappointed with the other members of this team. (rev)			
TMS: Coordination	coord1	Our team works together in a well-coordinated fashion			
	coord2	We accomplish our tasks smoothly and efficiently			
	coord3[a]	Our team has very few misunderstandings about what to do			
	coord4	There is often confusion in our team about how we will accomplish our tasks. (rev)	D	7 point Likert	Lewis (2003)
TMS: Credibility	cred1	I am comfortable accepting work suggestions from other team members			
	cred2	I am confident relying on the information that other team members bring into discussions			
	cred3[a]	I do not have much faith in other members expertise. (rev)			
	cred4	I trust that other members' task-related knowledge is credible			

Construct		Item		Scale	Source
TMS: Specialization	spec1	Each member of my team has special expertise			
	spec2[a]	I know which team members have expertise in specific areas			
	spec3	Different team members are responsible for expertise in different areas			
	spec4	The expertise of several different team members is needed to complete our deliverables			
Modularity	Mod1	The team's software has a highly modular architecture	PM	7 point Likert	Lau et al. (2007, 2009)
	Mod2	The team's software can be decomposed into separate, independent functional sub-units			
	Mod3	The team can change key component(s) of its software without redesigning others			
	Mod4	From a technical point of view, large parts of the team's software could be reused in other products			
External software quality	extq4	The capabilities of the software meet the needs of the team's customers (COMPANY internal or external)	PM	10 point frequency	Developed
	extq5	Overall, the team's software contributes to COMPANY's reputation as a high quality software company			
	extq6	The team delivers software that fully covers the requested functionality			
	extq7	The software the team delivers meets technical requirements			
Internal software quality	intq1	The team complies with done criteria	PM	10 point frequency	Developed
	intq2[a]	The software code is reusable			
	intq3	The software code is maintainable			
	intq4[a]	The software code is easily testable			
	intq5	The software code is clean (e.g., naming, structure, readability, formatting)			

(continued)

Table D.1 (continued)

Variable	ID	Indicator	Role	Scale	Adapted from
Attrition	Outflow	How many people have left the team during the last 12 months?	TL	Number	Developed
Team Size	tsize	How many people work on the team?	TL	Number	Developed
Task novelty	Novel1	Concerning the last 6 months, the team faced tasks for which there was a clearly known way how to solve them. (rev)	TL	7 point Likert	Nidumolu (1995)
	Novel2	Concerning the last 6 months, the team faced tasks for which the team's preexisting knowledge was of great help to solve them. (rev)			
	Novel3	Concerning the last 6 months, the team faced tasks for which the team's preexisting work procedures and practices could be relied upon to solve them. (rev)			
Task diversity	Div1	The team works on a broad spectrum of different tasks (new dev., maintenance, documentations, consulting others)	PM	7 point Likert	Developed based on Nidumolu (1995)
	Div2	The team faces very heterogeneous requirements			
	Div3	The team has to be familiar with details from many different software components (e.g., libraries, APIs)			
	Div4	The team works on various software layers in the technology stack (e.g., persistence, application logic, UI)			
Requirements volatility	Vol1	The software requirements the team works on were changing quite a bit during the last 3 months	PM	7 point Likert	Maruping et al. (2009a), Nidumolu (1995)
	Vol2	The software requirements the team works on will change quite a bit in the future			
	Vol3	The software requirements the team works on are quite different from those originally identified			

Continuous integration	CI1	Developers integrate new or modified code into our existing code base on a daily basis	TL	7 point Likert	Maruping et al. (2009a)
	CI2	We combine new code with existing code on a daily basis			
	CI3[a]	Our team has dedicated "integration phases" during which we integrate new or modified code of different developers. (rev)			
Refactoring	Ref1	How much of your development time do you roughly spend simplifying existing code without changing its functionality?	D	7 point Likert	Maruping et al. (2009a)
	Ref2	How much of your development time do you roughly spend identifying and eliminating redundancies in the software code?			
	Ref3	How much of your development time do you roughly spend improving the code quality?			
Code ownership	Own1	Anyone on this team is allowed to change any part of existing code at any time	TL	7 point Likert	Maruping et al. (2009a)
	Own2	Members of this team feel comfortable changing any part of the existing code at any time			
	Own3	If anyone wants to change a piece of code, they need the permission of the individual(s) that coded it. (rev)			

Notes: Respondent roles, *D* developer, *TL* team lead, *PM* product manager, *rev* reverse coded

[a]Removed due to low loading or high cross-loadings

7 point Likert: strongly disagree to strongly agree

10 point percent: 0–10 % to 90–100 %

10 point frequency: never (10 % of occurrences) – always (100 % of occurrences)

Table D.2 Pattern matrix: loadings and cross-loadings including 2nd order constructs

	pp	pcr	rel	mod	ci	ownshp	ref	tms	qual	tsize	instab	vol	div	nov	R/F	SE
PP1	**0.941**	−0.012	−0.028	−0.03	−0.01	−0.002	−0.009	0.03	0.014	0.106	0.021	−0.035	0.024	0.01	R	0.036
PP2	**0.931**	0.002	−0.039	0.053	−0.021	0.035	0.011	0	−0.057	0.065	0.02	0.007	0.043	0.029	R	0.04
PP3	**0.809**	0.012	0.077	−0.026	0.036	−0.037	−0.002	−0.035	0.049	−0.198	−0.047	0.032	−0.077	−0.045	R	0.047
PCR1	−0.024	**0.951**	0.035	−0.024	−0.025	−0.008	0.033	−0.051	0.004	−0.022	−0.014	−0.013	−0.022	0.021	R	0.054
PCR2	0.016	**0.952**	−0.037	0.016	0.015	0.017	−0.004	0.068	0.021	0	0.035	−0.028	−0.001	−0.011	R	0.051
PCR3	0.008	**0.954**	0.002	0.007	0.01	−0.009	−0.029	−0.017	−0.025	0.022	−0.021	0.041	0.023	−0.01	R	0.05
Rel1	0.039	−0.038	**0.882**	−0.037	−0.026	0.041	0.005	−0.035	−0.011	0.064	0.021	−0.016	0.041	−0.01	R	0.051
Rel2	−0.032	0.003	**0.9**	−0.015	−0.026	−0.024	0.016	0.009	0.09	−0.028	0.012	−0.016	−0.006	0.014	R	0.053
Rel3	−0.003	0.007	**0.925**	0.035	0.019	−0.016	−0.027	−0.026	−0.014	−0.008	−0.042	0.009	−0.048	−0.018	R	0.053
Rel4	−0.003	0.026	**0.917**	0.016	0.032	0.001	0.007	0.051	−0.063	−0.026	0.011	0.022	0.015	0.014	R	0.05
Mod1	−0.058	0.028	0.041	**0.845**	0.048	−0.091	−0.017	0.027	−0.03	−0.046	0.18	0.056	−0.034	0.05	R	0.03
Mod2	−0.027	0.021	−0.002	**0.884**	0.041	−0.023	0.011	0.028	0.088	−0.001	−0.112	0.18	−0.095	0.107	R	0.045
Mod3	0.05	−0.006	0.057	**0.861**	−0.116	0.024	−0.025	−0.036	0.032	0.098	−0.066	−0.2	0.079	−0.198	R	0.05
Mod4	0.038	−0.046	−0.101	**0.806**	0.029	0.095	0.032	−0.02	−0.099	−0.055	0.004	−0.043	0.056	0.04	R	0.035
CI1	−0.019	−0.032	−0.001	0.07	**0.979**	−0.003	0.006	−0.008	−0.027	0.041	0.014	−0.017	0.004	−0.029	R	0.057
CI2	0.019	0.032	0.001	−0.07	**0.979**	0.003	−0.006	0.008	0.027	−0.041	−0.014	0.017	−0.004	0.029	R	0.058
Own1	0.037	−0.033	−0.035	0.032	0.131	**0.888**	0.001	0.013	−0.057	−0.032	0.134	−0.082	0.035	0.094	R	0.039
Own2	−0.039	−0.109	0.014	−0.116	0.003	**0.801**	−0.016	0.026	0.224	0.085	−0.12	−0.009	−0.19	−0.021	R	0.035
Own3	−0.003	0.149	0.025	0.082	−0.151	**0.784**	0.014	−0.041	−0.163	−0.051	−0.03	0.102	0.154	−0.084	R	0.067
Ref1	0.002	0.002	−0.046	−0.001	0.005	0.046	**0.88**	0.006	0.026	0.022	0.102	−0.017	0.009	−0.037	R	0.054
Ref2	0.016	−0.017	−0.001	0.003	−0.034	−0.04	**0.879**	−0.071	0.038	−0.01	−0.046	0.026	−0.03	−0.028	R	0.07
Ref3	−0.018	0.015	0.048	−0.002	0.03	−0.007	**0.86**	0.066	−0.065	−0.011	−0.057	−0.009	0.021	0.066	R	0.046

															Type	SE
spec	−0.158	−0.082	−0.425	0.021	0.01	−0.057	0.033	**0.538**	−0.147	0.12	0.029	0.012	0.073	−0.017	F	0.099
cred	0.045	0.034	−0.005	0.016	−0.04	0.118	−0.021	**0.834**	−0.138	−0.042	−0.004	−0.085	0.076	0.084	F	0.077
coord	0.063	0.021	0.306	−0.033	0.037	−0.089	0	**0.761**	0.256	−0.038	−0.016	0.085	−0.135	−0.08	F	0.075
intq	0.027	0.028	0.038	−0.01	0.045	−0.098	−0.032	−0.073	**0.914**	0.001	−0.06	0.141	−0.153	−0.079	R	0.067
extq	−0.027	−0.028	−0.038	0.01	−0.045	0.098	0.032	0.073	**0.914**	−0.001	0.06	−0.141	0.153	0.079	R	0.052
Vol1	0.044	0.004	−0.005	0.056	−0.018	−0.008	0.008	0.029	0.026	0.048	0.045	**0.922**	0.013	−0.07	R	0.028
Vol2	−0.137	−0.036	0.009	0.087	0.042	0.049	0.037	−0.04	−0.016	0.082	0.019	**0.807**	−0.125	−0.015	R	0.045
Vol3	0.082	0.029	−0.002	−0.143	−0.021	−0.038	−0.044	0.007	−0.013	−0.13	−0.068	**0.852**	0.105	0.09	R	0.026
Div1	−0.076	0.086	0.138	−0.102	−0.073	−0.086	0.037	−0.095	0.082	0.276	0.009	−0.336	**0.654**	−0.087	R	0.076
Div2	−0.026	−0.086	0.019	0.078	0.028	0.008	0.003	−0.053	0.162	0.015	−0.093	0.067	**0.904**	0.013	R	0.039
Div3	0.031	−0.016	−0.06	0.041	0.076	−0.022	0.001	−0.007	−0.07	−0.157	0.004	0.161	**0.836**	0.032	R	0.073
Div4	0.062	0.046	−0.074	−0.051	−0.053	0.088	−0.036	0.151	−0.184	−0.082	0.097	0.033	**0.768**	0.024	R	0.093
Novel1	0.024	0.108	−0.017	0.061	−0.045	−0.032	−0.069	−0.017	−0.237	−0.026	−0.107	−0.07	−0.056	**0.826**	R	0.029
Novel2	−0.02	−0.016	0.005	−0.042	0.088	−0.06	0.038	−0.012	0.086	−0.128	−0.099	0.141	−0.092	**0.91**	R	0.04
Novel3	−0.002	−0.092	0.012	−0.015	−0.054	0.1	0.029	0.031	0.146	0.172	0.222	−0.087	0.161	**0.804**	R	0.054

Notes: Type R reflective, *F* formative; Loadings are unrotated and cross-loadings are oblique-rotated. Loadings greater than 0.5 in are in boldface Standard errors (SEs) are for loadings. All indicators load significantly ($p < 0.001$) on their respective constructs

Table D.3 Indicator weights including 2nd order constructs

	pp	pcr	rel	mod	ci	ownshp	ref	tms	qual	tsize	instab	vol	div	com	SE	VIF	ES
PP1	0.391	0	0	0	0	0	0	0	0	0	0	0	0	0	0.017	4.807	0.368
PP2	0.387	0	0	0	0	0	0	0	0	0	0	0	0	0	0.016	4.567	0.36
PP3	0.336	0	0	0	0	0	0	0	0	0	0	0	0	0	0.021	1.657	0.272
pcr1	0	0.35	0	0	0	0	0	0	0	0	0	0	0	0	0.021	4.792	0.333
pcr2	0	0.35	0	0	0	0	0	0	0	0	0	0	0	0	0.021	4.862	0.333
pcr3	0	0.351	0	0	0	0	0	0	0	0	0	0	0	0	0.021	5.03	0.334
Rel1	0	0	0.269	0	0	0	0	0	0	0	0	0	0	0	0.017	2.704	0.237
Rel2	0	0	0.274	0	0	0	0	0	0	0	0	0	0	0	0.016	3.104	0.247
Rel3	0	0	0.282	0	0	0	0	0	0	0	0	0	0	0	0.017	3.935	0.261
Rel4	0	0	0.279	0	0	0	0	0	0	0	0	0	0	0	0.018	3.619	0.256
Mod1	0	0	0	0.293	0	0	0	0	0	0	0	0	0	0	0.015	2.235	0.247
Mod2	0	0	0	0.306	0	0	0	0	0	0	0	0	0	0	0.015	2.643	0.271
Mod3	0	0	0	0.298	0	0	0	0	0	0	0	0	0	0	0.013	2.248	0.257
Mod4	0	0	0	0.279	0	0	0	0	0	0	0	0	0	0	0.015	1.846	0.225
CI1	0	0	0	0	0.511	0	0	0	0	0	0	0	0	0	0.031	6.228	0.5
CI2	0	0	0	0	0.511	0	0	0	0	0	0	0	0	0	0.031	6.228	0.5
Own1	0	0	0	0	0	0.434	0	0	0	0	0	0	0	0	0.022	1.972	0.385
Own2	0	0	0	0	0	0.392	0	0	0	0	0	0	0	0	0.028	1.565	0.314
Own3	0	0	0	0	0	0.384	0	0	0	0	0	0	0	0	0.023	1.493	0.301
Ref1	0	0	0	0	0	0	0.385	0	0	0	0	0	0	0	0.026	2.097	0.339
Ref2	0	0	0	0	0	0	0.384	0	0	0	0	0	0	0	0.023	2.084	0.338
Ref3	0	0	0	0	0	0	0.376	0	0	0	0	0	0	0	0.027	1.9	0.323

																SE	VIF	ES
spec (F)	0	0	0	0	0	0	0	0	0.344	0	0	0	0	0	0	0.067	1.07	0.185
cred (F)	0	0	0	0	0	0	0	0	0.533	0	0	0	0	0	0	0.037	1.305	0.445
coord (F)	0	0	0	0	0	0	0	0	0.486	0	0	0	0	0	0	0.056	1.237	0.37
intq	0	0	0	0	0	0	0	0	0	0.547	0	0	0	0	0	0.031	1.813	0.5
extq	0	0	0	0	0	0	0	0	0	0.547	0	0	0	0	0	0.041	1.813	0.5
TeamSize	0	0	0	0	0	0	0	0	0	0	1	0	0	0	0	0.034	0	1
instab	0	0	0	0	0	0	0	0	0	0	0	1	0	0	0	0.07	0	1
Vol1	0	0	0	0	0	0	0	0	0	0	0	0	0.414	0	0	0.015	2.741	0.382
Vol2	0	0	0	0	0	0	0	0	0	0	0	0	0.363	0	0	0.015	1.69	0.293
Vol3	0	0	0	0	0	0	0	0	0	0	0	0	0.383	0	0	0.018	2.083	0.326
Div1	0	0	0	0	0	0	0	0	0	0	0	0	0	0.258	0	0.041	1.89-	0.169
Div2	0	0	0	0	0	0	0	0	0	0	0	0	0	0.357	0	0.027	3.256	0.323
Div3	0	0	0	0	0	0	0	0	0	0	0	0	0	0.33	0	0.02	2.549	0.276
Div4	0	0	0	0	0	0	0	0	0	0	0	0	0	0.303	0	0.026	1.761	0.232
Novel1	0	0	0	0	0	0	0	0	0	0	0	0	0	0	0.383	0.024	1.789	0.316
Novel2	0	0	0	0	0	0	0	0	0	0	0	0	0	0	0.422	0.018	2.383	0.384
Novel3	0	0	0	0	0	0	0	0	0	0	0	0	0	0	0.373	0.017	1.647	0.3

Notes: F formative indicators, all others reflective, *VIF* indicator variance inflation factor, *SE* standard error, *ES* indicator effect size
All weights significant on their construct ($p < 0.001$); *P* values < 0.05 and VIFs < 2.5 are desirable for formative indicators

Table D.4 Structure matrix: unrotated loadings and cross-loadings of first order model

	pp	pcr	rel	mod	ci	ownshp	ref	cred	intq	vol	div	nov	spec	coord	extq
PP1	**0.941**	0.284	0.03	0.081	0.021	0.022	0.188	0.074	0.153	0.078	-0.112	0.024	-0.099	0.158	0.037
PP2	**0.931**	0.288	0	0.142	0.002	0.046	0.196	0.025	0.111	0.1	-0.111	0.053	-0.096	0.112	0.009
PP3	**0.809**	0.316	0.104	0.095	0.049	0.06	0.161	0.099	0.184	0.045	-0.182	-0.022	-0.131	0.172	0.095
PCR1	0.298	**0.951**	0.121	0.031	0.103	0.309	0.1	0.021	0.225	-0.035	-0.351	0.011	-0.159	0.164	0.097
PCR2	0.324	**0.952**	0.12	0.055	0.139	0.323	0.087	0.08	0.238	-0.047	-0.342	-0.036	-0.102	0.159	0.11
PCR3	0.316	**0.954**	0.104	0.033	0.126	0.306	0.06	0.04	0.217	0.008	-0.309	0.004	-0.152	0.163	0.074
Rel1	0.054	0.092	**0.882**	-0.047	-0.069	0.208	0.011	0.389	0.193	0.072	-0.04	-0.029	0.14	**0.522**	0.195
Rel2	0.021	0.104	**0.9**	0.005	-0.079	0.174	0.015	0.459	0.271	0.048	-0.074	-0.016	0.11	**0.562**	0.282
Rel3	0.05	0.132	**0.925**	0.041	-0.045	0.209	-0.01	0.438	0.254	0.05	-0.129	-0.022	0.094	**0.585**	0.236
Rel4	0.044	0.11	**0.917**	-0.013	-0.039	0.202	0.02	**0.504**	0.214	0.086	-0.074	-0.013	0.19	**0.571**	0.195
Mod1	0.064	0.012	0.013	**0.845**	-0.072	-0.038	-0.007	-0.011	0.266	-0.05	-0.152	0.131	-0.059	0.112	0.23
Mod2	0.139	0.114	0.052	**0.884**	-0.075	0.022	0.01	0.029	0.302	0.034	-0.22	0.225	-0.031	0.092	0.302
Mod3	0.095	0.018	0.036	**0.861**	-0.132	0.041	0.026	0.007	0.283	-0.295	-0.104	-0.119	-0.072	0.052	0.303
Mod4	0.103	-0.007	-0.122	**0.806**	-0.042	0.033	0.053	-0.069	0.197	-0.14	-0.109	0.091	-0.097	-0.052	0.183
CI1	-0.002	0.084	-0.086	-0.047	**0.979**	0.085	0.03	-0.052	0.015	-0.17	0.013	-0.137	0.025	-0.021	-0.046
CI2	0.052	0.169	-0.04	-0.14	**0.979**	0.109	0.032	-0.011	0.037	-0.131	-0.001	-0.097	-0.012	0.031	-0.004
Own1	0.053	0.282	0.142	0.022	0.203	**0.888**	0.101	0.068	0.02	-0.026	-0.26	-0.17	-0.082	0.037	0.059
Own2	0.004	0.248	0.242	0	0.075	**0.801**	0.064	0.139	0.145	0.01	-0.352	-0.187	-0.059	0.183	0.151
Own3	0.058	0.283	0.163	0.019	-0.048	**0.784**	0.092	0.083	-0.009	0.118	-0.164	-0.208	-0.109	0.057	-0.022
Ref1	0.175	0.09	-0.016	0.013	0.043	0.136	**0.88**	0.043	0.063	-0.025	-0.043	-0.183	-0.026	0.047	0.105
Ref2	0.186	0.05	-0.026	0.048	-0.007	0.058	**0.879**	-0.021	0.043	-0.025	-0.037	-0.127	-0.006	0.052	0.079
Ref3	0.172	0.087	0.07	-0.001	0.047	0.08	**0.86**	0.097	0.016	-0.008	-0.023	-0.064	0.059	0.1	0.073
cred1	-0.003	-0.018	0.279	0.029	-0.028	0.111	0.064	**0.745**	-0.019	-0.014	-0.014	0.02	0.204	0.235	0.043
cred2	0.124	0.069	0.442	-0.034	0.018	0.118	0.022	**0.84**	0.09	0.055	-0.039	-0.037	0.216	0.386	0.147
cred4	0.038	0.06	0.431	-0.018	-0.069	0.04	0.02	**0.752**	0.096	0.049	-0.057	0.01	0.177	0.399	0.142

intq1	0.143	0.157	0.18	0.199	−0.013	−0.05	0.061	0.031	**0.797**	−0.136	−0.01	−0.046	−0.144	0.201	**0.576**
intq3	0.128	0.171	0.198	0.372	−0.013	0.035	0.014	0.066	**0.926**	−0.033	−0.095	−0.076	−0.034	0.305	**0.586**
intq5	0.149	0.281	0.278	0.2	0.097	0.175	0.048	0.089	**0.808**	0.128	−0.261	−0.01	−0.06	0.351	**0.538**
Vol1	0.129	−0.003	0.095	−0.062	−0.15	0.055	0.016	0.049	0.052	**0.922**	0.064	0.112	0.095	0.079	−0.065
Vol2	−0.027	−0.038	0.036	−0.048	−0.104	0.105	−0.008	0.006	−0.044	**0.807**	−0.022	0.136	0.035	0.044	−0.183
Vol3	0.106	−0.028	0.048	−0.231	−0.141	−0.06	−0.068	0.046	−0.057	**0.852**	0.178	0.234	0.05	0.021	−0.211
Div1	−0.169	−0.197	−0.003	−0.167	0.014	−0.227	0.001	−0.037	−0.036	−0.186	**0.654**	−0.087	0.086	−0.084	0.131
Div2	−0.138	−0.354	−0.058	−0.033	0.006	−0.285	−0.042	−0.051	−0.035	0.105	**0.904**	0.048	0.073	−0.105	0.162
Div3	−0.084	−0.299	−0.143	−0.146	0.034	−0.3	−0.037	−0.077	−0.173	0.177	**0.836**	0.046	0.049	−0.195	−0.007
Div4	−0.089	−0.247	−0.063	−0.233	−0.037	−0.179	−0.042	0.02	−0.212	0.128	**0.767**	−0.012	0.113	−0.128	−0.075
Novel1	0.052	0.075	−0.103	0.084	−0.112	−0.191	−0.188	−0.03	−0.186	0.085	−0.072	**0.826**	−0.045	−0.179	−0.217
Novel2	0.039	0.014	0.005	0.077	−0.053	−0.214	−0.094	−0.009	0.052	0.233	−0.042	**0.91**	−0.027	−0.016	−0.004
Novel3	−0.036	−0.113	0.041	0.087	−0.145	−0.169	−0.084	0.028	−0.013	0.145	0.137	**0.804**	−0.009	−0.027	0.158
spec1	−0.089	−0.108	0.16	0.004	0.011	−0.069	0.002	0.258	−0.056	−0.016	0.052	0.018	**0.784**	0.121	−0.015
spec3	−0.061	−0.103	0.099	−0.074	0.011	−0.095	0.002	0.165	−0.078	0.124	0.099	−0.038	**0.836**	0.092	−0.064
spec4	−0.143	−0.144	0.058	−0.111	−0.004	−0.083	0.02	0.208	−0.087	0.063	0.091	−0.056	**0.842**	0.08	−0.017
coord1	0.136	0.156	**0.576**	0.006	−0.002	0.09	0.045	0.389	0.282	0.073	−0.141	−0.086	0.148	**0.87**	0.23
coord2	0.168	0.128	**0.512**	0.074	−0.03	0.06	0.105	0.367	0.342	0.05	−0.12	−0.041	0.101	**0.88**	0.29
coord4	0.11	0.152	0.491	0.08	0.049	0.134	0.042	0.363	0.237	0.021	−0.156	−0.092	0.05	**0.802**	0.25
extq4	0.05	0.144	0.249	0.265	0.038	0.07	0.081	0.115	**0.577**	−0.274	−0.058	−0.09	−0.021	0.296	**0.899**
extq5	0.086	0.125	0.261	0.251	−0.078	0.108	0.081	0.136	**0.602**	−0.07	0.086	−0.015	−0.073	0.279	**0.915**
extq6	0.028	0.115	0.176	0.131	0.019	0.024	0.109	0.088	**0.599**	−0.179	0.113	−0.078	−0.065	0.223	**0.894**
extq7	0.008	−0.049	0.197	0.431	−0.07	0.067	0.076	0.171	**0.588**	−0.088	0.097	0.102	0.026	0.268	**0.82**

Note: Loadings and cross-loadings are unrotated. Loadings greater than 0.5 in boldface

D.2   Post-Hoc Survey Analysis

Table D.5 Regression with error terms clustered by team

VARIABLES	(1) tms	(2) mod	(3) qual
mod			0.28***
			(0.10)
pcr			0.16**
			(0.08)
tms			0.18***
			(0.06)
modtms			−0.27***
			(0.06)
pcrtms			−0.13**
			(0.06)
ci			0.00
			(0.08)
ownshp			−0.01
			(0.11)
ref			0.02
			(0.04)
vol			**−0.06**
			(0.09)
pp	0.05	**0.12**	
	(0.04)	**(0.08)**	
rel	0.60***		
	(0.06)		
relpp	−0.16***		
	(0.05)		
div	−0.02		
	(0.04)		
novel	**−0.07**		
	(0.04)		
tsize	0.02		
	(0.05)		
instab	−0.04		
	(0.04)		
Constant	0.00	0.00	−0.00
	(0.04)	(0.11)	(0.09)
Observations	452	452	452
R-squared	0.40	0.01	0.27
Adjusted R-sq	0.39	0.01	0.26
F test	19.73	2.35	3.98
Prob > F	0.00	0.13	0.00

Robust standard errors in parentheses
Deviations from unclustered results in boldface
$*p < 0.1$; $**p < 0.05$; $***p < 0.01$

Bibliography

Aaltonen, A., & Tempini, N. (2014). Everything counts in large amounts: A critical realist case study on data-based production. *Journal of Information Technology, 29*(1), 97–110.

Ackroyd, S., & Fleetwood, S. (Eds.). (2000). *Realist perspectives on management and organisations*. Ontological explorations. London: Routledge.

Ågerfalk, P. J. (2013). Embracing diversity through mixed methods research. *European Journal of Information Systems, 22*(3), 251–256.

Aguirre-Urreta, M., & Marakas, G. (2013). Partial least squares and models with formatively specified endogenous constructs: A cautionary note. *Information Systems Research, 25*(4), 761–778.

Akgün, A., Byrne, J., & Keskin, H. (2005). Knowledge networks in new product development projects: A transactive memory perspective. *Information & Management, 42*(8), 1105–1120.

Akgün, A., Byrne, J., Keskin, H., & Lynn, G. (2006). Transactive memory system in new product development teams. *IEEE Transactions on Engineering Management, 53*(1), 95–111.

Alavi, M., & Leidner, D. (2001). Knowledge management and knowledge management systems: Conceptual foundations and research issues. *MIS Quarterly, 25*(1), 107–136.

Ambrose, P. J., & Chiravuri, A. (2010). A socio-cognitive interpretation of the potential effects of downsizing on software quality performance. *Information Systems Journal, 20*(3), 239–265.

Archer, M., Bhaskar, R., Collier, A., Lawson, T., & Norrie, A. (Eds.). (1998). *Critical realism: Essential readings*. London: Routledge.

Archer, M. S. (1995). *Realist social theory: The morphogenetic approach*. Cambridge: Cambridge University Press.

Archer, M. S. (1998). Realism and morphogenesis. In M. Archer, R. Bhaskar, A. Collier, T. Lawson, & A. Norrie (Eds.), *Critical realism: Essential readings* (pp. 356–382). London: Routledge.

Archer, M. S. (2010). Routine, reflexivity, and realism. *Sociological Theory, 28*(3), 272–303.

Argote, L., Beckman, S. L., & Epple, D. (1990). The persistence and transfer of learning in industrial settings. *Management Science, 36*(2), 140–154.

Arisholm, E., Gallis, H., Dyba, T., & Sjoberg, D. I. (2007). Evaluating pair programming with respect to system complexity and programmer expertise. *IEEE Transactions on Software Engineering, 33*(2), 65–86.

Austin, J. R. (2003). Transactive memory in organizational groups: The effects of content, consensus, specialization, and accuracy on group performance. *Journal of Applied Psychology, 88*(5), 866–878.

Avgerou, C. (2013). Social mechanisms for causal explanation in social theory based IS research. *Journal of the Association for Information Systems, 14*(8), 80–94.

© Springer International Publishing Switzerland 2016

K. Spohrer, *Collaborative Quality Assurance in Information Systems Development*,
Progress in IS, DOI 10.1007/978-3-319-25163-9

Avison, D., & Fitzgerald, G. (2006). *Information systems development: Methodologies, techniques and tools* (4th ed.). Maidenhaed: McGraw-Hill Higher Education.

Bacchelli, A., & Bird, C. (2013). Expectations, outcomes, and challenges of modern code review. In *Proceedings of the International Conference on Software Engineering*, San Francisco, CA, USA (pp. 712–721).

Bacharach, S. B. (1989). Organizational theories: Some criteria for evaluation. *Academy of Management Review, 14*(4), 496–515.

Bahli, B. (2005). The role of knowledge creation in adopting extreme programming model: An empirical study. In *ITI 3rd International Conference on Information and Communications Technology* (pp. 75–87).

Balci, B., Rosenkranz, C., & Schuhen, S. (2014). Identification of different affordances of information technology systems: An empirical study. In *Proceedings of the European Conference on Information Systems*, Tel Aviv, Israel.

Baldwin, C. Y., & Clark, K. B. (2006). The architecture of participation: Does code architecture mitigate free riding in the open source development model? *Management Science, 52*(7), 1116–1127.

Balijepally, V., Mahapatra, R., Nerur, S., & Price, K. H. (2009). Are two heads better than one for software development? The productivity paradox of pair programming. *MIS Quarterly, 33*(1), 91–118.

Balzert, H. (2009). *Lehrbuch der softwaretechnik: Basiskonzepte und requirements engineering* (3rd ed.). Heidelberg: Spektrum Akademischer Verlag.

Beck, K. (2000). *Extreme programming explained: Embrace change*. The XP series. Boston: Addison-Wesley Professional.

Begel, A., & Nagappan, N. (2008). Pair programming: What's in it for me? In *Proceedings of the Second ACM-IEEE International Symposium on Empirical Software Engineering and Measurement* (pp. 120–128), New York.

Beller, M., Bacchelli, A., Zaidman, A., & Juergens, E. (2014). Modern code reviews in open-source projects: Which problems do they fix? In *Proceedings of the 11th Working Conference on Mining Software Repositories* (pp. 202–211).

Bellini, E., Canfora, G., García, F., Piattini, M., & Visaggio, C. A. (2005). Pair designing as practice for enforcing and diffusing design knowledge. *Journal of Software Maintenance and Evolution: Research and Practice, 17*(6), 401–423.

Bernhard, E., Recker, J., & Burton-Jones, A. (2013). Understanding the actualization of affordances: A study in the process modeling context. In *Proceedings of the International Conference on Information Systems*, Milano, Italy.

Bernhart, M., Mauczka, A., & Grechenig, T. (2010). Adopting code reviews for Agile software development. In *Agile Conference, AGILE 2010* (pp. 44–47), Orlando, Florida, USA.

Bettenburg, N., Hassan, A., Adams, B., & German, D. (2013). Management of community contributions. *Empirical Software Engineering, 20*, 252–289.

Bhaskar, R. (1998a). *Possibility of naturalism*. London: Routledge.

Bhaskar, R. (1998b). The logic of scientific discovery. In M. Archer, R. Bhaskar, A. Collier, T. Lawson, & A. Norrie (Eds.), *Critical realism: Essential readings* (pp. 48–103). London: Routledge.

Bjørnson, F. O., & Dingsøyr, T. (2008). Knowledge management in software engineering: A systematic review of studied concepts, findings and research methods used. *Information and Software Technology, 50*(11), 1055–1068.

Bliese, P. D. (2000). Within-group agreement, non-independence, and reliability: Implications for data aggregation and analysis. In K. J. Klein & S. W. J. Kozlowski (Eds.), *Multilevel theory, research, and methods in organizations: Foundations, extensions, and new direction* (pp. 349–381). San Francisco: Jossey-Bass.

Boehm, B. W., Brown, J. R., & Kaspar, H. (1978). *Characteristics of software quality*. Amsterdam: North-Holland.

Boh, W. F., Slaughter, S. A., & Espinosa, J. A. (2007). Learning from experience in software development: A multilevel analysis. *Management Science, 53*(8), 1315–1331.

Bollen, K. A. (2002). Latent variables in psychology and the social sciences. *Annual Review of Psychology, 53*(1), 605–634.

Bosu, A., & Carver, J. C. (2014). Impact of developer reputation on code review outcomes in OSS projects: An empirical investigation. In *Proceedings of the 8th ACM/IEEE International Symposium on Empirical Software Engineering and Measurement* (pp. 33–42), Torino, Italy.

Brandon, D. P., & Hollingshead, A. B. (2004). Transactive memory systems in organizations: Matching tasks, expertise, and people. *Organization Science, 15*(6), 633–644.

Brusoni, S., & Prencipe, A. (2001). Unpacking the black box of modularity: Technologies, products and organizations. *Industrial and Corporate Change, 10*(1), 197–205.

Bygstad, B. (2010). Generative mechanisms for innovation in information infrastructures. *Information and Organization, 20*(3), 156–168.

Bygstad, B., & Munkvold, B. E. (2011). In search of mechanisms. Conducting a critical realist data analysis. In *Proceedings of the International Conference on Information Systems*, Shanghai, China.

Canfora, G., Cimitile, A., Garcia, F., Piattini, M., & Visaggio, C. A. (2007). Evaluating performances of pair designing in industry. *Journal of Systems and Software, 80*(8), 1317–1327.

Cannon-Bowers, J. A., & Salas, E. (2001). Reflections on shared cognition. *Journal of Organizational Behavior, 22*(2), 195–202.

Cannon-Bowers, J. A., Salas, E., & Converse, S. (1993). Shared mental models in expert team decision making. In J. J. N. Castellan (Ed.), *Individual and group decision making* (pp. 221–246). Hillsdale: Lawrence Erlbaum.

Cao, L., Mohan, K., Ramesh, B., & Sarkar, S. (2013). Adapting funding processes for Agile IT projects: An empirical investigation. *European Journal of Information Systems, 22*, 191–205.

Cenfetelli, R. T., & Bassellier, G. (2009). Interpretation of formative measurement in information systems research. *MIS Quarterly, 33*(4), 689–707.

Chemero, A. (2003). An outline of a theory of affordances. *Ecological Psychology, 15*(2), 181–195.

Chen, X., Li, X., Clark, J. G., & Dietrich, G. B. (2013). Knowledge sharing in open source software project teams: A transactive memory system perspective. *International Journal of Information Management, 33*(3), 553–563.

Child, J. T., & Shumate, M. (2007). The impact of communal knowledge repositories and people-based knowledge management on perceptions of team effectiveness. *Management Communication Quarterly, 21*(1), 29–54.

Chin, W. (1998). The partial least squares approach to structural equation modeling. *Modern Methods for Business Research, 295*(2), 295–336.

Choi, S. Y., Lee, H., & Yoo, Y. (2010). The impact of information technology and transactive memory systems on knowledge sharing, application, and team performance: A field study. *MIS Quarterly, 34*(4), 855–870.

Chong, J., & Hurlbutt, T. (2007). The social dynamics of pair programming. In *Proceedings of the 29th International Conference on Software Engineering* (pp. 354–363).

Chou, S.-W., & He, M.-Y. (2011). The factors that affect the performance of open source software development - The perspective of social capital and expertise integration. *Information Systems Journal, 21*(2), 195–219.

Cockburn, A., & Williams, L. (2002). The costs and benefits of pair programming. In G. Succi & M. Marchesi (Eds.), *Extreme programming examined* (pp. 223–247). Reading, MA: Addison-Wesley.

Cohen, J. (1988). *Statistical power analysis for the behavioral sciences*. Hillsdale, NJ: Lawrence Erlbaum.

Coman, I. D., Robillard, P. N., Sillitti, A., & Succi, G. (2014). Cooperation, collaboration and pair-programming: Field studies on backup behavior. *Journal of Systems and Software, 91*(0), 124–134.

Conboy, K., & Fitzgerald, B. (2010). Method and developer characteristics for effective Agile method tailoring: A study of XP expert opinion. *ACM Transactions on Software Engineering and Methodology, 20*(1), Article 2.

D'Adderio, L. (2011). Artifacts at the centre of routines: Performing the material turn in routines theory. *Journal of Institutional Economics, 7*(02), 197–230.

Daniel, S., Agarwal, R., & Stewart, K. (2012). The effects of diversity in global, distributed collectives: A study of open source project success. *Information Systems Research, 24*(2), 312–333.

Davern, M., Shaft, T., & Te'eni, D. (2012). Cognition matters: Enduring questions in cognitive IS research. *Journal of the Association for Information Systems, 13*(4), 273–314.

Dawande, M., Johar, M., Kumar, S., & Mookerjee, V. (2008). A comparison of pair versus solo programming under different objectives: An analytical approach. *Information Systems Research, 19*(1), 71–92.

Decuyper, S., Dochy, F., & Van den Bossche, P. (2010). Grasping the dynamic complexity of team learning: An integrative model for effective team learning in organisations. *Educational Research Review, 5*(2), 111–133.

DeSanctis, G., & Poole, M. S. (1994). Capturing the complexity in advanced technology use: Adaptive structuration theory. *Organization Science, 5*(2), 121–147.

Di Bella, E., Fronza, I., Phaphoom, N., Sillitti, A., Succi, G., & Vlasenko, J. (2013). Pair programming and software defects - A large, industrial case study. *IEEE Transactions on Software Engineering, 39*(7), 930–953.

Dibbern, J., Guttler, W., & Heinzl, A. (2001). Die Theorie der Unternehmung als Erklärungsansatz für das selektive Outsourcing der Informationsverarbeitung: Entwicklung eines theoretischen Bezugsrahmens. *Zeitschrift für Betriebswirtschaft, 71*(6), 675–700.

Dibbern, J., Winkler, J., & Heinzl, A. (2008). Explaining variations in client extra costs between software projects offshored to India. *MIS Quarterly, 32*(2), 333–366.

Dingsøyr, T., Djarraya, H. K., & Røyrvik, E. (2005). Practical knowledge management tool use in a software consulting company. *Communications of the ACM, 48*(12), 96–100.

Dingsøyr, T., Nerur, S., Balijepally, V., & Moe, N. B. (2012). A decade of Agile methodologies: Towards explaining Agile software development. *The Journal of Systems & Software, 85*, 1213–1221.

Domino, M., Collins, R., & Hevner, A. (2007). Controlled experimentation on adaptations of pair programming. *Information Technology and Management, 8*(4), 297–312.

Dourish, P. (2003). The appropriation of interactive technologies: Some lessons from placeless documents. *Computer Supported Cooperative Work, 12*(4), 465–490.

Dybå, T., Arisholm, E., Sjøberg, D. I., Hannay, J. E., & Shull, F. (2007). Are two heads better than one? On the effectiveness of pair programming. *IEEE Software, 24*(6), 12–15.

Dybå, T., & Dingsøyr, T. (2008). Empirical studies of Agile software development: A systematic review. *Information and Software Technology, 50*(9–10), 833–859.

Eco, U. (1983). Horns, hooves, insteps: Some hypotheses on three types of abduction. In U. Eco & T. A. Sebeok (Eds.), *The sign of three: Dupin, Holmes, Peirce* (pp. 198–220). Bloomington: Indiana University Press.

Edmondson, A. C., Dillon, J. R., & Roloff, K. S. (2007). Three perspectives on team learning. *The Academy of Management Annals, 6*, 269–314.

Edmondson, A. C., & McManus, S. E. (2007). Methodological fit in management field research. *Academy of Management Review, 32*(4), 1155–1179.

Eisenhardt, K. M. (1989). Building theories from case study research. *The Academy of Management Review, 14*(4), 532–550.

Ellis, A., Porter, C., & Wolverton, S. (2008). Learning to work together: An examination of transactive memory system development in teams. In M. London & V. I. Sessa (Eds.), *Work group learning: Understanding, improving, and assessing how groups learn in organizations* (pp. 91–115). New York, NY: Erlbaum Associates.

Ellis, A. P. J., Hollenbeck, J. R., Ilgen, D. R., Porter, C. O., West, B. J., & Moon, H. (2003). Team learning: Collectively connecting the dots. *Journal of Applied Psychology, 88*(5), 821–835.

Erickson, J., Lyytinen, K., & Siau, K. (2005). Agile modeling, Agile software development, and extreme programming: The state of research. *Journal of Database Management, 16*(4), 88–100.

Espinosa, J. A., Slaughter, S. A., Kraut, R. E., & Herbsleb, J. D. (2007). Team knowledge and coordination in geographically distributed software development. *Journal of Management Information Systems, 24*(1), 135–169.

Fægri, T. E., Dybå, T., & Dingsøyr, T. (2010). Introducing knowledge redundancy practice in software development: Experiences with job rotation in support work. *Information and Software Technology, 52*(10), 1118–1132.

Fagan, M. (1986). Advances in software inspections. *IEEE Transaction on Software Engineering, 12*(7), 744–751.

Faraj, S., & Azad, B. (2012). The materiality of technology: An affordance perspective. In P. M. Leonardi, B. A. Nardi, & J. Kallinikos (Eds.), *Materiality and organizing: Social interaction in a technological world* (pp. 237–258). Oxford: Oxford University Press.

Faraj, S., & Sproull, L. (2000). Coordinating expertise in software development teams. *Management Science, 46*(12), 1554–1568.

Fitzgerald, B., Hartnett, G., & Conboy, K. (2006). Customising Agile methods to software practices at intel Shannon. *European Journal of Information Systems, 15*(2), 200–213.

Fleetwood, S. (2005). Ontology in organization and management studies: A critical realist perspective. *Organization, 12*(2), 197–222.

Fleetwood, S., & Ackroyd, S. (Eds.). (2004). *Critical realist applications in organisation and management studies*. London: Routledge.

Flor, N. V., & Hutchins, E. L. (1991). A case study of team programming during perfective software maintenance. In *Empirical Studies of Programmers: Fourth Workshop* (p. 36).

Floridi, L. (2002). What is the philosophy of information? *Metaphilosophy, 33*, 123–145.

Floridi, L. (2005). Is semantic information meaningful data? *Philosophy and Phenomenological Research, 70*(2), 351–370.

Floridi, L. (2008). A defence of informational structural realism. *Synthese, 161*(2), 219–253.

Floridi, L. (2010). *Information: A very short introduction*. Oxford: Oxford University Press.

Floridi, L. (2011). *The philosophy of information*. Oxford: Oxford University Press.

Floridi, L., & Illari, P. (Eds.). (2014). *The philosophy of information quality*. Synthese library (Vol. 358). Heidelberg: Springer.

Foucault, M. (1980). *Power/knowledge: Selected interviews and other writings 1972–1977*. Brighton: Harvester Press.

Gagsch, S. (1980). Subsystembildung. In *Handwörterbuch der Organisation* (pp. 2156–2171). Stuttgart: Poeschel.

Gallis, H., Arisholm, E., & Dyba, T. (2003). An initial framework for research on pair programming. In *Proceedings of the International Symposium on Empirical Software Engineering* (pp. 132–142).

Gefen, D., Rigdon, E. E., & Straub, D. (2011). An update and extension to SEM guidelines for administrative and social science research. *MIS Quarterly, 35*(2), III–XIV.

Ghobadi, S. (2015). What drives knowledge sharing in software development teams: A literature review and classification framework. *Information & Management, 52*(1), 82–97.

Gibson, J. J. (1986). *The ecological approach to visual perception*. Hillsdale, NJ: Lawrence Erlbaum Associates.

Giddens, A. (1984). *The constitution of society: Outline of the theory of structuration*. Berkeley: University of California Press.

Gino, F., Argote, L., Miron-Spektor, E., & Todorova, G. (2010). First, get your feet wet: The effects of learning from direct and indirect experience on team creativity. *Organizational Behavior and Human Decision Processes, 111*(2), 102–115.

Goh, J. M., Gao, G. G., & Agarwal, R. (2011). Evolving work routines: Adaptive routinization of information technology in healthcare. *Information Systems Research, 22*(3), 565–585.

Gomes, P. J., & Joglekar, N. R. (2008). Linking modularity with problem solving and coordination efforts. *Managerial and Decision Economics, 29*(5), 443–457.

Goodhue, D. L., Lewis, W., & Thompson, R. (2012). Does PLS have advantages for small sample size or non-normal data? *MIS Quarterly, 36*(3), 891–1001.

Goodhue, D. L., Thompson, R., & Lewis, W. (2013). Why you shouldn't use PLS: Four reasons to be uneasy about using PLS in analyzing path models. In *Proceedings of the 46th Hawaii International Conference on System Sciences* (pp. 4739–4748).

Goodman, P. S., & Dabbish, L. A. (2011). Methodological issues in measuring group learning. *Small Group Research, 42*(4), 379–404.

Gopal, A., Espinosa, J., Gosain, S., & Darcy, D. (2011). Coordination and performance in global software service delivery: The vendor's perspective. *IEEE Transactions on Engineering Management, 58*(4), 772–785.

Grant, R. M. (1996). Prospering in dynamically competitive environments: Organizational capability as knowledge integration. *Organization Science, 7*(4), 375–387.

Gray, P. H. (2000). The effects of knowledge management systems on emergent teams: Towards a research model. *The Journal of Strategic Information Systems, 9*(2–3), 175–191.

Gray, P., & Meister, D. (2004). Knowledge sourcing effectiveness. *Management Science, 50*(6), 821–834.

Gregor, S. (2006). The nature of theory in information systems. *MIS Quarterly, 30*(3), 611–642.

Griffith, T., Sawyer, J., & Neale, M. (2003). Virtualness and knowledge in teams: Managing the love triangle of organizations, individuals, and information technology. *MIS Quarterly, 27*(2), 265–287.

Griffith, T. L., & Sawyer, J. E. (2010). Multilevel knowledge and team performance. *Journal of Organizational Behavior, 31*(7), 1003–1031.

Grunwald, R., & Kieser, A. (2007). Learning to reduce interorganizational learning: An analysis of architectural product innovation in strategic alliances. *Journal of Product Innovation Management, 24*(4), 369–391.

Guinan, P. J., Cooprider, J. G., & Faraj, S. (1998). Enabling software development team performance during requirements definition: A behavioral versus technical approach. *Information Systems Research, 9*(2), 101–125.

Gupta, N., & Hollingshead, A. B. (2010). Differentiated versus integrated transactive memory effectiveness: It depends on the task. *Group Dynamics: Theory, Research, and Practice, 14*(4), 384–398.

Hair, J., Black, W., Babin, B., & Anderson, R. (2009). *Multivariate data analysis*. Upper Saddle River, NJ: Prentice Hall.

Hanks, B., Fitzgerald, S., McCauley, R., Murphy, L., & Zander, C. (2011). Pair programming in education: A literature review. *Computer Science Education, 21*(2), 135–173.

Hannay, J., Sjoberg, D. I., & Dyba, T. (2007). A systematic review of theory use in software engineering experiments. *IEEE Transactions on Software Engineering, 33*(2), 87–107.

Hannay, J. E., Dybå, T., Arisholm, E., & Sjøberg, D. I. K. (2009). The effectiveness of pair programming: A meta-analysis. *Information and Software Technology, 51*(7), 1110–1122.

He, J., Butler, B. S., & King, W. R. (2007). Team cognition: Development and evolution in software project teams. *Journal of Management Information Systems, 24*(2), 261–292.

Heinrich, L. J., Heinzl, A., & Riedl, R. (2011). *Wirtschaftsinformatik: Einführung und Grundlegung* (4th ed.). Heidelberg: Springer.

Hemmer, E., & Heinzl, A. (2011). Where is the "I" in "IS research"? The quest for a coherent research stream in the context of human information behavior. In A. Heinzl, P. Buxmann, O. Wendt, & T. Weitzel (Eds.), *Theory-guided modeling and empiricism in information systems research*. Heidelberg: Physica.

Highsmith, J., & Cockburn, A. (2001). Agile software development: The business of innovation. *IEEE Computer, 34*(9), 120–127.

Hildenbrand, T. (2008). *Improving traceability in distributed collaborative software development a design science approach*. Informationstechnologie und Ökonomie (Vol. 33). Frankfurt: Peter Lang.

Hollan, J., Hutchins, E., & Kirsh, D. (2000). Distributed cognition: Toward a new foundation for human-computer interaction research. *ACM Transactions on Computer-Human Interaction, 7*(2), 174–196.

Hollingshead, A. B. (1998a). Communication, learning, and retrieval in transactive memory systems. *Journal of Experimental Social Psychology, 34*(5), 423–442.

Hollingshead, A. B. (1998b). Group and individual training the impact of practice on performance. *Small Group Research, 29*(2), 254–280.

Hollingshead, A. B. (1998c). Retrieval processes in transactive memory systems. *Journal of Personality and Social Psychology, 74*(3), 659–671.

Hollingshead, A. B. (2000). Perceptions of expertise and transactive memory in work relationships. *Group Processes & Intergroup Relations, 3*(3), 257–267.

Hollingshead, A. B. (2001). Cognitive interdependence and convergent expectations in transactive memory. *Journal of Personality and Social Psychology, 81*(6), 1080–1089.

Hollingshead, A. B., Gupta, N., Yoon, K., & Brandon, D. P. (2011). Transactive memory theory and teams: Past, present, and future. In E. Salas, S. M. Fiore, & M. Letsky (Eds.), *Theories of team cognition: Cross-disciplinary perspectives* (pp. 421–455). New York, NY: Taylor & Francis.

Houston, M. J., & Sudman, S. (1975). A methodological assessment of the use of key informants. *Social Science Research, 4*(2), 151–164.

Hsu, J. S.-C., Shih, S.-P., Chiang, J. C., & Liu, J. Y.-C. (2012). The impact of transactive memory systems on IS development teams' coordination, communication, and performance. *International Journal of Project Management, 30*(3), 329–340.

Huang, M. (2009). A conceptual framework of the effects of positive affect and affective relationships on group knowledge networks. *Small Group Research, 40*(3), 323–346.

Huber, P. J. (1967). The behavior of maximum likelihood estimates under nonstandard conditions. In *Proceedings of the Fifth Berkeley Symposium on Mathematical Statistics and Probability* (pp. 221–233), Berkley, CA, USA.

Huckman, R. S., Staats, B. R., & Upton, D. M. (2009). Team familiarity, role experience, and performance: Evidence from Indian software services. *Management Science, 55*(1), 85–100.

Hulkko, H., & Abrahamsson, P. (2005). A multiple case study on the impact of pair programming on product quality. In *Proceedings of the 27th International Conference on Software Engineering* (pp. 495–504).

Hutchby, I. (2001). Technologies, texts and affordances. *Sociology, 35*(2), 441–456.

Hutchins, E. (1995). *Cognition in the wild*. Cambridge, MA: MIT Press.

Ilgen, D. R., Hollenbeck, J. R., Johnson, M., & Jundt, D. (2005). Teams in organizations: From input-process-output models to IMOI models. *Annual Review of Psychology, 69*, 517–543.

Jackson, M., & Moreland, R. (2009). Transactive memory in the classroom. *Small Group Research, 40*(5), 508–534.

Janz, B., & Prasarnphanich, P. (2003). Understanding the antecedents of effective knowledge management: The importance of a knowledge-centered culture. *Decision Sciences, 34*(2), 351–384.

Janz, B., & Prasarnphanich, P. (2009). Freedom to cooperate: Gaining clarity into knowledge integration in information systems development teams. *IEEE Transactions on Engineering Management, 56*(4), 621–635.

Jarvenpaa, S. L., & Majchrzak, A. (2008). Knowledge collaboration among professionals protecting national security: Role of transactive memories in ego-centered knowledge networks. *Organization Science, 19*(2), 260–276.

Jones, E. E., & Kelly, J. R. (2013). The psychological costs of knowledge specialization in groups: Unique expertise leaves you out of the loop. *Organizational Behavior and Human Decision Processes, 121*(2), 174–182.

Kanawattanachai, P., & Yoo, Y. (2007). The impact of knowledge coordination on virtual team performance over time. *MIS Quarterly, 31*(4), 783–808.

Kang, K., & Hahn, J. (2009). Learning and forgetting curves in software development: Does type of knowledge matter? In *Proceedings of the International Conference on Information Systems*, Paper 194.

Karg, L. M., Grottke, M., & Beckhaus, A. (2011). A systematic literature review of software quality cost research. *Journal of Systems and Software, 84*(3), 415–427.

Keeling, M. (2010). Put it to the test: Using lightweight experiments to improve team processes. In *Agile processes in software engineering and extreme programming* (Vol. 48, pp. 287–296). Berlin: Springer.

Kettinger, W. J., & Li, Y. (2010). The infological equation extended: Toward conceptual clarity in the relationship between data, information and knowledge. *European Journal of Information Systems, 19*(4), 409–421.

Kilmann, R. H. (1984). *Beyond the quick: Managing five tracks to organizational success*. San Francisco, CA: Jossey-Bass.

Klein, H. K., & Myers, M. D. (1999). A set of principles for conducting and evaluating interpretive field studies in information systems. *MIS Quarterly, 23*(1), 67–93.

Klimpke, L. (2013). *Konzeption und Realisierung eines integrierten Mirkoblog-basierten Kommunikationsansatzes für die verteilte Softwareentwicklung*. Informationstechnologie und Ökonomie (Vol. 51). Frankfurt: Peter Lang.

Kock, N. (2013). *WarpPLS 4.0 user manual*. Laredo, TX, USA: ScriptWarp Systems.

Kock, N., & Gaskins, L. (2014). The mediating role of voice and accountability in the relationship between Internet diffusion and government corruption in Latin America and Sub-Saharan Africa. *Information Technology for Development, 20*(1), 23–43.

Kock, N., & Lynn, G. S. (2012). Lateral collinearity and misleading results in variance-based SEM: An illustration and recommendations. *Journal of the Association for Information Systems, 13*(7), 546–580.

Kotlarsky, J., & Oshri, I. (2005). Social ties, knowledge sharing and successful collaboration in globally distributed system development projects. *European Journal of Information Systems, 14*(1), 37–48.

Kotlarsky, J., Scarbroug, H., & Oshri, I. (2014). Coordinating expertise across knowledge boundaries in offshore-outsourcing projects: The role of codification. *MIS Quarterly, 38*(2), 607–627.

Kotlarsky, J., van den Hooff, B., & Houtman, L. (2015). Are we on the same page? Knowledge boundaries and transactive memory system development in cross-functional teams. *Communication Research, 42*(3), 319–344.

Kozlowski, S., & Bell, B. (2008). Team learning, development, and adaptation. In V. I. Sessa & M. London (Eds.), *Work group learning: Understanding, improving and assessing how groups learn in organizations* (pp. 15–44). New York, NY: Erlbaum Associates.

Kozlowski, S., & Klein, K. (2000). A multilevel approach to theory and research in organizations: Contextual, temporal, and emergent processes. In K. J. Klein & S. W. J. Kozlowski (Eds.), *Multilevel theory, research, and methods in organizations: Foundations, extensions, and new directions* (pp. 3–90). San Francisco, CA: Jossey-Bass.

Krcmar, H. (2005). *Informationsmanagement* (4th ed.). Berlin: Springer.

Kuhn, T. S. (1970). *The structure of scientific revolutions*. Chicago, IL: University of Chicago Press.

Larman, C., & Vodde, B. (2010). *Practices for scaling lean & Agile development: large, multisite, and offshore product development with large-scale scrum*. Boston, MA: Pearson Education.

Lau, A. K., Richard, C., & Tang, E. (2009). The complementarity of internal integration and product modularity: An empirical study of their interaction effect on competitive capabilities. *Journal of Engineering and Technology Management, 26*(4), 305–326.

Lau, A. K., Yam, R., & Tang, E. (2007). The impacts of product modularity on competitive capabilities and performance: An empirical study. *International Journal of Production Economics, 105*(1), 1–20.

Lee, A. S. (1991). Integrating positivist and interpretive approaches to organizational research. *Organization Science, 2*(4), 342–365.

Lee, A. S., & Baskerville, R. L. (2003). Generalizing generalizability in information systems research. *Information Systems Research, 14*(3), 221–243.

Lee, G., & Xia, W. (2010). Toward Agile: An integrated analysis of quantitative and qualitative field data on software development agility. *MIS Quarterly, 34*(1), 87–114.

Lee, G. K., & Cole, R. E. (2003). From a firm-based to a community-based model of knowledge creation: The case of the linux kernel development. *Organization Science, 14*(6), 633–649.

Leonardi, P. (2011). When flexible routines meet flexible technologies: Affordance, constraint, and the imbrication of human and material agencies. *MIS Quarterly, 35*(1), 147–167.

Leonardi, P. (2012). When does technology use enable network change in organizations? A comparative study of feature use and shared affordances. *MIS Quarterly, 37*(3), 749–775.

Leonardi, P. M., & Barley, S. R. (2010). What's under construction here? Social action, materiality, and power in constructivist studies of technology and organizing. *The Academy of Management Annals, 4*(1), 1–51.

Levesque, L., Wilson, J., & Wholey, D. (2001). Cognitive divergence and shared mental models in software development project teams. *Journal of Organizational Behavior, 22*(SI), 135–144.

Levina, N., & Vaast, E. (2008). Innovating or doing as told? Status differences and overlapping boundaries in offshore collaboration. *MIS Quarterly, 32*(2), 307–332.

Lewis, K. (2003). Measuring transactive memory systems in the field: Scale development and validation. *Journal of Applied Psychology, 88*(4), 587–604.

Lewis, K. (2004). Knowledge and performance in knowledge-worker teams. *Management Science, 50*(11), 1519–1533.

Lewis, K., Belliveau, M., Herndon, B., & Keller, J. (2007). Group cognition, membership change, and performance: Investigating the benefits and detriments of collective knowledge. *Organizational Behavior and Human Decision Processes, 103*(2), 159–178.

Lewis, K., & Herndon, B. (2011). Transactive memory systems: Current issues and future research directions. *Organization Science, 22*, 1254–1265.

Lewis, K., Lange, D., & Gillis, L. (2005). Transactive memory systems, learning, and learning transfer. *Organization Science, 16*(6), 581–598.

Li, Y., Jiang, J., & Klein, G. (2009). The role of team learning in enabling shared leadership in ISD teams. In *Proceedings of the Americas Conference on Information Systems*. Paper 182.

Liang, D. W., Moreland, R., & Argote, L. (1995). Group versus individual training and group performance: The mediating role of transactive memory. *Personality and Social Psychology Bulletin, 21*, 384–393.

Liang, J., & Mizuno, O. (2011). Analyzing involvements of reviewers through mining a code review repository. In *Joint Conference of the 21st International Workshop on Software Measurement and the 6th International Conference on Software Process and Product Measurement*, Nara, Japan.

Liang, T.-P., Jiang, J., Klein, G., & Liu, J.-C. (2010). Software quality as influenced by informational diversity, task conflict, and learning in project teams. *IEEE Transactions on Engineering Management, 57*(3), 477–487.

Lin, T.-C., Hsu, J. S.-C., Cheng, K.-T., & Wu, S. (2011). Understanding the role of behavioural integration in ISD teams: An extension of transactive memory systems concept. *Information Systems Journal, 22*(3), 211–234.

Lui, K. M., Chan, K. C., & Nosek, J. T. (2008). The effect of Pairs in program design tasks. *IEEE Transactions on Software Engineering, 34*(2), 197–211.

MacKenzie, S., Podsakoff, P., & Podsakoff, N. (2011). Construct measurement and validation procedures in MIS and behavioral research: Integrating new and existing techniques. *MIS Quarterly, 35*(2), 293–334.

Madeyski, L. (2006). Is external code quality correlated with programming experience or feelgood factor? In *Proceedings of the 7th International Conference on Extreme Programming and Agile Processes in Software Engineering* (pp. 65–74), Oulu, Finland.

Majchrzak, A., Faraj, S., Kane, G. C., & Azad, B. (2013a). The contradictory influence of social media affordances on online communal knowledge sharing. *Journal of Computer-Mediated Communication, 19*(1), 38–55.

Majchrzak, A., Jarvenpaa, S. L., & Hollingshead, A. B. (2007). Coordinating expertise among emergent groups responding to disasters. *Organization Science, 18*(1), 147–161.

Majchrzak, A., & Markus, M. L. (2012). Technology affordances and constraints in management information systems (MIS). In E. Kessler (Ed.), *Encyclopedia of management theory*. Thousand Oaks, CA: Sage Publications.

Majchrzak, A., Wagner, C., & Yates, D. (2013b). The impact of shaping on knowledge Reuse for organizational improvement with wikis. *MIS Quarterly, 37*(2), 455–469.

Malhotra, A., & Majchrzak, A. (2012). How virtual teams use their virtual workspace to coordinate knowledge. *ACM Transactions on Management Information Systems, 3*(1), 6. http://dl.acm.org/citation.cfm?doid=2151163.2151169

Mangalaraj, G., Nerur, S., Mahapatra, R., & Price, K. H. (2014). Distributed cognition in software design: An experimental investigation of the role of design patterns and collaboration. *MIS Quarterly, 38*(1), 249–274.

Markus, M. L., & Silver, M. S. (2008). A foundation for the study of IT effects: A new look at DeSanctis and poole's concepts of structural features and spirit. *Journal of the Association for Information Systems, 9*(10), 609–632.

Maruping, L. M., Venkatesh, V., & Agarwal, R. (2009a). A control theory perspective on Agile methodology use and changing user requirements. *Information Systems Research, 20*(3), 377–399.

Maruping, L. M., Zhang, X., & Venkatesh, V. (2009b). Role of collective ownership and coding standards in coordinating expertise in software project teams. *European Journal of Information Systems, 18*(4), 355–371.

Mc Call, J. A., Richards, P. K., & Walters, G. F. (1977). *Factors in software quality: Final report*. Information Systems Programs: General Electric Company.

Mc Connell, S. (2004). *Code complete - A practical handbook of software construction* (2nd ed.). Redmond: Microsoft Press.

McIntosh, S., Kamei, Y., Adams, B., & Hassan, A. E. (2014). The impact of code review coverage and code review participation on software quality: A case study of the Qt, VTK, and ITK projects. In *Proceedings of the 11th Working Conference on Mining Software Repositories* (pp. 192–201), New York, NY, USA.

McKinney, E. H., Jr., Charles, J., & Yoos, I. (2010). Information about information: A taxonomy of views. *MIS Quarterly, 34*(2), 329–344.

Miles, M. B., & Huberman, M. A. (1994). *Qualitative data analysis: An expanded sourcebook*. Thousand Oaks, CA: Sage Publications.

Mingers, J. (2001). Combining IS research methods: Towards a pluralist methodology. *Information Systems Research, 12*(3), 240–259.

Mingers, J. (2003). The paucity of multimethod research: A review of the information systems literature. *Information Systems Journal, 13*(3), 233–249.

Mingers, J. (2004). Real-izing information systems: Critical realism as an underpinning philosophy for information systems. *Information and Organization, 14*(2), 87–103.

Mingers, J. (2013). Prefiguring Floridi's theory of semantic information. *tripleC, 11*(2), 388–401.

Mingers, J., & Brocklesby, J. (1997). Multimethodology: Towards a framework for mixing methodologies. *Omega, 25*(5), 489–509.

Mingers, J., Mutch, A., & Willcocks, L. (2013). Critical realism in information systems research. *MIS Quarterly, 37*(3), 795–802.

Mingers, J. C. (1995). Information and meaning: Foundations for an intersubjective account. *Information Systems Journal, 5*(4), 285–306.

Mohammed, S., & Dumville, B. C. (2001). Team mental models in a team knowledge framework: Expanding theory and measurement across disciplinary boundaries. *Journal of Organizational Behavior, 22*, 89–106.

Mookerjee, V., & Chiang, I. (2002). A dynamic coordination policy for software system construction. *IEEE Transactions on Software Engineering, 28*(7), 684–694.

Moreland, R. L., & Myaskovsky, L. (2000). Exploring the performance benefits of group training: Transactive memory or improved communication? *Organizational Behavior and Human Decision Processes, 82*, 117–133.

Müller, M. M. (2004). Are reviews an alternative to pair programming? *Empirical Software Engineering, 9*(4), 335–351.

Müller, M. M. (2005). Two controlled experiments concerning the comparison of pair programming to peer review. *Journal of Systems and Software, 78*, 166–179.

Müller, M. M. (2006). A preliminary study on the impact of a pair design phase on pair programming and solo programming. *Information and Software Technology, 48*(5), 335–344.

Müller, M. M. (2007). Do programmer Pairs make different mistakes than solo programmers? *Journal of Systems and Software, (80*(9), 1460–1471.

Müller, M. M., & Padberg, F. (2004). An empirical study about the feelgood factor in pair programming. In *IEEE Metrics* (pp. 151–158).

Mutch, A. (2010). Technology, organization, and structure: A morphogenetic approach. *Organization Science, 21*(2), 507–520.

Myers, M. D., & Klein, H. K. (2011). A set of principles for conducting critical research in information systems. *MIS Quarterly, 35*(1), 17–36.

Nederhof, A. J. (1985). Methods for coping with social desirability bias: A review. *European Journal of Social Psychology, 15*(3), 263–280.

Nemanich, L., Keller, R., Vera, D., & Chin, W. (2010). Absorptive capacity in R & D project teams: A conceptualization and empirical test. *IEEE Transactions on Engineering Management, 57*(4), 674–688.

Nevo, D., Benbasat, I., & Wand, Y. (2012). Understanding technology support for organizational transactive memory: Requirements, application, and customization. *Journal of Management Information Systems, 28*(4), 69–98.

Nevo, D., & Ophir, R. (2012). Transactive memory and its application in IS research. In Y. K. Dwivedi, M. R. Wade, & S. L. Schneberger (Eds.), *Information systems theory* (pp. 41–58). Heidelberg: Springer.

Nevo, D., & Wand, Y. (2005). Organizational memory information systems: A transactive memory approach. *Decision Support Systems, 39*(4), 549–562.

Nidumolu, S. (1995). The effect of coordination and uncertainty on software project performance: Residual performance risk as an intervening variable. *Information Systems Research, 6*(3), 191–219.

Nonaka, I. (1994). A dynamic theory of organizational knowledge creation. *Organization Science, 5*(1), 14–37.

Nosek, J. T. (1998). The case for collaborative programming. *Communications of the ACM, 41*(3), 105–108.

Ohtsubo, Y. (2005). Should information be redundantly distributed among group members? Effective use of group memory in collaborative problem solving. *Applied Cognitive Psychology, 19*(9), 1219–1233.

O'Leary, M. B., & Mortensen, M. (2010). Go (con)figure: Subgroups, imbalance, and isolates in geographically dispersed teams. *Organization Science, 21*(1), 115–131.

Orlikowski, W. J., & Baroudi, J. J. (1991). Studying information technology in organizations: Research approaches and assumptions. *Information Systems Research, 2*(1), 1–28.

Oshri, I., van Fenema, P., & Kotlarsky, J. (2008). Knowledge transfer in globally distributed teams: The role of transactive memory. *Information Systems Journal, 18*(6), 593–616.

Pangsakulyanont, T., Thongtanunam, P., Port, D., & Iida, H. (2014). Assessing MCR discussion usefulness using semantic similarity. In *6th International Workshop on Empirical Software Engineering in Practice* (pp. 49–54).

Paulk, M. C. (2001). Extreme programming from a CMM perspective. *IEEE Software, 18*(6), 19–26.

Peltokorpi, V. (2004). Transactive memory directories in small work units. *Personnel Review, 33*(4), 446–467.

Peltokorpi, V. (2008). Transactive memory systems. *Review of General Psychology, 12*(4), 378.

Petter, S., Straub, D., & Rai, A. (2007). Specifying formative constructs in information systems research. *MIS Quarterly, 31*(4), 623–656.

Phongpaibul, M., & Boehm, B. (2006). An empirical comparison between pair development and software inspection in Thailand. In *Proceedings of the International Symposium on Empirical Software Engineering 2006*, Rio de Janeiro, Brazil.

Phongpaibul, M., & Boehm, B. (2007). A replicate empirical comparison between pair development and software development with inspection. In *First International Symposium on Empirical Software Engineering and Measurement* (pp. 265–274).

Plonka, L., Sharp, H., Van der Linden, J., & Dittrich, Y. (2015). Knowledge transfer in pair programming: An in-depth analysis. *International Journal of Human-Computer Studies, 73*, 66 78.

Plonka, L., & van der Linden, J. (2012). Why developers don't pair more often. In *5th International Workshop on Cooperative and Human Aspects of Software Engineering* (pp. 123–125).

Podsakoff, P., MacKenzie, S., Lee, J., & Podsakoff, N. (2003). Common method biases in behavioral research: A critical review of the literature and recommended remedies. *Journal of Applied Psychology, 88*(5), 879–903.

Poppendieck, M., & Poppendieck, T. (2003). *Lean software development: An Agile toolkit*. Boston, MA: Addison-Wesley.

Popper, K. R. (1959). *The logic of scientific discovery*. London, UK: Routledge.

Pozzi, G., Pigni, F., & Vitari, C. (2014). Affordance theory in the IS discipline: A review and synthesis of the literature. In *Proceedings of the 20th Americas Conference on Information Systems*, Savannah, GA.

Rai, A., Song, H., & Troutt, M. (1998). Software quality assurance: An analytical survey and research prioritization. *Journal of Systems and Software, 40*(1), 67–83.

Rau, D. (2005). The influence of relationship conflict and trust on the transactive memory performance relation in top management teams. *Small Group Research, 36*(6), 746–771.

Ravichandran, T., & Rai, A. (2000). Quality management in systems development: An organizational system perspective. *MIS Quarterly, 24*(3), 381–415.

Ren, Y., & Argote, L. (2011). Transactive memory systems 1985–2010: An integrative framework of key dimensions, antecedents, and consequences. *The Academy of Management Annals, 5*(1), 189–229.

Ren, Y., Carley, K., & Argote, L. (2006). The contingent effects of transactive memory: When is it more beneficial to know what others know? *Management Science, 52*(5), 671–682.

Rigby, P. (2011). *Understanding open source software peer review: Review processes, parameters and statistical models, and underlying behaviours and mechanisms*. Ph.D. thesis, University of Ottawa, Department of Computer Science.

Rigby, P., Cleary, B., Painchaud, F., Storey, M.-A., & German, D. (2012). Contemporary peer review in action: Lessons from open source development. *IEEE Software, 29*(6), 56–61.

Rigby, P., German, D., & Storey, M. (2008). Open source software peer review practices: A case study of the apache server. In *Proceedings of the International Conference on Software Engineering* (pp. 541–550), Leipzig.

Rigby, P. C., & Bird, C. (2013). Convergent contemporary software peer review practices. In *Proceedings of the 2013 9th Joint Meeting on Foundations of Software Engineering* (pp. 202–212).

Rigby, P. C., & Storey, M.-A. (2011). Understanding broadcast based peer review on open source software projects. In *Proceedings of the International Conference on Software Engineering* (pp. 541–550), Honolulu, HI, USA.

Ringle, C. M., Sarstedt, M., & Straub, D. (2012). A critical look at the use of PLS-SEM in MIS quarterly. *MIS Quarterly, 36*(1), iii–xiv.

Robert, L. P., Jr., Dennis, A. R., & Ahuja, M. K. (2008). Social capital and knowledge integration in digitally enabled teams. *Information Systems Research, 19*(3), 314–334.

Robey, D., & Anderson, C. (2013). Information technology, materiality, and organizational change: A professional odyssey. *Journal of the Association for Information Systems, 14*(7), 379–398.

Rogers, W. H. (1993). sg17: Regression standard errors in clustered samples. *Stata Technical Bulletin, 13*, 19–23.

Ronkainen, J., & Abrahamsson, P. (2003). Software development under stringent hardware constraints: Do Agile methods have a chance? In *Proceedings of the 4th International Conference on Extreme Programming and Agile Processes in Software Engineering*.

Rosenkranz, C. (2011). Information systems development as a social process: A structuration model. In *Proceedings of the International Conference on Information Systems*, Shanghai, China.

Rulke, D. L., & Rau, D. (2000). Investigating the encoding process of transactive memory development in group training. *Group & Organization Management, 25*(4), 373–396.

Ryan, S., & O'Connor, R. V. (2013). Acquiring and sharing tacit knowledge in software development teams: An empirical study. *Information and Software Technology, 55*(9), 1614–1624.

Rönkkö, M., & Evermann, J. (2013). A critical examination of common beliefs about partial least squares path modeling. *Organizational Research Methods, 16*(3), 425–448.

Salas, E., Fiore, S. M., Letsky, M. P. (Eds.). (2012). *Theories of team cognition: Cross-disciplinary perspectives*. London, UK: Routledge.

Salleh, N., Mendes, E., & Grundy, J. (2014). Investigating the effects of personality traits on pair programming in a higher education setting through a family of experiments. *Empirical Software Engineering, 19*(3), 714–752.

Salleh, N., Mendes, E., & Grundy, J. C. (2011). Empirical studies of pair programming for CS/SE teaching in higher education: A systematic literature review. *IEEE Transactions on Software Engineering, 37*(4), 509–525.

Sarker, S., Sarker, S., Kirkeby, S., & Chakraborty, S. (2011). Path to "Stardom" in globally distributed hybrid teams: An examination of a knowledge-centered perspective using social network analysis. *Decision Sciences, 42*(2), 339–370.

Sawyer, S., Guinan, P. J., & Cooprider, J. (2010). Social interactions of information systems development teams: A performance perspective. *Information Systems Journal, 20*(1), 81–107.

Sayer, A. (2000) *Realism and social science*. London: Sage.

Schilling, M. A. (2000). Toward a general modular systems theory and its application to interfirm product modularity. *Academy of Management Review, 25*(2), 312–334.

Schmidt, C. T., Kude, T., Heinzl, A., & Mithas, S. (2014). How Agile practices influence the performance of software development teams: The role of shared mental models and backup. In *Proceedings of the International Conference on Information Systems*, Auckland, New Zealand.

Schmidt, C. T., Spohrer, K., Kude, T., & Heinzl, A. (2012). The impact of peer-based software reviews on team performance: The role of feedback and transactive memory systems. In *Proceedings of the International Conference on Information Systems*, Orlando, Florida, USA.

Schmitz, P., Bons, H., & van Megen, R. (1982). *Software-Qualitätssicherung - Testen im Software-Lebenszyklus*. Braunschweig: Vieweg.

Schwaber, K., & Beedle, M. (2002). *Agile software development with scrum* (Vol. 18). Upper Saddle River, NJ: Prentice Hall.

Schöne, H. (2003). Die teilnehmende Beobachtung als Datenerhebungsmehtode in der Politikwissenschaft. Methodologische Reflexion und Werkstattbericht. *Forum Qualitative Sozialforschung, 4*(2), 168–199.

Schütz, A. (1970). *On phenomenology and social relations* (Vol. 360). Chicago, IL: University of Chicago Press.

Seidel, S., Recker, J., & vom Brocke, J. (2014). Sensemaking and sustainable practicing: Functional affordances of information systems in green transformations. *MIS Quarterly 37*(4), 1275–1299.

Senapathi, M., & Srinivasan, A. (2012). Understanding post-adoptive Agile usage: An exploratory cross-case analysis. *Journal of Systems and Software, 85*(6), 1255–1268.

Sessa, V. I., & London, M. (Eds.). (2008). *Work group learning: Understanding, improving & assessing how groups learn in organizations*. New York, NY: Lawrence Erlbaum Associates.

Sharp, H., & Robinson, H. (2006). A distributed cognition account of mature XP teams. In P. Abrahamsson, M. Marchesi, & G. Succi (Eds.), *Extreme programming and Agile processes in software engineering* (pp. 1–10). Berlin: Springer.

Sharp, H., & Robinson, H. (2008). Collaboration and co-ordination in mature eXtreme program-
    ming teams. *International Journal of Human-Computer Studies, 66*(7), 506–518.
Shaw, M., & Garlan, D. (1996). *Software architecture: An emerging discipline.* Upper Saddle River,
    NJ: Prentice Hall.
Simon, H. A. (1969). *The sciences of the artificial* (Vol. 136). Cambridge, MA: MIT Press.
Skerlavaj, M., Dimovski, V., & Desouza, K. C. (2010). Patterns and structures of intra-
    organizational learning networks within a knowledge-intensive organization. *Journal of
    Information Technology, 25*(2), 189–204.
Sommerville, I. (2010). *Software engineering* (9th ed.). Munich: Pearson Education.
Spohrer, K., Gholami, B., & Heinzl, A. (2012). Team learning in information systems development
    - A literature review. In *Proceedings of the European Conference on Information Systems*,
    Barcelona, Spain.
Spohrer, K., Kude, T., Heinzl, A., & Schmidt, C. T. (2013a). Peer-based quality assurance in
    information systems development: A transactive memory perspective. In *Proceedings of the
    International Conference on Information Systems*, Milan, Italy.
Spohrer, K., Kude, T., Schmidt, C. T., & Heinzl, A. (2013b). Knowledge creation in information
    systems development teams: The role of pair programming and peer code review. In *Proceed-
    ings of the European Conference on Information Systems*, Utrecht, Netherlands.
Stamelos, I., Angelis, L., Oikonomou, A., & Bleris, G. (2002). Code quality analysis in open source
    software development. *Information Systems Journal, 12*(1), 43–60.
Stoffregen, T. A. (2003). Affordances as properties of the animal-environment system. *Ecological
    Psychology, 15*(2), 115–134.
Strauss, A., & Corbin, J. (1998). *Basic of qualitative research: Techniques and procedures for
    developing grounded theory* (Vol. 2). Thousand Oaks, CA: Sage Publications.
Strong, D., & Volkoff, O. (2010). Understanding organization-enterprise system fit: A path to
    theorizing the information technology artifact. *MIS Quarterly, 34*(4), 731.
Strong, D. M., Volkoff, O., Johnson, S. A., Pelletier, L. R., Tulu, B., Bar-On, I., et al. (2014.) A the-
    ory of organization-EHR affordance actualization. *Journal of the Association for Information
    Systems, 15*(2), 53–85.
Stuckenberg, S. (2014). *Exploring the organizational impact of software-as-a-service on software
    vendors: The role of organizational integration in software-as-a-service development and
    operation.* Informationstechnologie und Ökonomie (Vol. 55). Frankfurt: Peter Lang.
Stuckenberg, S., Kude, T., & Heinzl, A. (2014). Understanding the role of organizational
    integration in developing and operating software-as-a-service. *Journal of Business Economics,
    84*(8), 1019–1050.
Su, C. (2012). Who knows who knows what in the group? The effects of communication network
    centralities, use of digital knowledge repositories, and work remoteness on organizational
    members' accuracy in expertise recognition. *Communication Research, 39*(5), 614–640.
Subramanyam, R., Ramasubbu, N., & Krishnan, M. S. (2012). In search of efficient flexibility:
    Effects of software component granularity on development effort, defects, and customization
    effort. *Information Systems Research, 23*(3), 787–803.
Sun, W. (2011). *The true cost of pair programming: Development of a comprehensive model and
    test.* Ph.D. thesis, University of Kansas.
Sutcliffe, A. G., Gonzalez, V., Binder, J., & Nevarez, G. (2011). Social mediating technologies:
    Social affordances and functionalities. *International Journal of Human-Computer Interaction,
    27*(11), 1037–1065.
Sutherland, A., & Venolia, G. (2009). Can peer code reviews be exploited for later information
    needs? In *31st International Conference on Software Engineering-Companion Volume, 2009*
    (pp. 259–262).
Sutton, R., & Straw, B. (1995). What theory is not. *Administrative Science Quarterly, 40*(3), 371–
    385.
Teasley, S., Covi, L., Krishnan, M., & Olson, J. (2002). Rapid software development through team
    collocation. *IEEE Transactions on Software Engineering, 28*(7), 671–683.

Thongtanunam, P., Tantithamthavorn, C., Kula, R. G., Yoshida, N., Iida, H., & Matsumoto, K. (2015). Who should review my code? A file location-based code-reviewer recommendation approach for modern code review. In *Proceedings of the 22nd IEEE International Conference on Software Analysis, Evolution, and Reengineering*, Montreal, Canada.

Thongtanunam, P., Yang, X., Yoshida, N., Kula, R., Camargo Cruz, A., Fujiwara, K., et al. (2014). ReDA: A web-based visualization tool for analyzing modern code review dataset. In *IEEE International Conference on Software Maintenance and Evolution* (pp. 605–608).

Tiwana, A. (2004). An empirical study of the effect of knowledge integration on software development performance. *Information and Software Technology, 46*(13), 899–906.

Tiwana, A., & Mclean, E. (2005). Expertise integration and creativity in information systems development. *Journal of Management Information Systems, 22*(1), 13–43.

Tomayko, J. E. (2002). A comparison of pair programming to inspections for software defect reduction. *Computer Science Education, 12*(3), 213–222.

Tsang, E. W. (2014). Case studies and generalization in information systems research: A critical realist perspective. *The Journal of Strategic Information Systems, 23*(2), 174–186.

Van Osch, W., & Mendelson, O. (2011). A typology of affordances: Untangling sociomaterial interactions through video analysis. In *Proceedings of the International Conference on Information Systems*, Shanghai, China.

Vanhanen, J. (2011). *Empirical assssessment of the adoption, use, and effects of pair programming.* Ph.D. thesis, Aalto University.

Vanhanen, J., & Lassenius, C. (2005). Effects of pair programming at the development team level: An experiment. In *International Symposium on Empirical Software Engineering*, Noosa Heads, Australia.

Vanhanen, J., & Lassenius, C. (2007). Perceived effects of pair programming in an industrial context. In *33rd EUROMICRO Conference on Software Engineering and Advanced Applications* (pp. 211–218), Lübeck, Germany.

Vanhanen, J., Lassenius, C., & Mantyla, M. V. (2007). Issues and tactics when adopting pair programming: A longitudinal case study. In *International Conference on Software Engineering Advances, 2007. ICSEA, 2007* (pp. 70–70), Cap Esterel, France.

Vanhanen, J., & Mäntylä, M. V. (2013). A systematic mapping study of empirical studies on the use of pair programming in industry. *International Journal of Software Engineering and Knowledge Engineering, 23*(09), 1221–1267.

Venkatesh, V., Brown, S., & Bala, H. (2013). Bridging the qualitative-quantitative divide: Guidelines for conducting mixed methods research in information systems. *MIS Quarterly, 37*(1), 21–54.

Vidgen, R., & Wang, X. (2009). Coevolving systems and the organization of Agile software development. *Information Systems Research, 20*(3), 355–376.

Vlaar, P. W. L., van Fenema, P. C., & Tiwari, V. (2008). Cocreating understanding and value in distributed work: How members of onsite and offshore vendor teams give, make, demand, and break sense. *MIS Quarterly, 32*(2), 227–255.

Volkoff, O., Strong, D., & Elmes, M. (2007). Technological embeddedness and organizational change. *Organization Science, 18*(5), 832–848.

Volkoff, O., & Strong, D. M. (2013). Critical realism and affordances: Theorizing IT-associated organizational change processes. *MIS Quarterly, 37*(3), 819–834.

von Hellens, L. A. (1997). Information systems quality versus software quality - A discussion from a managerial, an organisational and an engineering viewpoint. *Information and Software Technology, 39*(12), 801–808. Information System Quality.

Walsham, G. (1995a). Interpretive case studies in is research: Nature and method. *European Journal of Information Systems, 4*(2), 74–81.

Walsham, G. (1995b). The emergence of interpretivism in IS research. *Information Systems Research, 6*(4), 376–394.

Walsham, G. (2006). Doing interpretive research. *European Journal of Information Systems, 15*, 320–330.

Walz, D., Elam, J., & Curtis, B. (1993). Inside a software-design team: Knowledge acquisition, sharing, and integration. *Communications of the ACM, 36*(10), 63–77.

Wang, C. L., Ahmed, P. K., & Rafiq, M. (2008). Knowledge management orientation: Construct development and empirical validation. *European Journal of Information Systems, 17*(3), 219–235.

Wang, J., & Carroll, J. (2011). Behind linus's law: A preliminary analysis of open source software peer review practices in mozilla and python. In *International Conference on Collaboration Technologies and Systems* (pp. 117–124).

Wang, X., Conboy, K., & Pikkarainen, M. (2012). Assimilation of Agile practices in use. *Information Systems Journal, 22*(6), 435–455.

Ward, J., & Peppard, J. (2002). *Strategic planning for information systems* (3rd ed.). New York, NY: Wiley.

Waterman, M. G. (2014). *Reconciling agility and architecture: A theory of Agile architecture.* Ph.D. thesis, Victoria University of Wellington.

Wegner, D. M. (1987). Transactive memory: A contemporary analysis of the group mind. In B. Mullen & G. R. Goethals (Eds.), *Theories of group behavior* (pp. 185–208). New York, NY: Springer.

Wegner, D. M., Giuliano, T., & Hertel, P. T. (1985). Cognitive interdependence in close relationships. In *Compatible and incompatible relationships* (pp. 253–276). Berlin: Springer.

Wetzels, M., Odekerken-Schroder, G., & van Oppen, C. (2009). Using PLS path modeling for assessing hierarchical construct models: Guidelines and empirical illustration. *MIS Quarterly, 33*(1), 177–195.

Whetten, D. A. (1989). What constitutes a theoretical contribution? *Academy of Management Review, 14*(4), 490–495.

Williams, L., Kessler, R. R., Cunningham, W., & Jeffries, R. (2000). Strengthening the case for pair programming. *IEEE Software, 17*(4), 19–25.

Williams, L. A. (2000). *The collaborative software process.* Ph.D. thesis, Department of Computer Science, University of Utah.

Williams, L. A., & Kessler, R. R. (2000). All I really need to know about pair programming I learned in kindergarten. *Communincations of the ACM, 43*(5), 108–114.

Wilson, J. M., Goodman, P. S., & Cronin, M. A. (2007). Group learning. *Academy of Management Review, 32*(4), 1041–1059.

Winkler, D., & Biffl, S. (2006). An empirical study on design quality improvement from best-practice inspection and pair programming. In *Proceedings of the 7th International Conference on Product-Focused Software Process Improvement* (pp. 319–333), Amsterdam, The Netherlands.

Wong, S. (2008). Task knowledge overlap and knowledge variety: The role of advice network structures and impact on group effectiveness. *Journal of Organizational Behavior, 29*, 591–614.

Wray, S. (2010). How pair programming really works. *IEEE Software, 27*(1), 50–55.

Wynn, D., Jr., & Williams, C. K. (2012). Principles for conducting critical realist case study research in information systems. *MIS Quarterly, 36*(3), 787–810.

Yang, X. (2014). Social network analysis in open source software peer review. In *Proceedings of the 22nd ACM SIGSOFT International Symposium on Foundations of Software Engineering* (pp. 820–822), Hong Kong, China.

Yin, R. K. (2009). *Case study research.* Applied social research methods series (4th ed., Vol. 5). Los Angeles, CA: Sage.

Yoo, Y., & Kanawattanachai, P. (2001). Developments of transactive memory systems and collective mind in virtual teams. *The International Journal of Organizational Analysis, 9*(2), 187–208.

Yuan, Y. C., Fulk, J., & Monge, P. R. (2007). Access to information in connective and communal transactive memory systems. *Communication Research, 34*(2), 131–155.

Yuan, Y. C., Fulk, J., Monge, P. R., & Contractor, N. (2010). Expertise directory development, shared task interdependence, and strength of communication network ties as multilevel predictors of expertise exchange in transactive memory work groups. *Communication Research, 37*(1), 20–47.

Zachariadis, M., Scott, S., & Barrett, M. (2013). Methodological implications of critical realism for mixed-methods research. *MIS Quarterly, 37*(3), 855–879.

Zammuto, R. F., Griffith, T. L., Majchrzak, A., Dougherty, D. J., & Faraj, S. (2007). Information technology and the changing fabric of organization. *Organization Science, 18*(5), 749–762.

Zhang, X., Venkatesh, V., & Brown, S. A. (2011). Designing collaborative systems to enhance team performance. *Journal of the Association for Information Systems, 12*(8), 556–584.

About the Author

Kai Spohrer is a researcher in the field of Information Systems, with a particular focus on the role of technology in team-based software development and the implications of IT innovations for collaboration in organizations. From 2010 to 2015 he worked as a research and teaching assistant at the Business School's Department of General Management and Information Systems of the University of Mannheim, Germany. He was a visiting scholar at the Washington State University, Pullman, WA, USA in 2013. Previously, Kai Spohrer studied Information Systems and Computer Science at the University of Mannheim and at the Universidad Politécnica de Madrid, Spain. He received his Diploma (M.Sc.) in Management Information Systems from the University of Mannheim in 2010.

© Springer International Publishing Switzerland 2016
K. Spohrer, *Collaborative Quality Assurance in Information Systems Development*,
Progress in IS, DOI 10.1007/978-3-319-25163-9